Eli Saslow

TEN LETTERS

Eli Saslow has been a staff writer at *The Washington Post* since 2004. He covered the 2008 presidential campaign, wrote profile stories about Barack Obama, and then chronicled the president's life inside the White House. Saslow has won multiple awards for news and feature writing. He lives in Washington with his wife and daughter.

TEN LETTERS

The Stories Americans
Tell Their President

Eli Saslow

ANCHOR BOOKS
A Division of Random House, Inc.
New York

For Rachel

. . .

FIRST ANCHOR BOOKS EDITION, AUGUST 2012

Copyright © 2011 by Eli Saslow

The Library of Congress has cataloged
the Doubleday edition as follows:
Saslow, Eli.
Ten letters : the stories Americans tell
their president / by Eli Saslow. —1st ed.
p. cm.
1. Obama, Barack—Correspondence.
2. United States—Politics and government—2009–
3. United States—Economic conditions—2009–
4. United States—Social conditions—21st century. I. Title.
E907.S364 2011
973.932092—dc22 2011013838

Anchor ISBN: 978-0-307-74255-1

Author photograph © Steel Brooks
Book design by Pei Loi Koay

www.anchorbooks.com

CONTENTS

TEN LETTERS

"I lost my job, my health benefits and my self worth in a matter of 5 days."

The nightly briefing book arrived at the White House residence just before 8.00 p.m., hand-delivered to President Obama by a junior member of his staff. It was a large, three-ring binder that had been covered in black leather and stamped with the presidential seal, and Obama sometimes eyed it wearily and lamented the arrival of what he called his "homework packet." Each night brought another few hundred pages of policy memos and scheduling notes, another deluge of intelligence about two wars, terrorist plots, and the tumbling U.S. economy. Some documents Obama only skimmed. Others he set aside to read the next morning.

He opened the binder and reached for a thin purple folder—the one item that he always read, and usually read first. The contents inside the purple folder had become a fixture of his presidency, shaping his speeches and informing his policies. Senior advisers had referred to it by turns as Obama's "lifeline," "inspiration," "connection to reality," and "guide to what people really care about." On this evening, the folder had been labeled with the date: "January 8, 2010."

It was a snowy Friday night, the end of another long day at the end of another long week inside the White House. Obama and his family had recently returned from a ten-day trip to Hawaii, but he joked to friends that he already craved another vacation. In Washington, Obama had come back to a Republican resurgence that threatened the passage of his health-care bill; to the attempted terrorist bombing of a passenger flight over Michigan; to the latest American death in Afghanistan, from an explosion on January 3; to the mounting resistance of Tea Party protesters, some of whom marched across the street from his house and waved OBAMA = HITLER signs; to an approval rating of 50 percent and dropping, the lowest for a second-year president in more than half a century; to the increasingly feeble defense of his own press secretary, Robert Gibbs, who, on this day, had stood in front of eighty reporters during a regular briefing and said of his boss's current outlook: "I would say the president is worried about today and worried about the future."

Hours earlier, Obama had made a short statement of his own. It had once again fallen on him to deliver bad news, so he had entered the East Room of the White House at 2:45 p.m., displaying what had become some of his most familiar gestures—the body language of disappointment. He narrowed his eyes, pursed his lips, and offered a solemn nod once he reached the lectern. Another eighty-five thousand people had lost their jobs during the last month, he said. More than four million had lost jobs in the last year. Almost one million had given up on looking for work entirely. "Today's numbers," Obama said, frowning and squinting into the camera lights, "are a reminder that the road to recovery is never straight."

There were other reminders: the new gray hair spreading across the sides of Obama's head, the heavy creases running across his cheeks, and the dark circles deepening below his eyes. The president still looked remarkably fit for forty-eight years old, but some medical experts believed the last twelve months had aged Obama by two or three years. His cholesterol was climbing, and he continued to rely on the occasional cigarette to calm his nerves. Like all presidents, he described his responsibilities as never ending, and his aides conceded that they had underestimated the range of issues Obama would face during his first term. He had flown 152 times on Air Force One in the last year, visiting 30 states and 21 countries. He had given 160 news interviews, delivered 412 speeches, and spoken at 5 funerals. He had committed to a war in Afghanistan and received the Nobel Peace Prize. On an average day, he squeezed in a morning workout after his daughters left for school, rushed to a national security meeting at 8:30 a.m., and continued working virtually uninterrupted until nearly midnight. He usually spent the last two hours of his workday on a couch at home, where he fought off sleep and read the briefing book.

Now he opened the purple folder and glanced at the cover sheet.

"MEMORANDUM TO THE PRESIDENT," it read. "Per your request, we have attached 10 pieces of unvetted correspondence addressed to you."

Inside, Obama found crumpled notebook paper, smudged ink, sloppy handwriting, and misspelled words—a collection of ten letters from constituents that he considered his most important daily reading. One letter was from a grade-schooler asking for help on his spelling homework; another was from an unemployed mother demanding a job. Depending on the nature of each letter, Obama sometimes copied them for senior advisers, distributed them to members of his cabinet, or read parts aloud to his wife before bed.

He had first requested a sampling of ten letters on his second day as president, and the purple folder had come six days a week ever since, couriered to Obama even when he was away at Camp David or traveling abroad. The White House mail staff sorted through twenty thousand letters and e-mails addressed to Obama every day, screening for security threats, categorizing by topic, and then picking the most representative ten pieces for the purple folder. The letters chosen each day were the most intimate connection Obama had left to the people he governed. He believed the wide-ranging feedback—quick e-mails and thoughtful letters; congratulations and condemnations—offered him a unique view beyond the presidential bubble into what he called "the real America," a place of uncensored opinion. "I will tell you," Obama had said, laughing, "my staff is very evenhanded, because about half of these letters call me an idiot." He loved the give and take, aides said. He always read all ten letters and typically wrote back to one or two writers each day, usually responding by hand to those who offered articulate criticism or moving stories of hardship. Obama often said that the letters not only reminded him of why he had run for president; they also reminded him of all the work he had left to do.

But lately the tenor of the letters had changed, becoming darker. There were fewer glowing, post-inauguration thank-you notes and more missives addressed to "Dear Jackass," "Dear Moron," or "Dear Socialist." Former campaign volunteers wrote to express disillusionment; other people shared stories of how Obama's policies had failed them. Earlier in the day, during his somber speech in the East Room, Obama had spoken about the America now reflected back to him in the mail at the beginning of his second year in office. "In the letters that I receive at night," he had said, "I often hear from Americans who are facing hard times—Americans who've lost their jobs or can't afford to pay their bills. They're worried about what the future holds."

This had become the unmistakable message delivered each day inside the purple folder: America was struggling. Its president was struggling. Both desperately needed a better year ahead.

Obama reached into the folder on January 8 and removed the first letter. It was three pages long and written on lined notebook paper. He had always preferred handwritten notes to e-mails, believing them to be more thoughtful and to contain better stories. The return address showed Monroe, Michigan. The writing consisted of bubbly block letters, sometimes traced twice for emphasis. Obama started to read.

"Dear Mr. President," the letter began.

. . .

Jennifer Cline, twenty-seven, did not usually write letters, but she was not usually this bored. *Wheel of Fortune* had ended. *Jeopardy!* had ended. Her husband was out working the midnight shift, and her two sons had gone to bed. She sat in the living room of their small duplex in Monroe, Michigan, flipping aimlessly through the channels on her big-screen television. Obama's face appeared on the screen, and she set down the remote.

She had liked Obama ever since the beginning of his 2008 presidential campaign. He seemed more accessible than other politicians, she thought, and she viewed him as a contemporary. He had two young daughters; she had two young sons. He came from the middle class, and so did she. His campaign had converted her from a halfhearted Democrat into an advocate who stuck a sign in her front yard and argued with relatives who refused to vote for Obama because of his race. "He's more like us than any other politician," she had told them, but now the program on television gave her doubts. It was a holiday special about life inside the White House. She watched as Obama chased his dog across a manicured lawn, laughed with his daughters about their giant Christmas tree, tossed a football in the Oval Office, and stood next to a showcase of formal china. Jen looked around her own low-budget rental, with its faux-brick interior, milk stains on the television screen, white sheets draped over used furniture, and an aging pit bull snoring at her feet. She wondered: Does he really know what this life is like?

She reached across the coffee table and ripped a few pages from her eldest son's elementary-school notebook. She had always loved to write, once spending a year on an unpublished autobiography and keeping a regular journal during times of high stress. Lately she had been writing a lot in that journal. She began her letter in the top left corner—"Dear Mr. President"—and then skipped a line before writing again.

"Mr. Obama," she continued, "I am going to begin by telling you about my life over the past 2 years."

Where to start? She had been living in a two-story, riverside home with her boyfriend when the Michigan economy began to collapse in 2007. She lost her longtime job as a pharmacy technician in May of that year, downsized with three days' notice. Her mother, also a pharmacy tech, was laid off on the same day. Her boyfriend's new swimming-pool business sold two pools all summer, sunk $30,000 into debt, and was shuttered. The bank foreclosed on their house. Jen and her son, Brenden, moved into her parents' double-wide trailer in the Detroit suburbs, where her father, a mechanic, paid the bills even though his own work at the Chevrolet dealership had been cut to fifteen hours a week. A few days after she moved in, Jen found out she was pregnant with her second son.

In her letter to Obama, she reduced all of that to: "I lost my job, my health benefits and my self worth in a matter of 5 days."

She applied for a dozen jobs every week while working part-time as a bartender. Kohl's, a budget department store, asked her to come in for an interview, so she bought a new dress and showed up at the appointed time only to discover that it was a group interview shared with thirty-five other candidates. Home Depot offered her a job, but the store was forty-five miles away and the $7-an-hour wage was less than the cost of child care. Finally, late in 2008, Jen programmed a new number into her cell phone under the name MARVIN (Michigan Automated Response Voice Interactive Network), and called it to request unemployment assistance. She joked with other unemployed friends about throwing a MARVIN party since the android had become such a regular part of their lives. After Jen called a few dozen times, MARVIN granted her unemployment assistance of $850 a month.

In the letter, that became: "In Michigan, Mr. President, jobs are very difficult to land."

The $850 wasn't enough, not even close, so Jen used food stamps to buy groceries and credit cards to buy almost everything else. She got a card from Bank of America with a $3,000 limit and maxed it out within a few months. Interest and late fees mounted to a debt of $15,000 and Bank of America sued. So did another credit card company. And another. Soon Jen owed more than $50,000—debts to three credit card companies, two doctors' offices, a car dealership, and a community college.

Her skin started to break out in rashes, but she put off seeing a doctor because she no longer had health insurance. It was probably just stress, she thought. But the rashes kept spreading, so she applied for Medicaid and was repeatedly denied until, on her fourth visit to the caseworker, she pulled up her shirt in the middle of the office to reveal a series of deep red streaks on her chest and back.

That became: "I was then diagnosed with both melonoma and basal cell skin cancer and had to begin chemotherapy without health insurance."

Her letter was starting to feel like a downer, Jen thought, which was not what she had intended. She reached into her son's notebook and ripped out another page. She wanted to tell Obama about how she and her boyfriend, Jay, had finally gotten married in November and splurged on the open bar. How Brenden had secretly stashed away months of his allowance and offered to contribute $95 to the wedding reception. How, after radiation, two rounds of chemo, and some plastic surgery, doctors now believed she would outlast the cancer. How her husband had found a job working the midnight shift for Delta Air Lines, and how she had received a government Pell Grant to take classes toward a nursing degree at the local community college.

That became: "And in just a couple of years, we'll be in a great spot. We can both have a great job, and hopefully stop renting, and buy a home."

Jen had filled almost three pages in less than ten minutes, more a stream-of-consciousness journal entry than a formal note. She considered it unlikely that anyone would ever read it, let alone Obama, but she hardly cared. She felt the same way about the letter as she did about her unpublished autobiography: It was cathartic just to share her life story. "Hope this letter finds you in great health and happiness," she concluded. Then she signed her name at the bottom: "Jennifer Cline," which was what only bill collectors called her, but somehow "Jen" seemed too informal for the president. She had never been to Washington, and she looked up the zip code on the Internet. Then she grabbed a standard white envelope and addressed it to "The White House."

As Jen walked downstairs to the mailbox, she thought about the one item she had decided against including in the letter: She and Jay had begun to consider filing for bankruptcy. Jen had already been granted a Chapter 7 bankruptcy a year earlier, but Jay was still more than $60,000 in debt. Their combined annual income was $24,000. They had spent a few weeks running through the calculations and determined that, in a best-case scenario, it would take them forty years to pay off what they owed. Bankruptcy, which would erase almost all of Jay's debt, seemed like their only way out.

But the possibility filled Jen with shame. Going through the process once had been the low point of her adult life, and she dreaded doing it again with Jay. Bankruptcy was the last rung of failure, she thought. It was immoral, irresponsible, low-class. It was not something she wanted to share with the president. So she opened up the aluminum mailbox, dropped in her letter, and pulled up the red flag.

. . .

Three weeks later, Jen walked outside to get her mail on a freezing Tuesday afternoon. The aluminum box was positioned just off her front porch, but lately that had become a formidable distance worth traveling only once every few days. She felt nauseous from the latest round of chemo, or maybe from the constant diet of scrambled eggs and Twizzlers, the only foods she could consistently keep down while on the cancer medications. A thin layer of ice coated the wooden porch, and a cold wind whipped over from Lake Erie a few miles to the east.

Monroe had always felt like a bleak place, Jen thought, but never more so than now in late January, when winter had stolen the sun and turned the landscape colorless. Gray snow. Gray skies. Gray lake. Gray smokestacks framing downtown. She had moved here with Jay because it was better than living in the double-wide with her parents and because rent for the duplex cost less than $600 a month. But she and Jay despised almost everything about Monroe. The city of twenty-three thousand hugs Interstate 75 at its midpoint between Toledo and Detroit—once an ideal location for transportation and manufacturing, but lately the epicenter of the recession. Four major plants had closed in the last year. Monroe's unemployment rate had jumped to 17 percent. Petty crime was up. Violent offenses had doubled. Even before she began chemo, Jen had stopped going to local bars or jogging along the downtown river path, fearing for her safety. Their docile, aging family dog wore a spike-studded collar to intimidate would-be intruders even though his primary interests consisted of licking hands and receiving belly rubs. Jay and Jen sometimes took the dog and the boys for long drives out of town on weekends so they could explore the nicer Detroit suburbs and pick out homes they dreamed of one day buying.

Jen reached into the mailbox and pulled out half a dozen items. Ever since she had canceled her subscription to *Cosmopolitan* a few months earlier, the mailbox had become the sole property of Jennifer Cline, not Jen. Nothing good ever came. More reminders of a life in disarray arrived each day. She typically deposited the unopened mail on the kitchen table for Jay to look over, and he would flip through it quickly before shoving it all into a desk drawer, where it usually remained out of sight, if not entirely out of mind.

At first glance this stack looked like all the others, and Jen glanced over it quickly as she walked in from the porch. A credit card statement. Two doctor bills. An URGENT NOTICE from a collection agency. At the back of the stack was a big yellow envelope, stamped first class, and Jen turned it over to look at the address label. "The White House," it read, and Jen immediately thought: How did I get in so much trouble that now the president is involved?

She brought the envelope into the house and opened it at the kitchen table. Inside, she found two thin pieces of cardboard taped together. Protected in between the cardboard was another envelope, much smaller, and inside that envelope was a handwritten note in black ink, crafted on a white note card embossed with the presidential seal.

Then Jen remembered the letter she had written to Obama, and her hands started to shake. She lifted up the note card and held it under the light. "Jennifer," it began, but this one was not from a bill collector. There was cursive handwriting, smudged ink, and a signature with a sweeping *B* and *O* in the bottom right-hand corner.

Was it real? She thought so. She started to laugh, then scream before calming herself down to read.

"Jennifer—Thanks for the very kind and inspiring letter. I know times are tough, but knowing there are folks out there like you and your husband give me confidence that things will keep getting better."

Jen read the letter again, then for a third time, suddenly careful not to touch the ink. She packed it back into the envelope, reassembled the cardboard sleeve, and stored the package in a Kmart safe in her bedroom closet. She called to tell Jay, her parents, two friends, and a sister. "It's really from him," she said, again and again. And then: "I think it's a sign." Maybe her life would improve in 2010. Maybe the president understood. Maybe they mattered. Maybe they could find a way out of their mess and build something better.

Later that week, still feeling inspired, Jen sat down with Jay at their kitchen table. She held up a stack of unopened bills and collection notices that she had pulled out of the desk drawer. "It's too much," she said. "We're buried. We need a second chance." And so they agreed: There was only one way out, and they would take it. Jay would file for bankruptcy, and they would try to start over.

. . .

Jen's father came over one Sunday afternoon to build a basketball hoop for Brenden, and afterward Jen invited him in for spaghetti. He seemed to be in a good mood, she thought, so she sat down across from him. She had been dreading this conversation for more than a week, but this felt like the right time.

"Dad," she said, "I have some news you're probably not going to like."

"Uh-huh," he said.

"Jay and I have decided that he's going to file for bankruptcy. We're in so much debt that it would probably take us a hundred years to get out. It's not something I'm proud of, but we've got to give ourselves a fresh start. There's really no other option."

She looked across the table at her father and waited for his response. A year earlier, when she had told him she was filing for her own bankruptcy, he had stopped talking to her for three months, and now again Dan Knope stayed silent and fixed his eyes on his plate. He had been making his living for thirty years as a mechanic—"wrenching," he called it—and he wore a General Motors jacket with his name stitched over the right breast. His hands and feet were calloused and swollen; he suffered from chronic stiffness in his back and neck after thousands of hours spent lying under cars. Lately work at the dealership had been deadly slow—down from fifty-five hours a week to fifteen, but still Dan went for nine hours a day, waited by his alignment station, cleaned his tool kit, tried not to look at the clock, chatted with the other bored mechanics, and walked to the sales room for regular coffee breaks. The coffee was lousy but the walk was good. It gave him something to do. He was fifty-four, the oldest mechanic in the dealership by a decade, and his co-workers sometimes joked that he moved with a sluggishness better suited for a nursing home.

Yes, Dan agreed, that was probably true. Wrenching was young man's work. But it was work nonetheless, and he continued to do it.

He had never considered retirement, partly because it had never seemed like a realistic option. He and his wife, Joyce, had bought the double-wide trailer a few years back for $60,000, and now it was worth less than what they owed. Their credit card debt had skyrocketed as his hours plummeted, and they were digging out on a regimented payment plan. Dan thought he would keep wrenching into his sixties and then try for a job shaking hands at Walmart. A chair to rest his feet, air-conditioning, a lunch break—that sounded about like retirement to him. He had always done physical work, dropping out of high school to join the service and using his VA benefits to attend automotive trade school. He had fixed cars while Joyce worked as a pharmacy tech, and together they raised four kids on hourly wages. Just in case the kids didn't learn by example, Dan had often repeated one of his mottos: "Work hard and anything is possible." In the early 1990s, determined to teach the kids a lesson about stick-to-itiveness, he had gone back to high school three nights a week and earned a diploma he didn't need, posing for celebratory pictures in his cap and gown while wrapping his arm around Jen. Now, at the kitchen table, he looked up and met his daughter's stare.

"Bankruptcy?" he said, finally.

"There's no choice," Jen said again.

"Well, then I guess you're right. I'm not going to like it."

"But do you understand?"

"No, not really. You have always worked, and you and Jay can work your own way out of this. If you just file for bankruptcy, you're not paying anything back. It's making a joke out of the system. I don't believe in it."

Jen fell quiet. She wore fashionably torn jeans and curls of her hair fell over a green sweatshirt. Despite the cancer, radiation, plastic surgery, and the constant diet of Twizzlers, she still always made sure to look good. She had inherited her father's pride, but lately it had manifested itself primarily as shame. She felt guilty for being on unemployment and even worse when MARVIN called to offer her a fourteen-week extension on the $850 a month. Food stamps embarrassed her, so she often tried to use a cashier at the far corner of the grocery store where no one could see her pay. She believed in the principles of government assistance—they were the reason she usually voted for Democrats—but hated the idea of relying on them herself. They were meant for somebody else, she thought, somebody more desperate. She told friends that her family was living above the poverty line, even when she knew it wasn't. After her own bankruptcy hearing, she had gone to a bar and drank alone for one of the few times in her life, each successive margarita only amplifying her depression. And now, talking to her dad about bankruptcy again, she felt her eyes begin to well up and her stomach knot from a pain that had nothing to do with chemotherapy.

"I feel horrible," she said.

"I know," he said.

"Then why are you making me feel worse?"

"I'm not. I just want you to make the right decisions."

"But you're making me feel guilty."

They sat across from each other in the dining room that doubled as an office that tripled as a playroom. They had both endured rough times, and Jen had often persevered by relying on her father. Her eldest brother had been murdered in the 1990s, shot point-blank by a disgruntled guest whom he had kicked out of a house party, and Jen and her father had sat next to each other in a courtroom for weeks, crying during the trial and celebrating the murderer's guilty verdict.

Jen had sought her dad's advice when her first marriage ended in divorce after six months. The family had grown closer over the years, and Dan loved Jay and adored the two grandkids. He visited them every two or three days. Dan had already lost one child, and even now the grief resulting from that tragedy was only manageable when he was surrounded by his other kids. He took a deep breath and looked up from the spaghetti.

"Look, do what you have to do and get through it," Dan said. "You know we'll support you."

"Okay, thanks," Jen said. "Now let's talk about something else."

. . .

While Jen and Jay prepared to file for bankruptcy, Obama left the White House early one morning determined to prove that he understood problems like theirs. He walked across the South Lawn with an aide who carried his briefcase, and they climbed into a helicopter that flew over Washington's rush-hour traffic to a secluded airport in Virginia. Seven military officers waited at full attention on the tarmac, and Obama returned their salutes before walking up the carpeted stairs onto Air Force One. He spent the flight in a private suite with an office and a conference room. When the plane landed one hour later in Nashua, New Hampshire, a team of snipers watched from the roof of the airport hangar and a nineteen-car motorcade idled at the ready.

The purpose of Obama's visit was to connect with America's besieged working class, but his every movement indicated a life apart. This was the phenomenon he referred to, often derisively, as "the presidential bubble"—a feeling that he had been quarantined from the people he governed, forced to deal with an expanding public spotlight and a shrinking security perimeter that left him little personal space. All modern presidents faced a similar predicament, but none had been so closely guarded as Obama—the first black president, governing in the age of terrorism, with two wars continuing abroad. He had been given full Secret Service protection eighteen months before the 2008 election, the earliest ever for a presidential candidate, and aides who lauded Obama for his tranquillity had seen him fume over a succession of Secret Service restrictions. No more daily walks. No more personal e-mailing. No more spontaneous meals at restaurants. No more unscripted movements in public.

"It's the hardest thing about being president," Obama said shortly after taking office. "I mean, how do you stay in touch with the flow of everyday life?"

American leaders have strived for normalcy ever since the late 1700s, when the founders met in Philadelphia and decided it was essential for presidents to live like regular citizens so they could understand firsthand the problems of the people they governed. George Washington and Thomas Jefferson turned down architectural plans for a presidential palace in 1792 and instead asked for a president's house, one-fifth of the proposed size. Jefferson kept the doors of the mansion open so random visitors could come and go as they pleased, rifling through the artifacts of Lewis and Clark's journey and sometimes joining the first family for lunch. Andrew Jackson invited his inauguration crowd to celebrate inside the White House in 1829 and thousands came, breaking dishware and spitting tobacco juice on the floor until Jackson lured them back out by placing bowls of liquor and punch on the front lawn.

John Quincy Adams went for daily swims alone in the Potomac River. Martin Van Buren walked by himself in the nearby woods. Abraham Lincoln strolled unprotected through the city. Ulysses S. Grant received a $20 speeding ticket for racing his horse down M

Street. Near the time of the Civil War, a practice exam in a popular schoolbook captured the spirit of the presidency:

> *How are emperors and kings protected?*
> By great troops of guards; so that it is difficult to approach them.
> *How is the president guarded?*
> He needs no guards at all; he may be visited by any persons like a private citizen.

But then Lincoln was shot and killed during a play at Ford's Theatre while his lone army guard left his post to have a drink at a nearby bar. James Garfield was assassinated in 1881 while walking through a train station near Baltimore, and William McKinley was killed twenty years later while mingling with the crowd during an event in Buffalo. Finally, in 1906, after a raging debate in Congress about how to balance presidential safety with presidential accessibility, the Secret Service took charge of protecting the president and assigned twenty-seven men to the job.

Over the years, that number multiplied with each successive threat. After the bombing of Pearl Harbor, the Secret Service proposed camouflaging the White House, painting the windows black, and installing machine guns on the roof. Those suggestions were denied, but Congress voted to close the White House grounds to the general public and approved funds to increase the president's security staff to a hundred and forty. That number tripled in the aftermath of the Kennedy assassination, doubled again when a small plane crashed on the White House lawn in 1994, and doubled yet again after the terrorist attacks of September 11, 2001. By the time Obama flew to Denver in August 2008 to accept the Democratic nomination for president, more than a thousand Secret Service agents and five hundred FBI experts traveled along to ensure his safety. He was keenly aware that this created a problem: How could he connect and empathize with regular people if he was systematically separated from them?

"One of the things that I'm going to have to work on," Obama said, "is how to break through the isolation, through the bubble that exists around the president."

But a full year into his presidency, that bubble had evolved into much more than a personal nuisance. It had become a wedge that divided Obama from the public, from people like Jen and Jay.

As Obama arrived in New Hampshire, polls showed that one-third of Americans considered him to be "elitist." Nearly half believed he did not understand their problems. Almost two-thirds thought his economic policies had hurt the country or made no difference at all. His advisers had studied the data and discovered an obvious paradox: Obama was a president who had come from the middle class, and yet people still perceived him as being disconnected from it. The impression bothered Obama, but it drove his wife crazy. A few months earlier, while speaking at a high school in Indiana, Michelle had told the crowd: "When people talk about this elitist stuff, I say, 'Well, you couldn't possibly know anything about me.'"

As a means of reintroduction, the president had decided to launch a tour of working-class America early in 2010, making at least one trip out of Washington each week. His staff picked some of the country's most destitute places—many in swing states—and off Obama went, visiting farms and factories, diners and dive bars. To Elyria, Ohio, where he stopped in at Smitty's Place and split a burger with the mayor before paying with a crumpled $10 bill. To Tampa, Florida, where he spoke to a crowd about his own college debt and a family crisis that forced him to pull emergency money from his 401(k). To

Youngstown, Ohio, where he wore a flame-retardant jacket on a tour of a steel mill and posed for photos in front of a fire-breathing blast furnace. To Buffalo, New York, where his motorcade stopped at a bar for chicken wings and then passed by a billboard that read: DEAR MR. PRESIDENT, I NEED A FREAKIN' JOB. PERIOD. To Baltimore, Maryland, where he spoke from a makeshift podium inside a machine company, surrounded by blue-collar workers and their tools, and said, "I just like getting out of the White House, and then I like toolin' around companies that are actually making stuff."

And now, on this cold February morning, to New Hampshire. Obama stepped off Air Force One, walked ten paces, and ducked into the Beast, his custom-made limousine with armor-plated doors and pump-action shotguns, which had been flown in on its own special plane the night before. The limousine sped down the barricaded freeways, surrounded by its motorcade, and stopped at a quiet manufacturing park. Obama spent ten minutes inside one of the warehouses to tour a small business, pausing to study chemicals and admire machinery while a dozen photographers snapped pictures. Then the president disappeared back into the Beast, which traveled two miles to a high-school gymnasium.

This was the day's main event: a twenty-minute speech followed by a simple question-and-answer session in front of a crowd of three thousand. But Obama's own plan for the afternoon was much more involved. He hoped to connect with the unemployed despite holding the country's most prestigious job; to disparage Washington politics despite being a product of them; to have a self-described "direct conversation with the folks of New Hampshire," even while bomb squads waited on the high-school soccer field, Secret Service officers patrolled the gymnasium aisles, and fourteen television cameras zoomed in on his every move.

The owner of a local manufacturing business introduced Obama, who stepped onstage to a standing ovation. He took off his jacket and rolled up his sleeves. "I've had beers here at Peddler's Daughter, and I've manned the scoop at ice-cream socials from Dover to Hudson," Obama told the crowd, recalling his travels across New Hampshire during the presidential campaign. Gone was the president whose intellect could be mistaken for condescension and whose composure could seem like detachment. Now Obama started his speech with a series of jokes, dropping his g's and departing from scripted remarks to talk about "leakin' roofs" and "buyin' new curtains." He suggested that elected officials "stop playin' politics, get beyond the Washington game." He stuffed one hand in his pocket and referred to "folks" thirteen times, usually when he was attempting to empathize.

"We've gone through the deepest recession since the Great Depression, and folks here have had their lives uprooted by lost jobs and foreclosed homes, shuttered businesses, vanished savings," he said. "Many good, hardworking people who met their responsibilities are now struggling, in part because folks on Wall Street and people in Washington didn't meet their responsibilities. Now, these are the things that I hear about every day in the letters I get—from families going bankrupt; from small businesses crushed by their health-care costs. I am not going to walk away from these efforts. I am not going to walk away from these people."

He pounded his fist on the lectern for emphasis. When he finished his speech, he took questions from the crowd, calling on people "in the order of boy-girl, boy-girl," he explained. He answered questions about health care, energy efficiency, and government transparency. Then, after the sixth question, he held up his hand. "Sorry, but we're out of time," Obama said, even as hundreds of people continued to raise their hands. "Sorry," he said again, this time pointing apologetically to a cadre of aides and Secret Service agents who were motioning to the president and pointing at their watches. He stepped off the stage, lingering in the gym for a moment to shake hands and slap backs while his assistant, Reggie Love, followed behind with Obama's jacket and lip balm. Then eight Secret Service agents surrounded Obama and whisked him out a side entrance. He had been with the folks of New Hampshire for almost two hours, and their time was up. He climbed back into the Beast, back onto Air Force One, and back inside the bubble.

.   .   .

A few weeks later, Jay and Jen took their first airplane flight in years. Jen had finished chemo, and they could travel for free from Detroit by waiting for standby seats on Delta flights because of Jay's job. They scheduled a belated honeymoon to Arizona and Nevada since Jen had never been out West. They planned to stay with friends and cook their own meals, outlining a vacation that would cost less than $500 and provide them a break from budget crunching, the duplex, and the bleak Monroe winter. They drove to the airport in Detroit hoping to board the first plane with empty seats to Phoenix or Las Vegas. They ended up waiting through fifteen overbooked flights, eating five consecutive meals at the airport, and sleeping in the concourse for two nights before finally securing seats.

The eight-day vacation was great, but the trip back was just as brutal. They waited in Phoenix until Delta found empty seats on a plane to Memphis, which was as close as they could get to a flight home. From there, Jen and Jay rented a car and drove 720 miles through the night, making it back to Michigan just in time for Jay to report for his next graveyard shift at the airport. He worked graveyards the next three nights and woke up early on his day off to install his first swimming pool of the season. The job was in Riverview, a nice neighborhood south of Detroit, and Jay hauled loads of dirt in a wheelbarrow for nine hours while the owner supervised from a rocking chair on the porch. Jay stopped on his way home to pick up dinner for the family at Arby's. When he walked into the kitchen, Jen was waiting for him at the table, surrounded by financial forms and a manila folder labeled: "Bankruptcy."

"Really?" Jay said. "Do we have to deal with this right now?"

"Yes, because we're running out of time," Jen said. "The bankruptcy hearing is a few days away."

Jay dropped the Arby's bag on the table and slumped into a chair. "Okay," he said. "Let's get it over with. What do we need to do?"

"We should go through all this and make sure everything is here," Jen said. "Twenty minutes. Then we're done."

While they ate roast beef sandwiches, Jen pulled financial papers from the manila folder and studied them one at a time. The first was from the United States Bankruptcy Court, announcing case number 10-45682-wsd, for Jason Stanley Cline. He was filing for Chapter 7 bankruptcy, which, if granted, would erase all debts but remain at the top of his credit report for ten years. The next sheet was from the IRS, demanding unpaid tax payments of $5,051.84. Then came a bill for $10,672.67 from a videography class Jay had taken a few years back, which he had enjoyed but never put to practical use. Then a Sprint phone bill for $367; a doctor's bill to treat a dislocated shoulder for $679; and the papers for a used Dodge Charger, which Jay had bought after agreeing to an inflated interest rate of 24.24 percent.

The next stack of paperwork dealt mainly with Jay's pool business, debts that added up to more than $35,000. There were bills for pools he had bought but never sold and demands for rent he never had paid. There was a $15,000 lawsuit stemming from an incident when one of his employees had cracked the lining of a pool during installation, and Jay had been too broke to install a new one for the customer.

"So many bad memories," Jay said, leaning back from the table. "I hate looking at this stuff. What's the point? It just makes me feel like a loser."

"I know, but we're dealing with it now," Jen said. "That's all we can do. Won't it feel great to have it off your mind?"

"Yeah, it would," Jay said. "I just hope they grant us Chapter 7 and that's it."

"They will. They have to," Jen said. She gathered the paperwork and stuffed it back into the manila folder.

·   ·   ·

Two days later, they woke at six on the morning of the bankruptcy hearing, looking as if they had never slept. Jen had broken her ankle the day before in another stroke of bad luck when she tripped going down the stairs, and now all she could think about was Vicodin and a cigarette. Jay had a headache that was threatening to become a migraine. He walked out of their bedroom to discover three loads of unfolded laundry spread across the living-room floor, crusty dishes sitting on the kitchen table, and their youngest son, two-year-old Jayden, awake and wailing because of an earache.

Jay checked on the earache and then escaped with Jen to the back porch, where each had stored a half-smoked cigarette from the night before. This was their latest concession to the economic collapse: to smoke each Marlboro Medium in two shifts. The plan was meant to cut their consumption in half, but instead they were smoking twice as often, still burning $13 a day on two packs and wasting gas to drive ten minutes to a Walmart that offered the best cigarette prices. Jay smoked his half cigarette down to the edge of the filter and flicked it into the air.

"I don't know if I can do this," he said.

"You have to," Jen said.

"I've got five hours of work left to finish this pool. I've got the late shift tonight at the airport. We've got one kid screaming and another going on a field trip. You're hobbling around on crutches. My head is killing me. But I have to drop everything and drive all the way to Ann Arbor so I can prove that we're broke?"

"I'm sorry," Jen said. "There's no choice."

Jay went back inside and searched through his closet for an outfit. The last time he had dressed up was for their wedding, five months and fifteen pounds ago, and now his favorite pair of slacks refused to button. He found another pair of wrinkled khakis stuffed in the back of the closet and smoothed them with the iron. They fit, but he couldn't find a belt to match. He walked to the bathroom mirror and tried to knot a tie—once, twice, three times, and still the thing ended up dangling above his belly button. "Damn it," he said. He threw the tie back in the closet and went into the living room to show Jen his partial outfit.

"You look good," she said.

"I feel like an idiot," he said.

Jen went outside to smoke another half cigarette, and Jay disappeared into the closet again. This time, when he came out, he didn't ask for feedback. He was wearing skateboard shoes, jeans, a frayed cloth belt, an oversize Detroit Tigers T-shirt, and a baseball hat stained white with sweat marks. He tucked a cigarette behind each ear and grabbed his car keys. "This will have to work," he said, and then kissed Jen goodbye before she could object. He drove across the street to a Tim Hortons to order a "three and three," a coffee with three creams and three sugars. Then he pulled onto the highway and headed for Ann Arbor.

Jay kept the radio turned off while he drove and thought about

all the other times he had traveled this highway. He had lived in Ann
Arbor for a few years in his early twenties, dated a college girl, and
worked on swimming pools when the economy was booming. Customers often had paid him in cash, so he traveled with a stack of $20
bills in his pocket. He had celebrated a friend's birthday at the fanci-
est steak house in town, where waiters refolded his napkin when he
went to the bathroom and the $8 salad looked like yard debris. Now
he drove past that restaurant and parked in front of the courthouse.
Framed photos of Obama and Vice President Joe Biden hung on the
wall of the entrance, just beyond the metal detectors. Directly above
those photos was a printed sign: BANKRUPTCY PROCEEDINGS, it
read, with an arrow pointing up the courthouse stairs.

Jay followed the sign to a second-floor lounge where bankruptcy
hearings had taken place every Wednesday for a year because the
courtroom was always overbooked. The bankruptcy lounge looked
like the waiting room of a doctor's office, with fake flowers at the
entrance, four televisions hanging from the ceiling, and back issues
of *Fortune* magazine an ironic choice spread across coffee tables.
Forty chairs were arranged around the room. The bankruptcy officiate, essentially the judge, sat in a tailored suit at a white folding
table, which was wedged next to a humming refrigerator where court
employees stored their lunches.

"This is like fast-food court," Jay said as he looked for a seat.

He found a chair near the back of the room and surveyed the
people sitting around him. There was an elderly black man wearing
mismatched tennis shoes, one red and one white; a motorcyclist in
a Harley-Davidson T-shirt with an unkempt, grizzly beard; an obese
woman whose jeans, worn too low, forced mounds of flesh to spill into
plain view. Later Jay would learn that many of these people had been
advised by their lawyers to look as destitute as possible, reinforcing

the impression of bankruptcy. It was the unspoken rule of bankruptcy court: Dress to depress, not to impress. In his stained baseball hat, Jay was the most dapper client in the room.

His lawyer, whom he had never met, arrived twenty minutes late, mumbled an apology about "bad bankruptcy traffic," and pulled Jay into the hallway for a consultation. "Thanks for coming, sir," Jay said. The lawyer had his hair slicked back with gel, and he casually tossed a pen into the air with his right hand. "Sure, sure," he said. "Glad to help." It was a good day for the lawyer. He would represent four of the other people filing for bankruptcy, earning $1,300 per case. Jay and Jen had already started sending him monthly checks as part of a payment plan, incurring one new debt in an attempt to erase all the others.

"So, remind me again why are you filing?" the lawyer asked.

"Lots of reasons," Jay said, "but mainly because my pool business went under."

"Really? I thought you guys made a lot of money in pools. My brother just bought an inground pool, and it's costing him thirty grand."

"We didn't get many orders like that," Jay said.

The lawyer shrugged and handed Jay a one-page form to fill out before he faced the bankruptcy officiate. Jay grabbed a pen and started to write. Under 2008 income with spouse, he wrote: "$14,000." Under 2009 income: "$23,025." He checked a few boxes, signed the bottom of the form, and handed it back to the lawyer.

"Okay," the lawyer said. "Here's how this is going to go. The officiate will call us up, and he'll ask you a few questions. Keep your answers short and polite. There shouldn't be anything too confusing. If it all goes well, you'll be granted your bankruptcy. Don't be nervous. I do this all the time. Trust me. This is a piece of cake."

Jay nodded and they went back into the lounge, where the officiate stood to announce the beginning of the proceedings. The room
fell silent. Jay leaned forward in his seat to listen. One by one, people
filing for bankruptcy walked to the front of the room and sat across
from the officiate at the white table. They raised their right hands,
swore under oath, and offered their testimony—the soundtrack of a
recession.

Case One: "The primary reason I'm filing for bankruptcy is that
I was the owner-operator of a truck business. That went bad. Now I
have no truck and no business."

Case Two: "The only money we have coming in right now is from
my youngest son who lives with us and gets disability. Also, my girlfriend of twenty years sometimes tends bar, but that's not much."

Case Three: "I'm in sales, and there's no commission anymore. I
sell copiers and printers. It's a full-time job. A full-time job. And, sir,
I only made $11,000 last year."

Case Four: "My son is on welfare and not doing so good, so now
I'm supporting all five of the grandkids."

Thirty minutes into the hearing, the bankruptcy officiate stood
up from the table and called for "Jason Stanley Cline." Jay walked
to the front of the room with his lawyer and they sat side by side at
the white folding table. The officiate, Doug Ellmann, stared back at
them. He was a muscular man with a crew cut, a clenched jaw, and
dark circles under his eyes. He had been processing bankruptcy cases
every other Wednesday for twenty-one years, supervising what he
called a "nonstop parade of misery" from 8:00 a.m. to 4:00 p.m. It
had always been a hard job, but lately Ellmann had started to wonder
if it was becoming untenable. Bankruptcy cases were at an all-time
high, with more than 1.57 million people filing for it nationally during the twelve-month period ending on June 30, 2010—an increase

of 20 percent over the previous year, which had also set a record. Ellmann dreaded Wednesdays, enduring them only because he rushed
directly from bankruptcy hearings to a martial arts class that, he said,
helped "release all that anger and tension built up after hearing about
the suffering and misery in the world."

He had processed 1,700 bankruptcies in 2009, his busiest year
ever, and he was on pace to work 50 percent more in 2010. The prepa-
ration for each case required 60 pages of paperwork, but no amount
of groundwork made the face-to-face meetings any easier. People filing for bankruptcy seemed more desperate than ever, he thought, and
more likely to snap. They shouted. They cried. They slammed their
fists on the table. Lately Ellmann had been forced to call in the court
marshal to handle a violent outburst about once a month. He thought
of his job as similar to that of an emergency room physician. "After a
while, you've seen a lot of the same pain and suffering," he said. "You
know the stories. People are sick, unemployed, homeless. Every case
is depressing. I don't want to say you become jaded, necessarily, but
you have to look at their problems objectively and move forward in an
efficient manner to the next case."

Now Ellmann looked across the table at the next case: Jason Stanley Cline, case number 10-45682-wsd.

"So," Ellmann said, "what caused the bankruptcy?"

"I went into business at a bad time, in a bad location, and a lot of
my debts stem from that," Jay replied.

Ellmann looked down and studied Jay's bankruptcy filing. Not
long ago, Ellmann had believed that most bankruptcies resulted
from "avoidable mistakes," but now he wasn't so sure. He saw in
Jay's paperwork a familiar combination of bad luck, declining wages,
housing foreclosure, and unemployment—the story of Michigan's
economy at the beginning of 2010. Sometimes Ellmann studied a

case and thought immediately of a favorite expression: "There but for the grace of God go I." He continued to do his job, he said, because the paycheck kept him on the right side of the white table. He looked across at Jay.

"Is everything you filed here accurate?" Ellmann asked.

"Yes, sir," Jay said.

"Then I have no further questions. That completes your exam."

Jay stood up and walked out of the courtroom. The lawyer followed him into the hall and squeezed his shoulder. "No further questions means they're going to grant you the bankruptcy," the lawyer said. Jay nodded. He shook the lawyer's hand, walked out to his car, and drove back to Monroe. He called Jen from the road. "It's done," he said. "Let's celebrate."

They met at a Mexican restaurant in Monroe, where the lunch entrees cost $4.95 and came big enough to split. Jen leaned her crutches against the wall and wrapped her arms around Jay when he pulled into the parking lot. They smoked their half cigarettes and then went inside to order, a beer for him and a margarita for her. It was 11:15 a.m. Jay had to work later that night at the airport; Jen had to take Jayden to the doctor to check on his earache. The restaurant was empty. Mariachi music played in the background. They sat on the same side of the booth, holding hands. Jay took off his hat, smirked, and raised his glass.

"To bankruptcy," he said.

"To bankruptcy," she said.

"To fresh starts," he said.

"To fresh starts," she said.

"To 2010," he said.

"To 2010," she said.

CHAPTER 2

"My own path to the presidency was met with many challenges."

Stefan Johnson's link to the president began with a simple nickname. Obama. That's what Stefan's teachers and classmates started calling him early in 2008. He had the same pointed ears, same skin tone, same hand gestures, and the same measured manner of speech. There were worse things a black kid could be called at a Catholic high school in South Philadelphia—worse things he *had* been called. So, sure. Obama. He embraced it.

As the 2008 presidential campaign wore on, Stefan began to notice some other similarities. Like him, Obama was a black man who had been abandoned by his father, raised by a single mother, and brought up as an outsider in private schools. Like him, Obama sometimes had grown up poor and subsisted on food stamps. Stefan, seventeen, had always paid attention to politics, but he started devouring information about Obama, reading his autobiographies,

buying copies of *Jet* magazine that featured him on the cover, and saving newspaper clippings about his campaign. He went by himself to
an Obama rally late in 2008 and waited three hours to hear a twenty-
minute speech. More than thirty-five thousand other people came,
and Obama implored the audience to "shed cynicism, doubts, and
fears and believe in the possibility of America again." Inspired, Stefan
signed up to volunteer at Obama's local campaign office and devoted
his weekends to making cold calls. He knew little about Obama's politics, so he made his pitch for Obama as a role model. "He's somebody
we can all look up to," Stefan told strangers who picked up the phone.
"He's inspirational enough to bring this country back together."

Stefan had earned a reputation at Roman Catholic High School
for being "standoffish and quiet," he said, but during the election
he finally started to engage. He wore an Obama button to school and
debated politics with his peers and teachers. Many of his classmates
supported Republican John McCain, and each year the school organized a field trip to Washington so students could participate in an
anti-abortion rally. Stefan was his school's first outspoken Obama
supporter, and his reputation skyrocketed along with Obama's:
unknown in 2007, promising in 2008, and coming into his own in
2009. On the day of Obama's inauguration, teachers and classmates
congratulated Stefan in the hallways and teasingly referred to him as
"Mr. President."

A few months later, Stefan started thinking about becoming a
politician himself. He had sometimes imagined running for president of Roman's class of 2010, but it had always seemed implausible.
No black Catholic had ever been elected student body president in
Roman's 120-year history. Presidents were usually white kids from
the suburbs or Italians from downtown. In a city subdivided by
neighborhoods and ethnicities, Stefan was the ultimate outsider. a

black kid in South Philly, surrounded mostly by Italians, Mexicans, Cambodians, and the Irish immigrants who lived half a mile from his house on Second Street, where the racism was so legendary that Stefan had only dared visit the Irish section once or twice. Most of the other black students at Roman came from West Philly, and they tended to vote for student president as a bloc. Whites voted for whites. Asians voted for Asians. Only football and basketball players had any chance at crossover appeal, and Stefan played neither. Every once in a while, a rich kid bought his way into office by handing out fancy T-shirts and bumper stickers, but that option didn't exist for Stefan, whose mother was unemployed and two months behind on his tuition bills.

And yet Obama had arrived out of nowhere to become president, Stefan thought, so why not him? He borrowed his idol's campaign slogan—"Hope and Change for a Better Roman Catholic"—and posted flyers across the school. Seven candidates ran against him. He borrowed a suit jacket and wore a flag pin during his campaign appearances and wrote speeches that mimicked Obama's pacing and echoed his theme of inclusiveness. "Roman can be a melting pot of unique cultures—black, white, Asian, and Hispanic," Stefan said. And then, in his final campaign speech: "I'm running to be the president for people from different classes and different backgrounds, from Tracks 1, 2, and 3, and even from different neighborhoods. So vote for me, Stefan Johnson."

Improbably, they did, electing him by a margin of six votes out of eight hundred ballots cast. The results surprised nobody more than Stefan, who had been so sure of defeat that he had never told his mother he was running. But the other three elected student council members—white, Hispanic, and Asian—signified the prescience of Stefan's campaign message. "The United Nations," other students

called the group. Their student council picture was hung on a wall at
the entrance of the marble-and-granite Gothic building, right down
the hall from portraits of the thirteen superintendents in Roman's
history, a row of white, graying, solemn-looking men that dated back
to the 1800s. "People probably think we rigged the election to become
the poster child for diversity," said Father Joseph Bongard, the superintendent in 2010. "But this is the great thing about the age of Obama.
It's a sign of the times."

Stefan embraced the presidency not so much as a job but as a new
identity. He used his sudden popularity to forge a group of friends
from across social cliques, playing in weekend basketball games in
West Philly and taking the city bus to attend parties in the suburbs.
He started a school recycling program, increased alumni donations,
and collected school supplies to send to Guatemala. He improved his
grades from mediocre to good. Most of all, he vowed to focus more on
his future and less on his past. No more fights with his mother about
how her diminishing income had forced them to move six times in the
last eight years, each time to a smaller apartment. No more brooding
about his father, who had been in jail since Stefan was born, serving
two life sentences for abetting in a murder. His father communicated
from prison only through infrequent letters about the Philadelphia
Eagles and the 76ers, even though Stefan rooted for the Baltimore
Ravens, Orlando Magic, and Philadelphia Phillies. Lately Stefan had
decided it was best not to respond, and his father's letters had become
increasingly pleading. "I would like to know why you don't write me
or send me a phone number so I can call you," one read. "Once again,
send me a phone number. I repeat, send me a phone number."

Early in 2010, Stefan decided to sit down and write to someone
else instead—a role model who had yet to fail him. He was midway
through his tenure as school president, and Father Bongard suggested

he write a letter about his experiences to Obama. Stefan agreed that a thank-you note would be appropriate. He sent along a picture of himself making a speech while wearing the suit jacket and flag pin, and he typed up a letter on his laptop until he filled a page. "I know you are busy, so I did my best to keep this brief," he wrote.

> *Just a few months ago, I embarked on a journey that would lead me to become the first African-American Catholic Student Council President since my high school's founding in 1890. My own path to the presidency was met with many challenges. I believe that my hardest transition was when I transferred from an inner city public school to a small private school; it was a completely different environment. I think that I struggled at times, to find myself.*
>
> *As President sometimes I am burdened with things I can't do which are completely out of my control. But I still enjoy being President. When I took the job, I realized that it wasn't going to be all good. But it's hard when you try to change things that are out of your control. Thank you President Obama, for inspiring me to do great things. You have been more of an influence than I can ask.*

A few months later, he received a short, handwritten reply from Obama himself—"Stefan, we are very proud of you, so keep it up"—and his mother laminated the note card and framed it in the living room. A Philadelphia newspaper wrote a story about his success and his exchange with the president. Classmates voted him Most Likely to Become President in the yearbook, and they signed Stefan's copy with effusive testimonials: "My favorite Prez!," and "Even better than the real Obama," and "Thanks for breaking friend barriers and track barriers to truly unite the Class of 2010."

He graduated with honors. His commencement speech ended in

a standing ovation. La Salle University in Philadelphia offered a substantial scholarship, and he planned to become one of the first in his
family to graduate from a four-year college. He would double major
in political science and communications. One day, he planned to run
for Congress.

But then, within weeks of receiving Obama's letter, Stefan learned
about a major hitch.

As graduation neared, his unemployed mother was still struggling to afford to buy a copy of his high-school diploma. The balance
of her bank account had dropped down to $28. They were on the verge
of being evicted. So how, Stefan wondered, could his mother possibly
afford to supplement La Salle's scholarship and help put him through
college?

·   ·   ·

For seventeen years, Monica Johnson had managed to send her son to
summer camps and good schools by working two jobs, living in cheap
apartments, and bartering with bill collectors. She considered herself a "master at getting by," she said, and she took pride in providing for Stefan without ever letting him glimpse the toll involved. "It's
just what us single mothers do," she liked to say. But now, at the worst
possible time, her delicate balancing act was verging on collapse.

She had been laid off as a secretary in the middle of 2008 and
let go from her second job as a receptionist a few months later. She
had signed up for unemployment assistance and spent the last year
scraping by on $1,600 a month, only to learn one month before Ste-
fan's graduation that her payments would not be renewed. The government had cut back on unemployment programs during the middle
of the recession, and Obama's attempt to extend payments across the
country had stalled in Congress. Now Monica was searching the clas-

sifieds and applying for secretarial jobs, even though she doubted
anyone would hire a secretary "who is forty-nine, tired, and over-
weight," she said. She was watching C-SPAN for the first time in her
life to track the congressional hearings on unemployment extensions, praying that the confusing back and forth between Obama and
the Senate would somehow result in a check destined for her mailbox.
She was fighting insomnia, gaining a pound a week, and struggling
with depression. She kept the shades to their row house drawn and
stayed inside most of the day. Instead of volunteering at her church
to distribute food to the homeless, as she had before, she was bringing church food home for herself. The cable company had threatened
to stop service, and the electric bill was a month overdue. One afternoon, while Stefan was away at school, Monica picked up the phone
and called the local unemployment office.

"I'm getting ready to be homeless," she told the caseworker on
the other end of the line. "I'm not trying to make you feel sorry for me,
but it's the truth. I don't know what to do. The stress is killing me."

But by the time Stefan came home from school each afternoon,
Monica had hidden the collection notices, turned off C-SPAN, and
reopened the shades. This was graduation time—Stefan's time—so
she worked harder than ever to maintain the façade. She decorated
the outside of their house in Roman school colors: gold-and-purple
trim around the windows, balloons dangling above the gutters, and
elaborate ribbon forming a trail up the stairs. Their two-story house
sat in the middle of a littered block in a run-down neighborhood,
a place where graduating from any high school counted as a major
accomplishment. Graduating from a Catholic school as class president was an event that merited gloating, Monica thought. She taped
two gigantic photos of Stefan to the front window, one of him wearing
his cap and gown and the other taken in his prom tuxedo, and then

splashed gold-and-purple glitter around the images. Their happy house could be seen from two blocks away.

To celebrate on graduation weekend, Monica reserved a special room at Phillips Seafood and invited thirty-five members of the extended family to dinner. Stefan tried to convince her that the party was unnecessary, that he would be happy with a backyard barbecue, but Monica insisted. "We both worked too hard for this to let it just pass by," she said, and so Stefan agreed. Monica had also graduated from a Philadelphia-area Catholic school, and she had spent the last six years paying $5,100 for Stefan's annual tuition. He had attended public schools through seventh grade, but Monica had vowed to provide him with a topnotch high-school education. Roman had denied his first application, but Monica had gone to the school's office and pleaded for his admission. She had paid the tuition by abandoning her risky plan to run a jewelry boutique and taking on two jobs as a secretary, even though the work could be tedious. She and Stefan had almost never gone out to fancy dinners.

So they would celebrate. They dressed up, drove downtown, and gathered after graduation with distant aunts and uncles at the Phillips Seafood in the lobby of the Sheraton Hotel. They ordered $8 starter salads, $25 salmon, and toasted to Stefan. They lingered in the wood-paneled dining room for more than three hours. Some of the relatives offered to help pay when the bill arrived, but Monica waved them off. "Oh no, it's nothing," she said, but actually it was a little more than $1,600, which she could only afford to pay by borrowing $250 from her mother and the rest from her father. She promised to pay him back but warned that it might take awhile. She already had a long list of more urgent debts.

Stefan's graduation had come with a series of extra expenses: $1,000 for overdue tuition, $250 for class pictures, $100 for a yearbook, $175 for an end-of-year retreat, and a $300 "graduation fee" that included Stefan's cap and gown. Monica had tried to bargain with the school's billing department and then resorted to avoiding its phone calls for weeks at a time. "Owing $160 feels like owing a million when you don't have it and you don't know how you ever will," she said. The school required monthly payments, but Monica joked that her schedule had become more like biannual. Stefan did not find this funny; it looked bad for the class president to be so delinquent on payments, he said. The school had withheld his cap and gown because of overdue fees until hours before his commencement address, and Monica had only afforded his final tuition payment because of an unexpected, unannounced, last-minute $750 scholarship from teachers and staff that seemed suspiciously like an act of charity.

But they had made it. He had graduated. That was all that mattered.

Monica's relief lasted only a few days. Stefan's college acceptance letters had piled up in the mail: Hofstra, La Salle, and Pittsburgh—all charging upward of $40,000 a year. Stefan liked Hofstra best, but it provided no financial aid. "No way," Monica said. "We'll both be in debt for the rest of our lives." He also liked Pittsburgh, where he imagined himself packed into the student section at a big-time sporting event, waving at the cameras on ESPN. "Too far away," Monica said. "When would I see you?" That left only La Salle, a medium-size school in northwest Philadelphia that cost $44,000 a year. La Salle had offered Stefan a full scholarship to cover tuition. It shared the same Catholic principles taught at Roman. It was the only school that made sense, so Stefan made plans to enroll.

Meanwhile, Monica continued to gain weight, stare at the ceiling all night, and track the congressional debates on C-SPAN. Left uncovered by La Salle's scholarship were meals, textbooks, and rent

for a dorm room—expenses that would exceed $10,000 a year. The
rent on their row house was due in a few days, which meant another
$1,020 that Monica didn't have. Her job search so far had resulted in
two days of work for a temp agency, which had tentatively scheduled
her next shift for two months down the road. The only other hope
for quick cash was a reinstatement of her unemployment assistance,
which would result in more than $2,400 in back payments. "That's
my only way out," she said.

But she always had distrusted the government, and she felt particularly unsure about Obama. Did he have the fortitude to push
extended unemployment through a divided Congress? She doubted
it. She had voted for Hillary Clinton during the 2008 presidential
primaries because she thought Clinton had more experience and
more political savvy than Obama. Stefan had protested that an Obama
presidency would be more historic and more inspirational, but
Monica had only shrugged. "Voting for color is stupid," she had said.
Then, later, when Stefan was out of range: "Maybe he can afford to be
a dreamer, but I can't." She depended on politics not for role models
or inspiration but for results, and it was results she needed now.

. . .

Obama needed results, too, and for six long weeks he had failed to
make any headway. He had spent much of the late spring advocating
for a nationwide extension of unemployment assistance only to watch
Republicans in the Senate stall for several weeks and then vote it
down three times. More than 2.3 million of the country's most destitute people had already lost their payments, and 50,000 more joined
the ranks of desperation each day. Americans who had lost their jobs
during the recession now had no source of income—no way to pay the
mortgage or buy food. It was a national disaster, Obama said, and it
had also started to become a disaster for his presidency.

The economy had shown a few signs of stabilizing during the first months of 2010, and Obama had made a series of speeches celebrating steady gains by the stock market and incremental job growth in each of the last five months. But he had always heralded the unemployment rate as the ultimate indicator of economic strength, and by this measure the recession continued to drag on into the summer. The nationwide rate held steady at just under 10 percent; 17 percent of blacks and 13 percent of Latinos remained unemployed. Half of all unemployed people had been looking for work for at least six months, and one-quarter had been out of work for more than a year.

The recession had made the government's standard twenty-six-week unemployment plan vastly insufficient, and Obama and his aides initially assumed Congress would extend the payments with little debate. Over the last thirty years, it had become customary for Congress to extend unemployment during even minor downturns when the unemployment rate hit 7 percent. The Senate had voted for extensions fifteen consecutive times, always quickly and always with support from both Republicans and Democrats. Even in March 2010, when Obama had last pushed for an unemployment extension, the measure had passed easily through the Senate with seventy-eight votes, including nineteen cast by Republicans.

But now, in late June, both parties had begun strategizing for the midterm elections in November, and Republicans had united behind the theme of limited government spending. The unemployment extensions would add another $34 billion to the national deficit, which had just topped $13 trillion the previous month. Republicans in the Senate united at the Capitol to make a joint public statement about "wasteful government spending," and then voted against the extension three times, defeating it by a single vote and making Obama look powerless in the process.

As the Republican strategy hardened, so too did Obama's frustration, aides said. He not only believed that extending unemployment was a moral imperative; he also thought it could help propel the economic recovery. Some studies had shown that increasing unemployment assistance was one of the best ways to boost consumer spending. People who received unemployment tended to spend the payments quickly out of necessity, buying household essentials and groceries, whereas other government stimulus tactics like tax cuts and lump-sum checks sometimes went to wealthier people who set the money aside in savings accounts and mutual funds. Obama blamed the delay on politicking and gridlock in Congress. It was the same pattern that had made him dislike being a senator in the first place, he told aides— except at least now he had more authority to fight back.

As Monica and nearly three million others entered their second month without assistance, Obama and his staff began targeting Republicans with uncharacteristic vitriol. Robert Gibbs held two press briefings in which he opened by arguing for an extension of unemployment assistance, and Obama devoted two of his weekly radio addresses to the same topic. "Gridlock as a political strategy is destructive to the country," he said in late June. And then, in another radio address a few weeks later, after the Senate had voted against the extension again: "Too often the Republican leadership in the United States Senate chooses to filibuster our recovery and obstruct our progress. After years of championing policies that turned a record surplus into a massive deficit, including a tax cut for the wealthiest Americans, they have finally decided to make their stand on the backs of the unemployed."

Finally, on July 19, Obama invited three unemployed workers to the White House to help make what would amount to his final argument. He met with them in the Oval Office for a few minutes and then led them to a press conference in the Rose Garden. Obama stood at the podium, flanked by a laid-off maintenance worker from New

York, a former Honda car dealer from New Jersey, and an unemployed beautician from Virginia who now paid her monthly rent by borrowing from her father. "It's time to stop holding workers laid off in this recession hostage to Washington politics," Obama said. "It's time to do what's right—not for the next election but for the middle class." After his speech ended, Obama's press assistants led the unemployed workers through a series of interviews on the White House lawn. Jim Chukalas, the former car dealer, stood in the same tan suit he had worn while walking door to door to ask for jobs ever since being laid off in September 2008. "We've cut back on everything we can cut back on," he said.

Two days later, the Senate gathered to vote on unemployment for a fourth time. Carte Goodwin, a Democrat from West Virginia, had just been appointed to the Senate to fill the seat of Robert Byrd, who had recently died. Goodwin walked up to the clerk and cast his vote first, supporting unemployment extensions and essentially guaranteeing the Democrats of their sixtieth vote. But even still, Republicans stalled the voting for thirty hours, the maximum time allowed, to make one last statement of opposition.

Back inside the White House, Obama and his aides postponed their celebration to lambaste the Republican tactic as spiteful and reckless. Because of bureaucratic delays, it would be another two days before Obama could sign the final bill and another month before state governments could process and mail the new unemployment checks. Now that process would be drawn out for another day while Republicans stalled the vote.

"These people can't afford another thirty hours," Gibbs said.

. . .

By midsummer, Monica had run out of both money and ideas. She was elated that Congress had passed the extension, but her back payment of almost $3,000 from the government was not scheduled to arrive for another month. "I might be living in a shelter by then," she said. She had come up with an innovative, long-term financial plan after talking to a foster-care agency about housing a couple of eight- and nine-year-old kids once Stefan left for college. The agency paid a monthly stipend of $750 per kid or even more for those with behavioral issues, and Monica figured she could handle a lot. She didn't want to be alone in the house once Stefan left, anyway. It was a way to do "God's work while paying the bills," she said, and mothering had always come naturally to her.

But that solution hardly helped now, with the cable and phone already cut off, the rent a week overdue, and the landlord stopping by every few days to threaten eviction. Monica's insomnia was worse than ever, and during a long succession of sleepless nights she had stared at the ceiling and come up with only one solution. It was the last thing she wanted to do. One weekday in late June, she called a close girlfriend and told her about the plan. "It's going to break my heart, but I have to do it this afternoon," Monica said. Then she hung up the phone, sat on the stairs, and waited for Stefan to come home so she could have one of the most difficult conversations of her life.

Stefan had just started his summer job at a nearby swimming pool, and lately he had been working forty hours a week as a supervisor for the lifeguards. The job was a grind; Philadelphia had decided to staff its swimming pools around the clock to discourage break-ins and vandalism, and part of being a supervisor meant occasionally working the 10:00 p.m. to 6:30 a.m. shift. Stefan was the only black supervisor and also the only one under thirty, which he believed undercut his authority at a once-segregated pool still visited mostly by Irish and Italians. But the job paid $500 a week for ten weeks, and Stefan passed his long hours at work by spending the money in his head. He'd make $5,000 by summer's end, enough to finally buy a

used car, maybe visit a friend living in Europe, and even have some
spending money left over for his first semester of college.

He opened the front door to the row house after a morning shift
in late June and saw his mother sitting on the stairs. She looked like
she had been crying, he thought. He had almost never seen her cry.

"Ma, what's wrong?" he asked.

"I'm sorry," she said. "I never wanted you to have to deal with
this, but I need your help."

"Sure," he said. "What is it?"

"I'm out of money," she said, "and we need to pay the rent."

Stefan was quiet for a moment. He had known they were in trouble; they were always in trouble. But his mother had almost never
asked him to pay for anything. They had always scraped by, and now
he was so close to being raised and gone. In just a few more months he
hoped to be living in a dorm room, and maybe then his mother could
move in with relatives and never have to worry about making the rent
again.

"Sure," he said finally. "I can help."

He had yet to receive his first paycheck of the summer, so later
that afternoon he went to the bank and withdrew the balance of his
savings account. He had a little more than $1,200, most of it gradu-
ation money from friends and relatives, all of it just enough to cover
one month of overdue rent. Stefan wrote a check to Monica, and she
wrote a check to the landlord. She promised Stefan that she would
pay him back, but he waved her off. "It's no big deal," he said. He had
nothing to spend it on anyway, he told her. It was an easy lie to tell,
and for a while it seemed to make his mother feel better.

.   .   .

A few days later, as the prospect of Stefan's freshman year neared,
he and his mom woke up before dawn to take an express train across

town for their first trip together to La Salle University. The school required a final enrollment commitment and a down payment by the end of the month, and Stefan had yet to press his mother for either. He wanted her to see the place first. Now the school was hosting its Day One, an orientation for new students and their parents, and Stefan and Monica were supposed to arrive by 8:00 a.m. La Salle had promoted the day as "an eight-hour introduction to college life," and Stefan had been looking forward to it for weeks. But as they left their row house to walk ten blocks to the train station, Monica looked considerably less enthused. "Why does this thing have to happen so early?" she said. She wore gray sweatpants, a bandanna over her hair, and dark sunglasses to cover sagging eyes. She had failed to sleep again the night before. An old knee injury had been bothering her lately—probably because of the added weight, she guessed—and she could not afford the cost of a cortisone shot. She walked five steps behind Stefan on the sidewalk, limping dramatically.

"Slow down," she said. "This knee is killing me."

"Hurry up," he said. "We're going to be late."

They rode in silence, thinking about the day ahead. Stefan wanted to make a good first impression, come away with some new Facebook friends, maybe even meet a girl. This was the moment when he would begin building a reputation from scratch; he was no longer the Roman class president or the kid whose mother struggled to pay the high-school tuition bills. He wore a blue T-shirt, knee-length cargo shorts, and black shoes. Aviator-style sunglasses dangled from the neck of his T-shirt. It was a preplanned outfit specifically designed not to look preplanned. He wanted to come off to his new classmates as relaxed, confident, and cool—even if he felt like none of the above.

Monica sat across the aisle from him on the train, closed her eyes, and thought about money. She had read that the first bill to La

Salle would be due at the beginning of August, almost a full month before Stefan started school. On top of the free tuition, he had won another $5,000 community scholarship toward his room and board, but Monica guessed that still left at least $5,000 uncovered. And what about furniture for his dorm room, a television, clothes, or a new computer? She hoped to learn the financial specifics during orientation. How much did she owe? To whom? For what? By when? At least once she knew, she could try to borrow and barter with a goal in mind.

They got off the train in North Philly, climbed a set of stairs, walked past a row of towering maple trees, and arrived at La Salle. Monica had not been to the school in years, and she took off her sunglasses to survey the campus. All around were pristine white sidewalks, brick buildings, manicured grass quadrangles, wooden benches, and deep-blue ponds. The sun had come out, and birds chirped loudly enough to mask the sounds of city streets. Other people walked by them toward the orientation, smiling families who had traveled to La Salle from twenty-seven states. A disc jockey on the quad played uplifting, 1990s soft rock. Volunteers handed out free doughnuts and coffee. One La Salle employee walked up to Stefan and handed him a yellow T-shirt inscribed with the names of every prospective student in the class of 2014, and he found his printed on the back.

"It's beautiful here," Monica said, now barely limping, walking beside Stefan. "I can't believe we're still in Philadelphia."

"I know," Stefan said. "I told you this place was great."

They followed the rest of the families into an auditorium and took two seats near the middle of the theater. Jim Moore, dean of student life, stood alone onstage and spoke into a microphone. "Welcome to the beginning of the next phase of your life," he said. "You made a big decision and a big commitment to be in this room today." He started a slideshow that introduced the class of 2014—"a group that showcases our diversity," he said. It included students fluent in Ukrainian, Russian, and Spanish; a renowned accordion player; a professional dream interpreter; the fifth in line for the throne of Istanbul; and a Haitian teenager displaced by the earthquake. When the slideshow finished, Moore divided the students into groups of fifteen and dismissed them from the auditorium. Parents and students would be separated for the rest of the day, he said. Stefan stood up to walk out, and Monica grabbed his hand.

"You okay?" she asked.

"Yeah," he said. "You okay?"

Monica nodded, and Stefan headed to the quad to join his assigned orientation group. He formed a circle with fifteen other freshmen and their senior group leader, who suggested they start by playing icebreaker games. To Stefan, the teenagers around him looked like another handpicked advertisement for campus diversity: eight girls and seven guys; eleven white and four black; nine from Pennsylvania and six from out of state. Like Stefan, each freshman had created an outfit to cultivate the desired first impression. A kid with a Mohawk and an eyebrow piercing interrupted the group leader to ask if he could smoke a cigarette. A muscular teenager from the New Jersey shore wore a tight tank top and a baseball cap cocked sideways on his head. A soccer player was dressed head to toe in Adidas. A girl from Colorado wore a floral-print dress and kicked her sandals off into the grass.

Their first task was to go around the circle and name favorite movies—a throwaway game that had never before generated such anxiety and deep thought. The kid with the eyebrow piercing said that actually he preferred music to movies, mostly '70s and '80s punk rock like the Ramones, but if forced to choose a movie then probably his favorite was *Fear and Loathing in Las Vegas* because Raoul Duke reminded him of himself. The muscled teenager from the Jersey shore liked *The Hangover* because he also liked to "knock back a few beers and get hazy," he said, and he had seen the film, "I don't know, dude, like seven or eight times." The girl from Colorado believed that *An Inconvenient Truth*, the Al Gore documentary about climate change, was a movie that "opens your eyes and changes your life." They circled around to Stefan, who swayed side to side with his left hand buried deep in his pocket. Favorite movie? Favorite movie? He liked so many. Now only one could define him. He cleared his throat. "My name is Stefan," he said, "and I guess my favorite movie is *Head of State*, that comedy where Chris Rock becomes the first black president." The rest of the group chuckled and nodded their heads in affirmation. It was the perfect choice—funny, topical, slightly obscure, and with a touch of political heft. Stefan smiled as the next fidgety eighteen-year-old stepped forward and cleared her throat.

When they finished the icebreaker, the senior group leader walked them across campus to meet with academic advisers who would help them sign up for their fall classes. Stefan hurried for an empty seat between the soccer player and a well-dressed girl from North Philly. A middle-aged man in a jacket and tie stood at the front of the room. He told each freshman to sign up for five classes worth a total of sixteen credits. He told them to expect three hours of homework for every hour spent in class. He told them that the best students at La Salle treated their studying like a mandatory day job. "This is serious stuff," he said.

Stefan already knew he wanted to double major in communications and political science, so he flipped through a course book and started filling out his schedule. He wanted morning classes so he could apply for a job and work in the afternoon, and he hoped to keep his schedule entirely clear on Fridays. He picked Spanish, Intro to

Politics, Communications, and Freshman Forum. Before he could pick a fifth class, the academic adviser called the group's attention back to the front of the room.

"Okay, here's the big question," the adviser said. "How much do you think it costs to go to school here for one year?"

"How should I know? My parents are paying," one girl said.

"About thirty thousand," said another.

"Fifty thousand," said a third.

Stefan sheepishly raised his hand, and the adviser pointed at him. "It costs $44,420," he said.

"That's right," the adviser said. "It costs about $44,000 to attend La Salle University for one year." He turned on a slide projector and placed two transcripts on the screen. One transcript showed four consecutive years of straight A's; the other listed one D, three F's, and a series of withdrawals. "There are two paths you can take once you leave this room," the adviser continued. "This kid here, he aced his freshman year, graduated with honors, and took a job at a big accounting firm. Then there's this student, who failed after one year, with a zero GPA, zero credits earned, and $44,000 spent. We have thirty freshmen like that every year. Try to imagine how their parents felt."

Meanwhile, across campus, Monica was also being cautioned on the risks of her investment. The parents had been divided into small groups, and now Monica sat in the back row of a classroom and listened to an expert speak about university technology. She wrote down dollar figures while he talked. Students had the best chance to succeed in college, he said, if they bought a university-sold laptop ($650), a network cable ($75), antivirus software ($50), and a four-year insurance plan ($125). To avoid a lawsuit ($7,000) resulting from a child who downloaded music illegally on the Internet, it was wise to invest in at least one iTunes gift certificate ($100).

The next speaker handed out a piece of paper that detailed the choice between two meal plans: a seven-day, unlimited access pass to the dining hall ($2,980), or fourteen meals a week ($2,295). Stefan had a sensitive stomach—he struggled to digest pork, beef, and cheese—and Monica had always worried about his nutrition. She circled the unlimited meal option but then noticed a small notation in italics at the bottom of the page. *Listed price is per semester.* "Dear God," she whispered. "Are they eating gold?" She crossed out the unlimited option and circled fourteen meals a week.

La Salle was happy to accept credit cards for all payments—"We take American Express, MasterCard, or Discover, just like any store in the mall," the presenter said—but credit card payments would include an additional flat charge of 2.75 percent. Parents could pay an enrollment fee ($55) in order to then have their other payments automatically deducted each month from a bank account. Or they could send lump-sum checks to pay in full for each semester. In either case, La Salle "strongly recommended" its tuition-refund plan for dropouts ($359 per year) in case "your child's educational experience does not go as you hoped."

The session ended and Monica stood up, feeling dizzy. The next seminar on her schedule was entitled "Alcohol Use and Abuse: What Your Student Is Doing at 2 a.m.," but right now that sounded like a relief. She grabbed her notebook and walked across the hall to the alcohol class with the rest of the parents. On the dry-erase board at the front of the room, a diagram depicted increasing levels of drunkenness, from the DUI limit, to vomiting, to blackouts, to loss of consciousness, to death. Above the graph the instructor had written a message: "Compared to the national average, our students began drinking earlier, got drunk earlier, and have more family members with drinking problems." The parents entered the room quietly and slumped into their chairs. Monica sat in the front row. A substance-abuse counselor clapped his hands to welcome them.

"Okay, great! Thanks for coming," he said. "How's your first day here at La Salle?"

Nobody answered.

"Let me guess," he said. "You all just came from the money talk."

"Yep," Monica said. She curled her mouth into a wry smile and looked back over her shoulder at the rest of the parents. "And now we could all use a drink."

The parents laughed, and so did the instructor. The alcohol presentation lasted forty-five minutes, and then the parents walked back across campus to the auditorium to reunite with their children for the final event of the day. Monica sat down with two other single mothers and watched the door, looking for Stefan. "I hope he's okay," she said. A minute later, he walked into the auditorium flanked by a young man wearing Adidas and a well-dressed, pretty girl. The three of them were laughing. Stefan caught his mother's eye and flashed her a thumbs-up. She waved back. He walked to the front of the auditorium and sat with the rest of the students in a section labeled "Class of 2014."

The dean of students came onto the stage again. "I can already tell you are a special group," he said. He dimmed the lights and started another slideshow. It was a collection of photographs taken during orientation—images that showed Stefan and his group standing in a circle on the quad, touring their future dorm rooms, and filling out their schedules. A soft-rock ballad from 1997 called "Save Tonight" played on the auditorium speakers. Monica watched the slideshow and listened to the lyrics, which described the pain involved in saying goodbye to a loved one before moving away.

It was a sappy song, Monica thought—ridiculous, even. But she couldn't help feeling moved. It was true. Stefan would be gone soon, headed on to the next phase of his life. He had made all the right choices for eighteen years, and so had she. Now he was going to college. College! For a few minutes, she considered the accomplishment without thinking about the money it would involve. She thought about how she wanted to stop at the bookstore to buy a La Salle T-shirt and sweatpants, no matter how much they cost. She thought about saving extra copies of the orientation program and starting a college scrapbook for Stefan. She thought about coming back to La Salle for parents' weekends, random visits, and award ceremonies. She thought about throwing another graduation party in 2014.

They would make it work, she decided. No matter what it took, she would find a way to get him through these next four years, just like she'd found a way to get him through the last eighteen. He would commit to enroll at La Salle. She would use the first chunk of his scholarship for the down payment and take out a $5,000 loan to pay for his meal plan. A friend from church would buy his books. Stefan would take two jobs. Monica would continue to look for work while borrowing money from relatives.

The song ended, and the dean dismissed the students. Stefan walked to the back of the auditorium and found Monica still idling in her seat. She stood up and wrapped him into a hug.

"What was that for?" he asked.

"For nothing," she said.

"Are you ready to go, or do you want to look around more?" he said.

"We can go," she said. "We'll be back."

.   .   .

A few weeks before Stefan began his freshman year at La Salle, he boarded a train early one Saturday morning for a short trip to Washington. One of Obama's aides had also read Stefan's letter to the president and decided to invite him on a special tour of the White House. He was told to choose four people to join him for the trip, so he invited his mother, grandmother, a high-school friend, and Father Bongard. They left Philadelphia at 6:00 a.m. and rode business class on the Amtrak train. Stefan wore khaki pants and a tucked-in polo shirt; his mother wore a black dress with a white necklace and matching earrings. They stopped for breakfast at Washington's Union Station, walked outside into the late-summer heat, and hailed a yellow cab.

"Please take us to 1600 Pennsylvania Avenue," Stefan told the driver. And then, just to clarify: "We're going to the White House."

Ten minutes later, their cab pulled up to the curb of Pennsylvania Avenue and dropped them off in the middle of the mob scene. It was a Saturday in late July, the heart of tourist season, and hundreds of people crowded onto the barricaded street in front of the White House. Gay rights demonstrators shouted through megaphones. War protesters camped in tents on the scorched grass in a park across the street. Capitol Police officers with a gun attached to each hip patrolled on horseback. Children from a German summer camp jockeyed with a Japanese tourist group for the best viewing positions in front of the White House, posing for pictures, peering at the grounds through binoculars, and pushing up against the wrought-iron fence. A police officer rode over on his horse. "Stay back," he yelled. "Stay back. Nobody goes within three feet of the fence."

Stefan was going in. He walked up to a security gate with his small group, and they told the guards their names, birth dates, and social security numbers. The White House had already run background checks, and the guards cleared all five members of Stefan's party. They passed through one metal detector and then another security checkpoint before walking through the fence. A White House assistant greeted them and introduced herself as their private tour guide.

Stefan had been to the White House once before, for a shotgun tour with a gigantic school group in eighth grade. They had hurried through the White House in ten minutes and then raced along to Arlington National Cemetery, a few Smithsonian museums, and the national monuments before driving back to Philadelphia that same night. This time, he entered via the East Wing, passing a marble fountain and the first lady's vegetable garden before walking down the long hallway of the East Colonnade. It was typically quiet for a Saturday; Obama was out playing golf and the house was closed to big tour groups. Their footsteps echoed off the tile floor.

They walked into the president's library, stood under a gilded wood chandelier, and admired a 1796 portrait of George Washington. Then they climbed upstairs to the Green Room, where James Madison had signed the country's first declaration of war in 1812; to the Blue Room, where Obama had entertained leaders from seventeen countries; to the Red Room, where the walls were covered in satin and Obama had sometimes sat on the couch making last-minute edits to his speeches.

Finally, they proceeded past a collection of presidential portraits and into the East Room. It was one of the most famous spaces in the White House, where Richard Nixon had announced his resignation and where the coffins of Abraham Lincoln and John F. Kennedy had been placed for viewing after their assassinations. Stefan walked across the oak parquet floors to the far side of the room, his eyes locked on a lectern adorned with the presidential seal. He recognized it as the scene of some of the most important moments of Obama's presidency—prime-time press conferences and speeches pushing for the extension of unemployment payments. Stefan turned to face the tour guide.

"Can I stand up there?" he asked.

"Sure," the guide said.

He walked up to the lectern and looked out at the room, notic-ing the old Steinway grand piano sitting in the corner and the heavy golden curtains around the windows. He imagined the room full, and he pictured himself speaking to the crowd. Maybe he would be back here someday, he thought. It was unlikely, sure. But with all that had happened lately, he felt as though anything were possible.

The tour guide continued into the next room, and Stefan's mother and grandmother called for him to keep up. He had his own big moments ahead. College would start in a few weeks, and with it would come new friends, new interests, and probably a new nickname. He stepped down from the lectern, knowing that this marked the end of one of his life's great moments. But now he also realized something else: There would be so many more in the years ahead.

CHAPTER 3

"Thank you from my son, Doug, a lieutenant serving in Afghanistan."

Obama wrote his most personal responses to members of the military and their families, people whose lives had been upended by the wars in Iraq and Afghanistan. Such letters were often placed at the front of his purple folder so he would read them first. The president occasionally asked junior aides to compile research about a soldier so he could better personalize his response. He sometimes signed letters about the war with his first name only, writing: "Sincerely, Barack."

He told friends that letters about war were the most difficult to read—and also the hardest responses to write. One mother mailed him a letter the day after her son died in Afghanistan, because, she wrote, "I just want you to know what kind of hero he was." Others expressed relief at escaping combat or detailed their struggles with Don't Ask, Don't Tell or post-traumatic stress disorder. But the most gripping letters sent by military families reflected the uncertainty of war itself: The service members' stories were continuing to unfold, their fate still in doubt.

It was that uncertainty which had tortured Polly Chamberlain for five months. Her only son, Doug, was serving in a remote area of Afghanistan as a second lieutenant in the marines, and she had heard from him just once since his tour began. She hung a picture of Doug in full uniform on her refrigerator in Richmond, Virginia, and kept his handwritten letter—their only wartime correspondence—near her bed so she could read it again and again: "Mom, I must admit I am pretty homesick," he had written. "There is no rest here, even when I get to sleep."

Everything made her think about Doug, and sometimes the worrying became too much to bear. She walked down the main hallway of her house with one eye closed to avoid seeing a picture of Doug as a little boy posing next to Mickey Mouse at Disneyland, his hair sweaty and tousled, his innocent grin revealing teeth still too big for his head. The picture had always reminded her of one of their greatest days together. Now it represented all she had to lose. On the calendar in her kitchen she had marked off the months of Doug's eight-month tour as they passed, because doing something active gave her a false sense of control. November. December. January. February.

And now March, the month of Polly's fifty-fifth birthday. It was a landmark occasion, the official entry into her golden years, but all she wanted was to move on to April. She had no desire to celebrate. She worried about Doug. Her only other child, Anne, had recently moved to attend college in Maryland, so Polly was living alone in Richmond. She spent her birthday at work, sitting at her desk in a small not-for-profit corporation. A few hours into the day, her cell phone rang.

For the last five months, Polly had reacted to each cell-phone call with two thoughts in quick succession. It could be Doug! And then, just as she felt her heart begin to race: It could be news about Doug.

She carried her cell phone everywhere and sometimes checked her voice mail even when it displayed no messages. Now she stood up from her desk, paced across the room, and stopped next to a window where she usually had good service. She punched a button on her phone and answered. "Hello," she said.

The reception was scratchy and the volume faint, but she could tell from the first word that it was her son. "Happy birthday," he said. "Doug!" she yelled. He explained he had only five minutes to talk. Polly wanted to sob and tell him how much she loved and missed him, but she knew that would only make the call more difficult for him. She asked how he was doing. He told her that he was fine, that he loved her, that she shouldn't worry, and that he couldn't wait to come home. Then he said goodbye before the line went dead.

Polly sat back down at her desk, too excited to work. She felt overcome with gratitude. She called her daughter: Doug was safe! She called Doug's wife: He sounded good! She wanted to tell everyone, to write a thank-you letter to the universe. Later that night, back on the computer at her house, she pulled up a blank document on her computer and started to write. She had adored Obama since early in the 2008 presidential campaign, and lately she had felt sorry for him when she read about the foundering wars, the faltering economy, and the Tea Party's surging popularity. Obama had started to look old, she thought. Did he ever hear anything good? She decided to put his name at the top of the page and make this a thank-you note to him. "Dear Mr. President," she wrote.

> *I would like to say Thank You.*
>
> *I would like to say Thank You from my son, Doug, a lieutenant in the United States Marine Corps and presently serving in Afghanistan. He knows how much his family and friends love and support him, but he also knows that he is supported by his government.*

Thank You from his brand-new wife, Kris, who waits anxiously for her husband to come home, and who has a network of support from her larger family, the Marine Corps.

Lastly, I would like to Thank You for myself . . . I am only one small voice among millions, but my Thank You is very large. Please remember that, when there are so many of us talking at you, MANY of us are actually saying Thank You.

Polly printed the letter on green stationery bordered by red flowers and sent it to the White House. Several weeks later, she received a short, handwritten response in Obama's hand: "Thanks for the thoughtful letter," Obama wrote on a signature note card, before asking Polly to thank Doug for his "service to our country." Polly read the two-sentence letter again and marveled at the irony. She had an easier time communicating directly with the president than she did with her own son.

She placed Obama's note in her bedroom next to Doug's letter, in a drawer where she also stored her children's baby teeth and a curl of Doug's hair. It had been three weeks since his phone call, and her gratitude had given way to the same gnawing uncertainty. So many questions echoed in her head and nobody—not even the president— could answer them. Was Doug okay? Would he make it home? Would he be different when he returned? Would his new marriage withstand the stress of this separation? What was he feeling right now, far away in the desert of Afghanistan, while she sat in Richmond, Virginia, holding the president's letter?

. . .

He was lonely.

Second Lieutenant Doug Toulotte, thirty-one, had spent five

months in Afghanistan, and already it was beginning to feel like the only place he had ever known. He was in charge of a twenty-six-man platoon that roamed the desert in search of Taliban fighters and drug runners, but sometimes weeks passed with no sign of the enemy. Out here there were only camels and snakes, the infinite blue sky and a relentless sun. Doug studied the empty horizon through binoculars while on lookout each day and slept on the ground at night next to one of the platoon's four light-armored vehicles, called LAVs. In his sleeping bag, he sometimes imagined his journey home and connected the dots between the desert and the one-bedroom apartment he shared with his wife in Annapolis, Maryland: a twenty-mile drive to the nearest marine outpost, a helicopter transport to another military base, and flights to Kyrgyzstan, western Europe, Maine, California, and finally Baltimore. Suffering from the same sense of isolation, some other marines in Doug's battalion had begun referring to Afghanistan as "the moon."

The platoon had been given one satellite phone for calling home, but it had broken less than a week into the deployment. A quarter-inch piece of plastic had snapped off the battery charger, a maddeningly basic malfunction that had left the phone permanently dead and the marines essentially cut off from the outside world. Doug had been able to borrow a phone from another platoon about once every three weeks, but he was only allotted ten minutes and the calls usually dropped long before his time ran out. He had spoken with his mother once and his new wife five or six times. He tried to send occasional e-mails from a military base that had spotty Internet service, but, more often than not, he typed in the addresses of friends and relatives at the top of the page and then stared at a blank screen. How, he wondered, could he possibly bridge the gap between these two worlds, between home and the moon? It was not always possible, he decided. So he made a habit of keeping his mass e-mails simple and upbeat.

> Ladies and Gents—I'm coming to you from the future! I'm
> 10 hours ahead and found a spot where I could send a quick
> email. Don't respond because I won't be able to check it!

He had wanted to be in the military for his entire adult life, enlisting to become a pilot in the marines in 2001 while in college at Virginia Tech, only to blow out his knee and lose his spot a few months later. It had taken him six years to rehabilitate the knee and work his way through college, and by then the marines considered him too old to be a pilot. He was nearing thirty and building a life that terrified him—a job selling insurance, an apartment in the suburbs, a string of mediocre relationships. Only the military, he believed, could restore his sense of purpose. So he signed a series of age and medical waivers, joined the infantry as a reservist, and moved into the barracks with junior marines a decade younger.

One month before he started training, a mutual friend introduced him to a nursing student from Florida named Krissy. They fell in love during a succession of three-hour phone calls, became engaged on a snowboarding trip to Vermont, planned a wedding, and booked a two-week honeymoon to Hawaii. But the marines accelerated Doug's deployment, so he and Krissy squeezed in the wedding and canceled the honeymoon. They spent ten days together as newlyweds, moving into an apartment in Annapolis, combining finances, filling out wills, and teaching Krissy how to load and shoot a short-barrel shotgun to defend herself against intruders. On the day before he deployed, Doug came back from running an errand at the hardware store to find Krissy sobbing uncontrollably on the couch. "I just changed my name and moved across the country and now you're leaving," she said. "I don't have friends. I don't even have a job."

"I know I'm asking for a lot," he said. "But this is something I have to do. It will be over soon. It will be worth it."

But now he sometimes wondered: Was it?

I hope you all enjoy your Christmas! Please eat a little extra and drink a little more for me and the rest of us over here. And of course—keep the letters and packages coming! Every time they arrive it's like Christmas all over again!

Doug's twenty-six marines were all infantrymen between the ages of twenty and twenty-four. Some had volunteered to deploy on short notice so they could fight during the peak of the war; all but two had joined after September 11, 2001, expecting to fight. They had spent two years training to survive suicide bombers, improvised explosive devices, and firefights. Each marine carried a helmet, four armored plates, two tourniquets, burn dressing, a rifle, a pocketknife, and at least 180 rounds of ammunition. Superiors had routinely told them that action in Afghanistan was on the rise, casualties had increased, and Obama would soon be adding more troops to escalate the war. Some expected to step into a live-action video game. During their first nights in the desert, a few had thought up a potential slogan for the battalion: "Putting bullets in bad guys."

But five months later, their war had instead become a slow and steady routine. They were farther south in Afghanistan than any other U.S. troops, sometimes isolated from the rest of the war by more than fifty miles. They woke up each morning before dawn and burned their trash so the Taliban would not be able to follow their tracks. On the best days, after one of the marines had received a care package from

home, they would cook pancakes and summer sausage by holding a
shovel over the trash fire. Then they moved into position on another
hillside with sweeping views of the Helmand River and the Pakistani
border. They remained on watch for twenty-four hours before packing up their gear, driving a few miles to a new hillside, and beginning
the routine again. Lieutenants congratulated Doug's platoon for scor-
ing a tactical success: the Taliban, spotting the platoon's LAVs on the
horizon, limited its movement around the border. But for Doug and
his men, this also created a practical dilemma. What were they supposed to do with so much empty time?

> Nothing beats the adrenaline rush of hauling through the des-
> ert in an LAV in hopes of catching some unsuspecting Taliban
> "in the act." My Marines are still in great spirits, and continue
> to execute any of the missions I task them with.

The gunner started playing Sudoku. The medic listened to his
iPod while taking naps. Doug started a journal and read whatever he
could borrow from members of his platoon, tearing through magazines, trashy novels, and books about World War II and the Hell's
Angels.

While a few marines took turns surveying the desert on one-hour
lookout shifts, the rest of the platoon gathered in the shade behind
the tanks. They played six-hour games of categories—"Okay, now
let's name female movie stars"—and invented a way to play home-run
derby by swinging at rocks with a tent pole. They complained end-
lessly about their flavorless, military-issued food; about the hun-
dred-degree days that soaked them with sweat and the windy nights
that left them wet and shivering; about the poisonous snakes that
crept into their sleeping bags, boots, and flak jackets; about the lucky

marines stationed nearby at Camp Leatherneck, who slept in beds, ate soft-serve ice cream from a cafeteria, and talked nightly to their girlfriends on Skype.

Most of all, they complained about the boredom.

"This is bullshit."

"Where's the goddamn Taliban?"

"Why won't those bastards fight us?"

"When are we finally going to get some action?"

"What a waste of time."

"Counterinsurgency sucks."

We're kicking arse over here and starting to see immediate results. Our focus is still strong and we have every intention of taking the fight straight to the doorstep of the enemy (and sometimes inside).

Doug had been taught during officer training that it was impossible to satisfy junior marines, and he thought of that lesson as their complaints intensified. He was removed from his men by military rank, age, and maturity, but he shared some of their impatience. He tried to ease his mind by rereading intelligence reports about how his platoon was disrupting the Taliban and reminding himself that it would be better to return home with twenty-six bored marines than with twenty-one. He woke his men at odd hours and quizzed them on Taliban strategy to keep them alert. "Get complacent for a second and it can get you killed," Doug told his platoon, and every so often the men experienced a burst of action that proved him right. They detained forty-five suspected insurgents who were racing across the desert in two pickup trucks and found Taliban orders hidden inside the seats. They seized 6,100 pounds of black tar opium and 130 pounds of processed heroin. Then, a few weeks later, they found and destroyed 5,000 pounds of marijuana seeds.

On one terrifying afternoon, Doug had been shaving his face with a razor behind one of the tanks and studying his reflection in a hand-held mirror when an explosion echoed across the desert. BOOOOM. That noise meant one of three possibilities. Either a fellow marine had found a Taliban weapons stash and destroyed it; another platoon had run into an IED; or the enemy had fired a rocket that was still traveling in midair. Doug realized it was the third by the sound—a faint whistle that built to a shriek and then to the deafening roar of an approaching freight train. "Get the fuck down! Rocket!" he screamed, before diving to the ground. The Taliban sometimes fired rockets from as far away as four kilometers. The weapon was potentially deadly but also wildly inaccurate—it could kill several men or miss its target by a kilometer—and for three miserable seconds Doug imagined the possibilities. Would he die quickly, like the three marines from another platoon who had been blown up by a suicide bomber a few days earlier? Would he have his face and legs torn off, like they had? Would it hurt? Would his men know how to fight back without him? How pissed would Krissy be if she found out he had died because he'd been outside of the tank to do his mandatory daily shaving, risking his safety to follow a meaningless military protocol?

BOOOM. The ground shook from a second explosion, and Doug turned his head around to locate the blast. The rocket had landed long, charring the desert. He was alive. Alive by a few hundred yards.

Later that night, his heart still racing and his mind clear, Doug lay awake and thought about the war. He had come to Afghanistan seeking purpose and clarity, but instead he had a collection of disconnected snapshots. War was the American flag they had flown in defiance above their LAV after the rocket landed long. It was the ratty, diseased

cat that had tried to sneak into his platoon's sleeping bags until finally
one of the young marines, awoken one too many times, had solved the
problem with an ax. It was the intelligence reports containing photographs of marines killed in action, which were passed along to Doug
because of his rank but which he chose not to open. It was endless
boredom. It was intermittent terror. It was awe-inspiring sunsets,
star-filled skies, and beautiful lightning storms that made him miss
Krissy more than anything else. It was Afghanistan, a different world,
indescribable, the moon.

> This is probably dumb to say, but don't worry too much
> about me! I have 26 Marines in my platoon, and 136 Marines
> in my company to help keep me safe. I'll be home before you
> know it!
> Fighting the good fight . . .
> Love, Doug

. . .

As the end of Doug's deployment neared, Obama decided to make
his first visit to Afghanistan as commander in chief. He cut short a
weekend with his family at Camp David and boarded Air Force One
at ten on a Saturday night, dressed in slacks and a dark sweater. The
entire trip would be executed under the cover of darkness, and it had
been kept secret to ensure Obama's safety. Hamid Karzai, the Afghan
president, had been notified of the trip only hours earlier, and now
his aides rushed around the palace in Kabul to prepare a red-carpet
entry, an arrival ceremony with the color guard, and a formal state
dinner. Junior White House assistants and a small contingent of traveling media were given even less notice; they remained clueless as to
the destination even while they boarded the plane, forced to surren-

der their cell phones to the Secret Service before they were briefed about the trip at cruising altitude.

Obama was going to Bagram Airfield, into the heart of a war zone, twelve hours and forty-six minutes across the world.

Some of Obama's critics believed the trip was long overdue. The ongoing battle in Afghanistan—"Obama's War," some called it—had become a centerpiece of his time in office, and yet he had visited twenty-three other countries first. He had won the presidency in part by casting himself as a fierce critic of the invasion of Iraq (a "dumb war," he said) and a proponent of action in Afghanistan (the "good war"). He had committed more than 30,000 additional U.S. troops to the fight, most of them infantrymen trained for the front lines. Casualties had more than doubled under his watch—from 155 Americans in 2008 to 317 the following year—and the toll continued to rise.

Obama had angered Republicans and military leaders by sometimes appearing to treat the war less like an ongoing reality than an exercise in critical thought. In the fall of 2009, governing with typical deliberateness, Obama had spent more than three months contemplating whether or not to send more service members into Afghanistan. He had assembled twenty-five religious leaders to converse with him about the morality of war and then researched opinions on combat by Winston Churchill, Martin Luther King Jr., Reinhold Niebuhr, and Saint Thomas Aquinas. He had read *Lessons in Disaster*, a book about the Vietnam War, and asked his aides to prepare forty intelligence reports detailing military strategy. He had assembled a cadre of national security advisers for ten meetings, including one that lasted more than eleven hours. He had flown in the middle of the night to Dover Air Force Base to greet the flag-draped coffins of eighteen Americans killed in action and wandered through a sea of white headstones in Section 60 of Arlington National Cemetery, where service members who died in Afghanistan and Iraq are buried.

When he finally made his decision in December 2009, announcing he would swell the war with thirty thousand more troops in hopes of winning and then withdrawing quickly, he had spoken primarily of the "solemn responsibility" of being a commander in chief. Ben Rhodes, one of the speechwriters charged with helping craft Obama's remarks about the war, recounted his boss's instructions in an interview with *The New York Times*: "He was very clear we were not going to beat our chests," Rhodes said, "and we were not going to treat war as a glorious endeavor to be celebrated."

So how, then, could the commander in chief connect with and inspire a group of tired, beleaguered troops during a six-hour, overnight trip to Afghanistan? He had rarely interacted directly with troops during the first year of his administration, visiting Iraq once and making a few speeches at West Point, where the cadets had always treated him with a polite yet distant formality. Soldiers rarely wrote letters to Obama or spoke with him casually because they considered it disrespectful within the chain of command to offer criticism or feedback to a superior. Emotional connections with military members had instead become the territory of the First Lady, who had visited bases and convened roundtables to generate support for military families.

Obama landed at Bagram at 8:00 p.m. local time, changed into a dark suit, and boarded a military helicopter for Kabul. He met with Karzai for forty minutes at the presidential palace, ate a late dinner with local politicians, and then flew back to the air base. This time, 2,500 troops were waiting for him in an airplane hangar, standing in their military fatigues, awake beyond their military curfew at 11:25 p.m. Thousands more, like Doug, slept out in the desert and continued with their missions, only learning about Obama's trip days later. Back in Richmond, Polly saw a tidbit on the news about the speech, and the dark images of midnight in Afghanistan only reinforced the distance. For her, it was still early afternoon.

"How's it going, Bagram!" Obama said, waving as he entered the hangar and strode to a blue podium. "You know, it turns out that the American people let me use this plane called Air Force One, so I thought I'd come over and say hello."

Obama had changed outfits again, and this time he was wearing a brown leather bomber jacket adorned with the presidential seal on one breast and an American eagle on the other. It was the same jacket that the staff of Air Force One had given each president for the last forty-plus years, and Lyndon Johnson, Richard Nixon, and George W. Bush had all worn it while addressing wartime troops. It looked particularly like a prop on Obama, who had spoken at antiwar rallies only a few years earlier, and whose closest personal connection to the military was his maternal grandfather, Stanley Dunham, who had fought in World War II. As Obama stood before the troops in Bagram, he tugged at the jacket's sleeves and smoothed its zipper.

He started his speech with a five-minute list of people he wanted to thank—leaders in all three branches of the military, America's allies, and the citizens of Afghanistan—before clearing his throat and turning his attention to the troops. "My main job here today is to say thank you on behalf of the American people," he said, and then, during the next fifteen minutes, he spoke about combat with a new conviction. He described the war in the exact terms he once asked his speechwriters to avoid: It was a moral imperative—a glorious endeavor to be celebrated.

I know it's not easy. You're far away from home. You miss your spouses, your family, your friends. Some of you, this is your second or your third or your fourth tour of duty . . . If I thought for a minute that America's vital interests were not served, were not at stake here in Afghanistan, I would order

you all home right now . . . I anguish in thinking about the
sacrifices that so many of you make.

There's going to be setbacks. We face a determined enemy.
But we also know this: The United States of America does not
quit once it starts on something. You don't quit. The American
armed services does not quit. We keep at it, we persevere and
together with our partners we will prevail. I am absolutely
confident of that.

Al Qaeda and the violent extremists who you're fighting
against want to destroy. But all of you want to build, and that
is something essential about America. They've got no respect
for human life. You see dignity in every human being. They
want to drive races and regions and religions apart. You want
to bring people together and see the world move forward
together. They offer fear, in other words. You offer hope.

By the time Obama finished his twenty-minute speech, the
troops' polite applause had turned to stomps and whistles. They
pressed toward the stage, and Obama shook hands for a few minutes.
Next he stopped by a hospital on the base to visit with injured troops
and made one final appearance at a military cafeteria, where a dozen
service members turned off a basketball game on television and stood
in line to shake his hand. He returned to Air Force One just after 1:00
a.m., still wearing his bomber jacket, ready for another twelve-hour
flight that would put him home before his family returned from Camp
David.

As Obama's plane rose safely into the air, the Taliban fired a
rocket toward Bagram. The familiar noise echoed across the base:
BOOOM! The ground shook, emergency alarms sounded, and the war
continued.

.   .   .

Doug was supposed to return home in less than four weeks, and Krissy had started to feel nervous. In the two years since she met her husband, she had never spent more than fifteen consecutive days with him. Theirs had always been a long-distance relationship—Florida and Maryland, Virginia and Florida, Maryland and Afghanistan— but never before had she felt this isolated. She was alone in a one-bedroom apartment in Annapolis, a city where she knew nobody. Doug had called six times in the last eight months and e-mailed only once every week or so. Her main connection to him had become a nondescript voice mail that he had left on her answering machine just before he deployed, which she had saved and replayed a dozen times when she was desperate for the sound of his voice. "Hey, it's me. Uh, I guess I missed you." They had occasionally exchanged pictures through e-mail, and a few weeks earlier she had clicked open the most recent image to see a man who looked gaunt and serious, his face hidden by sunglasses and a rifle slung over his left shoulder. She had stared at the picture for almost a full minute. Was it really her husband?

The last eight months had been the slowest and most difficult of her life, but she had learned to manage. Early in Doug's deployment, after a few weeks with no word from him, she had done a Google search for "Afghanistan and marine and dead," resulting in an Internet deluge of tragedy and gore that turned her concern into panic. She had cursed herself for indulging her imagination and vowed never to search online again. After that, she had decided to avoid hearing about Afghanistan, the war, the marines. "Doug is just at work," she had told herself, repeating the mantra over and over, and sometimes it helped. But the days still crawled by, and the holidays were most depressing of all. She had sent an e-mail to Doug just before Christmas:

Hey babe—I've just been feeling really lonely the last few days.
I just can't help but be jealous of all the wives that get regular
phone calls. They're always saying things like, "the sound
of his voice makes everything better," or, "hearing my husband say HI is the most wonderful sound in the world," and
corny shit like that. I just don't care to hear about it . . . Bah-
humbug.

I have a feeling that I'm going to get a little emotional and
opt out of some of the festivities. I don't want to celebrate
anything. I don't want to be thirty. I don't want any gifts. I just
want it to be June.

She wrote to him again on Valentine's Day.

Geez! No flowers?!?! lol! That's OK. Your sister and I boycot-
ted Valentine's Day by pigging out on chocolate and going to
see the movie Dear John. So, it wasn't a total loss. ;)

I've been thinking about a lot of things lately . . . Our
engagement. The night we met. The night we tried to make-
out on the beach and got rained on. Etc. . . . I think about you
all the time, babe. I can't wait until you get home and we can
make some more memories TOGETHER!

She had tried to pass the time by sending e-mails to Doug every
few days and embracing her new role as a military wife. She brokered
a deal with one of Doug's ex-girlfriends over a condo Doug and the
ex-girlfriend owned together, visited a financial counselor to sort out
Doug's college debt, and became best friends with her sister-in-law,
Anne, seeing her a few times every week. She traveled to Richmond
to celebrate her thirtieth birthday with Polly, bonding with her new
mother-in-law by looking at pictures of Doug and listening to sto-

ries about his childhood. Doug had left Krissy in charge of a saltwater
fish tank, so she adopted his obsession as her own, mastering tem-
peratures, nitrates, and pH levels and then setting up a second tank
to surprise him. She passed a grueling nursing exam and applied for
dozens of jobs only to amass a stack of rejection letters. "I WANT TO
WORK!" she wrote in an e-mail to Doug after five months of unemployment. "I WANT to make some money! I hate feeling like such a
loser." So she decided on a whim to put on a business suit and drive
to a local hospital, where she idled in the waiting room, talked her
way into an interview, and then turned the interview into a job as an
emergency room nurse.

"Babe, you are one strong woman," Doug had written back, con-
gratulating her.

Except now, with Doug finally about to come home, she was actually a mess—a tangle of self-doubt, guilt, and anxiety.

She thought back on the last year and obsessed over her imperfections: the money she spent at the bar while he drank water in the
desert; the precious phone calls wasted on small talk about work and
grocery shopping because her mind suddenly went blank when she
heard his voice; the love letters that she labored over but that still
ended up reading like cheesy greeting cards; the security questions
required for Doug's online bank account—City of birth? Elementary
school?—that left her stumped. She wondered: While he was risking his life, had she been a dead weight on the marriage? Would he
still love her? To prepare for his return, she organized and cleaned
the apartment, scheduled a hair appointment, joined a gym and exer-
cised five times a week.

As the marines' tentative return date neared, Krissy was invited
to a seminar at Fort Detrick to prepare families for the homecoming. She picked up Anne, and they drove the seventy miles, passing
through Frederick, Maryland, turning into the base, and winding

down a dirt road. They parked in a sprawling lot and followed signs
to a gym. Several tables had been set up just inside the entrance, one
for doughnuts and coffee and others labeled "Health Care," "Veteran
Benefits," "Alcohol and Drug Issues," and "PTSD." The lobby was
filled with other wives, some carrying babies decked out in marine
T-shirts, others showing off pictures of their husbands and trading
war stories from Afghanistan heard during video chats on Skype.
"Doug is just at work," Krissy told herself. She grabbed the informational packets off the tables without looking and walked into the gym,
sitting near the back with Anne.

Presenters rotated onto the stage to speak about military benefits, finances, and veteran affairs. Then a chaplain lectured about
PTSD. "If they were gone for ten months, it will take them ten months
to get back to normal," he said. And then: "Everyone comes back with
some damage." And then: "There will be some distance. Don't expect
them to tell you everything. Give them space."

Krissy had heard enough. She looked over at Anne. "Doug's not
going to be like this, right?" she said. She tuned out the rest of the
presentation and started to flip through the stack of papers she had
collected in the lobby. She reached first for a comic book, fun and
colorful, thirty-six pages introduced on the cover by the cartoonlike
drawing of an airplane and a title: *Coming Home: What to Expect, How
to Deal When You Return from Combat*. She opened the comic book and
started to read. The beginning depicted a veteran on his first night at
home, sleeping fitfully on the floor and clutching a baseball bat while
his gorgeous wife slept alone in the bed. The veteran heard a noise
and jumped to his feet, grabbing the baseball bat and flexing biceps
covered with barbed-wire tattoos. His eyes radiated a deep red. "It's
just the garbage truck and the baby crying," his wife said, alarmed.

Krissy's stomach dropped. She turned to the next page.

Now the veteran, a look of disdain on his face, was holding his crying baby. "Jeez—what's wrong with him!" the veteran said. Now he was handing the baby back to his wife and leaving to go out to a bar with his military friends. Now he was driving like a maniac, swerving all over the road. Now he was downing another beer, and another, and another. Now he was back home, looking menacing, glaring at his wife, and flexing his muscles. Now the wife was telling him, "I don't even know you anymore." Now she was taking the baby and leaving. Now the veteran was attempting suicide, downing an entire bottle of prescription pills and passing out on the couch.

Krissy put down the magazine and turned to Anne. "Let's go," she said.

They left the seminar two hours early, drove back to Annapolis, and went straight to a downtown bar for few drinks. Anne tried to comfort Krissy by joking about the comic book. "Doug's not going to be doing Rambo cartwheels across the living room," she said. "This is my brother, not some psychotic stranger on steroids."

Krissy smiled and nodded, but when she returned home to the empty apartment a few hours later she was fighting back tears. She looked at wedding pictures and thought about the night she and Doug had first met. They had been out with a group of mutual friends, and Doug had been too nervous to say anything to her until they stood up at the end of the night to say goodbye. Doug knew already that he liked Krissy, and he knew this was his last chance to make an impression. He leaned in to hug her, opened his mouth . . . and suddenly licked the side of her face from chin to temple like a dog. "Gotcha!" he had shouted, laughing and running away, and she had chased him across the street before leaning over and laughing hysterically. She had fallen in love with him because he was fun, goofy, and sensitive. Now the marines had prepared her to expect the exact opposite when he got home. Stoic. Silent. Aloof. Angry.

It was all too much to hold in. She decided to send Doug an e-mail, even if he did not get a chance to read it until he returned home.

> Hey crazy man—
>
> I've been thinking about what you're going through over there. Are you OK? Are you dealing with things OK? Is there anything I can do to help? I really need your feedback on how this "homecoming" is going to work . . . What do I need to do to help you transition back home? Your mom had mentioned that you talked to her briefly about some of the changes you've experienced already. Apparently you said, "I'm going to be a changed man when I get home." What does that mean, babe? Is that a bad thing, good thing or neither? I'm scared, and I need to know how to help. Please talk to me. I'm here for you, babe. It's my job as your wife.
>
> Love always . . .

. . .

Doug and his battalion flew home on Memorial Day, stopping to refuel in Kyrgyzstan and western Europe, buying cold beers at an airport in Maine, and then continuing on to California to spend a few final days sorting through gear and turning in their weapons. Krissy decided to travel to the West Coast to greet him. She requested vacation from her new job, stayed with relatives in Orange County, and drove to the military base at 8:00 p.m., an hour before Doug was scheduled to land. His flight was delayed by a volcanic-ash cloud and then again by headwinds. Krissy waited alone in a parking lot near the base, sitting in the driver's seat of her rental car, checking her watch, and touching up her makeup in the rearview mirror.

Forty minutes passed. An hour. Two. Krissy went to a nearby Waffle House for dinner and came back to the parking lot. Doug's plane finally landed, but she continued to wait. He had warned her that, as a second lieutenant, he would have to help junior marines turn in their weapons and fill out paperwork after the plane landed. Krissy tried to relax. She reclined in her seat and closed her eyes. Two hours later, she woke up and saw a young marine approaching the car next to hers. A pretty woman rushed out of the car, wearing high heels, a slinky dress, and a heart-shaped diamond ring. She sprinted toward the marine, shrieking, jumping into his arms, touching his face, squeezing his shoulders, shrieking again, and kissing his cheeks while a professional photographer followed behind with a camera to capture the reunion. Krissy looked at the clock on the dashboard. Almost 3:00 a.m.

Where the hell was Doug?

Her cell phone rang. "Hello," she said, her voice tired and groggy.

"Hi." It was Doug, speaking in the same casual baritone she had replayed again and again on her message machine. "Where are you?" he said.

"I'm here waiting," she said.

"Oh. Okay. Well, where are you in the parking lot? I've got all this gear to carry to the car."

She explained how to find the car, but she hung up the phone and felt her heart drop. Eight months she'd been waiting—eight months and now seven more hours in this dark parking lot—and he was worried about how far he had to carry his bags? What about the romantic greeting, the shriek, the kiss? She got out of the car and started walking to meet him. It was cold outside, and she hadn't slept in twenty hours. She saw Doug walk into the parking lot carrying his bags. He was more handsome than she remembered. She felt her heart quicken and tried to calm herself by pulling in a deep breath. "I can't

belleve you were worried about your bags," she said. Doug wrapped
her into a long hug, and she helped him load his gear into the trunk.
"I love you," she said.

They sat quietly in the car, unsure what to do next. She was nervous. So was he. She reached out to hold his hand, then dropped it
because it felt too forced. They passed a couple of awkward hours
together, ordered Chinese takeout, and checked into a nearby Holiday Inn at 5:00 a.m. Doug had to report back to the base to finish his
work two hours later. Krissy took a commercial flight back to Maryland. Doug was forced to stay another day before flying home with the
battalion for its official homecoming at Fort Detrick.

He left California for Maryland on a Saturday afternoon, and this
time seven relatives had come to Fort Detrick with Krissy to greet him.
Polly had driven from Richmond, wearing a red shirt and an American flag bandanna tied around her neck, and she waited alongside
Anne. Doug's grandmother had brought snacks that she had made
and frozen on the day Doug deployed, a symbolic gesture, but now
the cheese looked strange and nobody wanted to eat it. The parking
lot was filled with a few hundred people, all crowded into a makeshift holding pen marked off with yellow caution tape. They jockeyed
for position, stood on their tiptoes, and watched for the busloads of
marines to arrive. A band played the national anthem. Families waved
balloons and handmade signs. People chanted, "USA! USA!" Finally,
just after 5:00 p.m., three nondescript tour buses rounded the corner
and pulled into the parking lot.

Dozens of marines streamed off the buses, and relatives screamed
out their names and pushed against the caution tape. Polly saw Doug
walk off the bus, carrying two seabags and wearing wraparound Oak-
ley sunglasses and full military fatigues. The sleeves of his shirt were
rolled up to reveal his biceps. He looked skinnier than she remem-

bered, but also more self-assured. "Doug!" she yelled. "Doug! Doug!
Doug!" He couldn't hear her. All around people were reuniting, crying, laughing, and high-fiving. A marine met his baby for the first
time. Another proposed. The crowd surged through the caution tape,
and Polly and Krissy started moving toward the buses, and suddenly
Doug was in front of them, squeezing his mother and sister into hugs,
putting his arm around his grandmother, and kissing Krissy while
touching her cheek.

"It's over," he said. "I'm home."

They stood in a semicircle around Doug and chatted in the parking
lot for a while. Polly wanted to touch him constantly and she reached
out for his arm. "You look good," she said. "You really look good." She
hadn't felt so relieved since Doug's phone call on her birthday, and
now she told him about her letter to Obama and the president's handwritten response. Doug laughed in disbelief. He wanted to read the
letter someday, he said.

But right now he was jet-lagged and overwhelmed, so after
twenty-five minutes Polly suggested he go home and rest. She had
made the two-hour drive from Richmond alone in her hot car, her
head swimming with all those questions for Doug that had been stored
up over the last eight months. She had been reading books Doug recommended, *Making the Corps* and *On Killing*, and building a list in her
head of the things she wanted to know about his time at war. But now
none of it seemed to matter. He was whole. He was home. He was safe.

"Go home and get some rest," she said. "You're back. We'll have
the rest of our lives to catch up."

. . .

For the first few weeks, everything went well enough. Krissy and Doug
studied a calendar and figured out that he would have a minimum of

eighteen months before he had to deploy again, since he was in the military reserves. Doug bought a Nintendo Wii, threw a welcome-home party at a local bar, started to look for a job in law enforcement, and fixed up his motorcycle. Then one morning while Krissy was still asleep, he started to stomp around their apartment, clambering in the kitchen and cursing loud enough to wake her up. She got out of bed and went into the living room, where Doug was now sitting on the couch and watching cartoons.

"What's the problem?" she said.

"Nothing," he said, continuing to stare straight ahead at the TV.

"Come on. Really. You woke me up. Now I'm here. What's wrong?"

"Well, actually, a lot of things," he said, and then he listed them, spilling his frustrations for ten minutes. He had spent years taking care of a saltwater fish tank and suddenly could not remember what time to feed the fish. He felt like a stranger in his own house, unable to remember where anything was, and by the way, where did they keep the goddamn tinfoil? How come so many of his friends and in-laws, when they saw him for the first time, patted him on the back and said, "Hey! Welcome back! How was it?" like he'd been on some kind of Caribbean cruise? Worse was the one relative who had stopped by and told him that "Wow" his deployment had "just flown by," and he had smiled, reminded himself to stay calm, and then told her that twelve hours in the desert felt like three months Maryland time, so no—actually, no—time had not flown by, not at all. What was wrong with these people, anyway? Why weren't they asking him more questions about the war, about what it was like? Didn't they care? Why, on the day he showed Krissy the entire slideshow of his pictures from Afghanistan, did she suddenly interrupt him and open her own computer to show Doug a drawing one of her grade-school nieces had done on his behalf? Why wasn't she hugging him more, holding him, grabbing his hand in public like she had done before he left? Weren't they supposed to be newlyweds?

Then there were the daily annoyances: the drivers in Annapolis who careened across the road like idiots, oblivious to the consequences, honking at him because he was going too slowly on the highway since he was still used to traveling at thirty miles an hour and standing with his head outside of the tank and scanning for IEDs. And the people at the grocery store, who clogged up the aisles and obsessed over organic labels, this ingredient or that, while he threw anything and everything into the cart, ecstatic not to be bartering for onions, eggs, and potatoes at an Afghan bazaar. He felt like he was still divided between two worlds, between home and the moon. Before he left the house to run errands, he always thought he was forgetting something, and he would touch his pockets and try to figure out why they felt so light. Wallet. Phone. Keys. What else? What else? And usually it took him a few minutes before he realized—wait, that was everything. He didn't need body armor, tourniquets, or his rifle.

"Wow, I didn't know," Krissy said. "I thought you were adjusting really well."

"Sometimes I am," Doug said. "Sometimes I'm not."

"We're dealing with a lot," Krissy said. "Maybe we should consider some counseling."

"I don't want to talk to a stranger," Doug said. "I just want to talk to you."

So they slowly started talking. She asked him about the war; he let her read his journal. She told him when she needed space; he told her when he wanted more affection. She encouraged him to journal more about the war, and he started thinking about writing a book. They bought a dog, a 120-pound bull mastiff, and named him after a military tank. Friends invited them to go camping, but they spent most of their time home alone together, committed to "figuring each other out," Doug said, "and learning how to be married."

There were still problems. Every once in a while, Krissy treated Doug like he was the damaged veteran she had read about in the PTSD comic book and tried to shield him from violent TV shows or news about the war. He told her not to act like he was some "messed-up kid in an after-school special." They sometimes escaped into their own cell phones or video games because it was easier than talking. But they also laughed about how they had proved the old adage true: Yes, the first year of marriage was, in fact, the hardest. He started to refer to Krissy as "the Wife." She called him "the Husband."

A month after he returned home, they began looking at houses. They found one in the suburbs near Annapolis, a fixer-upper on a quiet street with a big yard, four bedrooms, and good schools nearby—the kind of place that made Doug see into his future. "This is it," he said on their first tour of the house. "It's the perfect place for our family." A few weeks before their first anniversary, they met with a real estate agent and signed the papers.

They moved into the house as the war raged on. Obama sent more troops to Afghanistan, fired the top general, spoke at more funerals, and started withdrawing soldiers. Doug monitored the progress of the war, but he focused more on redoing the floors, fixing up the yard, and putting in new bathrooms. Polly drove up to visit every few months—her new perspective on distance made the two-hour drive seem easy. Doug mourned the suicide of a stepbrother, attended friends' weddings, interviewed with the FBI, and eventually took a temporary job guarding against shoplifters for Home Depot. Afghanistan felt farther and farther away. He told Krissy that he hoped the war would end before his turn came up for another deployment. After all, this was home, and that was the moon.

(TOP) Deb Corbin, one of fifty mail analysts in the White House Correspondence Office, sorts through letters addressed to the president. Each analyst works for twelve hours a day and reads about 400 letters, helping divide the mail into seventy-five subject categories. (© Linda Davidson/*Washington Post*)

(BOTTOM) In the White House Correspondence Office Cisco Robinson looks through letters and drawings sent by children. The mailroom staff processes about 20,000 letters and e-mails each day before picking ten pieces that will be delivered to the president in a purple folder. (© Linda Davidson/*Washington Post*)

(TOP) The Michigan economy cost Jen and Jay Cline their jobs and forced them into a small duplex apartment with their two sons. They wrote to Obama about their plight and eventually filed for bankruptcy, believing it was their only hope for a fresh start.

(BOTTOM) Second Lieutenant Doug Toulotte returns home from the war in Afghanistan and is greeted by his mother, Polly, and sister, Anne. Polly exchanged letters with the president midway through Doug's tour, when she was wracked with anxiety.

(TOP) Stefan Johnson selects his freshman-year classes at La Salle University in Philadelphia. With his father in prison and his mother unemployed, Stefan sought inspiration from the president, ran for class president of his high school, and then earned a full scholarship to college.

(BOTTOM) After Stefan Johnson graduated from high school as class president, his mother celebrated by decorating their apartment in a rundown section of South Philadelphia. At the same time she worried about how to help him pay for college when she had $28 in her bank account.

(TOP) Natoma Canfield, a cleaning woman in Ohio, swallowed at least eleven pills every day during her fight against leukemia. Doctors gave her a 30 percent chance to live. She began treatment despite worrying about how she could pay for it with no health insurance.

(BOTTOM) Natoma Canfield relied heavily on her sister, Connie Anderson, while suffering from leukemia. Both women became central in the president's push for health-care reform. Connie introduced Obama at a rally; Natoma received a celebratory note from the president after his health-care bill became law. "I couldn't have done it without you," he wrote.

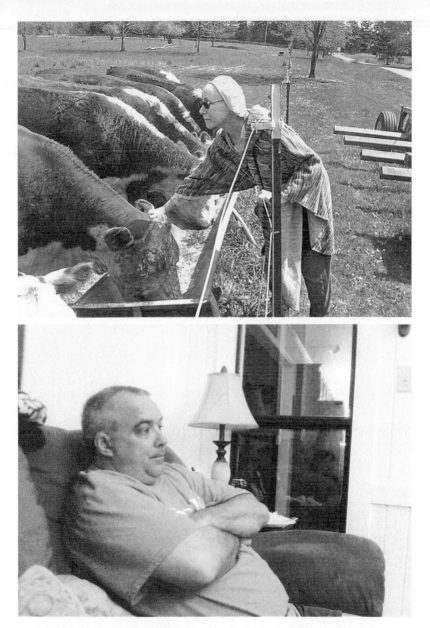

(TOP) Natoma Canfield lost many things to leukemia, including her hair, her appetite, and more than thirty pounds.

(BOTTOM) Thomas Ritter sits in his house in Plano, Texas, and watches Fox News in the room he calls the "man cave." An ardent conservative, Thomas sent an e-mail expressing his frustrations to the White House and then spent a few hours in disbelief when he received a two-page response written in the president's sweeping cursive.

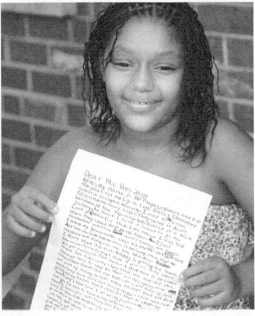

(TOP) Lucy Gutierrez and her family considered moving from their home in Kingman, Arizona, after the state passed a controversial immigration law. A U.S. citizen herself, Lucy had relatives who feared deportation. She also faced a tidal wave of racism. "Where is the America I thought I knew?" she asked the president.

(LEFT) Na'Dreya Lattimore, a fifth grader in Covington, Kentucky, sent this handwritten letter to the president, which he shared with the country during a major speech about education. Na'Dreya's school district ranked dead last out of 174 districts in Kentucky. "I know you are busy," she wrote to Obama, "but I could really use your help on this." (© *Cincinnati Enquirer*/Patrick Reddy)

(LEFT) Hailey Thatcher catches a fish off the coast of Suwannee, Florida, where his family has owned land for forty-five years. Fishing has been inconsistent in Suwannee since the BP oil spill, which threatened to destroy a place that is "just ingrained in me," Thatcher said.

(BOTTOM) Hailey Thatcher poses with his grandparents in a picture that still hangs on the wall of the family fishing trailer. Not much had changed for decades at their property in Suwannee—until the BP oil spill threatened to change everything.

(TOP) Jon Santos films his video for the "It Gets Better" project, a collection of messages for gay teens contemplating suicide. He spoke about being bullied in high school and coming out to his father, stories he also shared in his letter to the president.

(BOTTOM) Jessica Duran looked all over New York for a job in order to help support her mother, who had suffered homelessness, domestic abuse, and unemployment since moving to the U.S. from the Dominican Republic in the late 1990s. Jessica asked the president: "What would you do if it was your mom out there being treated like that?"

 CHAPTER 4

"I simply can no longer afford to pay for my health care costs!!"

Obama had read thousands of letters since becoming president, and aides privately worried that the mail might leave him discouraged or numb. People tended to write their president when circumstances turned dire, sealing a prayer into an envelope as a matter of last resort. What resulted each day inside Obama's purple folder was an intimate view of hard luck and personal struggle, a wave of desperation capable of overwhelming the senses.

But Obama was a writer himself, the author of a policy book and a memoir, and he had an eye for writing and an appreciation of good stories. He learned more about key issues from some letters than he did from his own staff. "They tell a story that is much more powerful than just some abstract policy briefing," he said. He particularly liked letters that were unflinching and detailed—letters that allowed him to glimpse beyond the bubble. On a Tuesday in early February, he opened the purple folder and paused over a letter that stood out immediately. It was loaded with specific numbers, boldface words, and consecutive exclamation marks. Obama asked his staff secretary to make twenty copies and distribute them around the West Wing. He knew this letter had heart. He knew it had power.

What he could not have known, at least not yet, was that this letter-writer's story was only beginning, and that it would change the course of his presidency during the coming weeks.

Natoma Canfield was a fifty-year-old cleaning woman who lived alone outside Medina, Ohio, a distant suburb of Cleveland. She owned a small house on a rural road, where two cats kept her company and chickens and deer milled around the five-acre backyard. She spent her free time admiring antique cars, dressing in costumes for Renaissance festivals, and caring for the livestock on a nearby farm. Every Saturday night, she walked over to a neighbor's house to play pinochle. She almost never watched TV, and she rarely followed politics. When she did, she tended to side with Republicans.

She had divorced and become self-employed fifteen years earlier, forcing her to find her own health insurance. It had been a miserable process made worse because she was diagnosed with carcinoma in the early 1990s, marring her application with what insurance companies termed a "preexisting condition." Doctors had treated the cancer and told her she was healthy, but insurance companies still wanted nothing to do with her. She called every major company to see if any would take her, and only Anthem said yes. It offered a high-risk policy at an inflated rate, and Natoma paid it for the next thirteen years by working long hours and limiting her spending.

Then, at the beginning of 2009, when the recession had cut her cleaning business in half, she received a letter notifying her that Anthem had increased her insurance premiums by 25 percent, raising her payments to more than $500 a month. She thought about canceling her policy, but living without insurance terrified her. If she got sick, she could go into debt and lose her house—the only place she had ever lived, designed and built by her father in 1958. It was too big of a risk, she decided, so she kept her insurance and cut everything else, canceling long-distance phone service, signing up for food stamps, taking a second job at a catering company, asking a charity to pay one of her electric bills, negotiating down her trash bill, canceling the newspaper, and making her own greeting cards and presents to distribute at Christmas. She kept meticulous track of her medical expenses throughout 2009: She paid $6,075.24 in premiums, $2,415.26 for medical costs, $1,500 in prescriptions, and $225 in copays. Anthem paid only $935.32 on her behalf.

Early in 2010, Anthem sent another letter. Even though Natoma had upped her deductible to the maximum of $2,500 to lower her monthly costs, Anthem had decided to raise her premiums again—this time by 40 percent. Two days after she received the news, Natoma began a letter of her own. She had read about Obama's plan for health-care reform in the newspaper, but her letter was less a targeted plea to the president than a mass mailing to anyone and everyone with power. She typed "cc: everyone" at the top of the page and forwarded the letter to city politicians, state leaders, and Anthem executives. But she directed her language squarely at Obama because he had the most power of all. She wrote:

> As a responsible individual, I have struggled to maintain my
> individual coverage and have increased my deductible and out of
> pocket-limits in an attempt to control my cost and keep my health
> insurance.
>
> In 2009 my insurance company received $6075.24 in premiums

*and paid out only $935.32! Incredibly I have just been notified that
my premium for 2010 has been increased over 40% to $8496.24
($708.02 per month)!!!! This is the same insurance company I have
been with for over 11 cancer free years!!! I need your Health reform
bill to help me!!! I simply can no longer afford to pay for my health
care costs!! Thanks to this incredible premium increase demanded
by my insurance company, January will be my last month of insurance.*

A few weeks after she sent her letter, Natoma received an envelope in the mail from Washington. It arrived protected by two sheets
of cardboard, and inside she found a note card embossed with the
presidential seal. "Natoma," wrote the president in sweeping black
script. "Thanks for your letter. It's because of folks like you that we
are still fighting to get health care done!" Surprised to see Obama's
signature at the end of the letter, Natoma took the note card to Hobby
Lobby and had it framed for $28. It was a nice memento, she thought,
but it did nothing to change her circumstances. She called Anthem
and canceled her insurance, assuming that was the end of it.

A few days later, the White House called. A woman introduced
herself as an assistant to the president, and she told Natoma that
Obama wanted to read her letter aloud during a private meeting
with insurance executives, including the CEO of Anthem. The president hoped her letter would convince executives that their practices
were immoral, the assistant said. Did Natoma mind if the president
shared it? "Of course not," Natoma said, feeling vindicated. And for
the next two days, her phone rarely stopped ringing. Reporters called
to request interviews, photographers asked to take her picture, and
a congressman from Ohio offered his support. The woman from the
White House called back. Sometime soon, she said, Obama hoped to
fly Natoma to Washington to meet with him in person.

Anticipating that trip one Sunday at the beginning of March, Natoma went to a salon in downtown Medina to have her hair colored and styled by a friend who offered to do it for free. Before the appointment ended, one of her cleaning clients called her cell phone. He needed help dealing with a pregnant cow. Natoma drove over to the farm, parked her car, and started running toward the cow. After five steps, she was out of breath. She felt dizzy. Her ears rang. Her vision blurred, then turned black. She collapsed into a chair outside of the barn, and the owner ran over to see what was wrong.

"Do you need an ambulance?" he said.

"What's an ambulance?" she said.

The owner called for help, and Natoma awoke ten minutes later to the sound of sirens. It took another minute for her to piece together her predicament. She was lying on a stretcher in the back of an ambulance. Two paramedics leaned over to check her vitals. She had no insurance. She couldn't afford this. She looked up at the paramedics and started to speak. "Let me explain," she said. It had been a crazy week. Reporters had been calling. She was getting ready to go to the White House. "I'm probably just stressed and tired," she said. "I'm fine." But the paramedics continued with their work, and the ambulance roared on toward the hospital.

. . .

The president had always believed in the power of narrative, but rarely had he latched on to a story quite like Natoma's. The debate over his plans for health-care reform, now almost a year old, could be complicated, numerical, nuanced, and boring. Two Senate committees and three House of Representative panels had worked for months to craft legislation. Edits, compromises, and last-minute additions had resulted in a final bill of 2,409 pages. Natoma, meanwhile, had managed to humanize the debate in a one-page letter, providing all the elements of populist storytelling that Obama loved. There was the protagonist: a hardworking cleaning woman trying to do right. The antagonist: a billion-dollar insurance company greedy for more money. And a difficult choice: drop her insurance or risk losing her house.

Obama believed the outcome of health-care reform would profoundly affect the entirety of his presidency, and most lawmakers in Washington agreed. Pass the bill and he could become a historic president, generating the momentum to push more of his ambitious ideas through Congress. Fail and he would appear weak, even powerless. "Is the Obama presidency at stake here? Yes, it is," said Congressman Dennis Kucinich, a Democrat from Ohio who had run against Obama in the 2008 presidential primary. Jim DeMint, a Republican senator from South Carolina, was even more blunt. "If we're able to stop Obama on this, it will be his Waterloo," he said. "It will break him."

Obama had made health care his top priority during his first year in office only to watch legislation stall in Congress and nearly die when Scott Brown, a Massachusetts Republican, won a special election to the Senate in January and diluted the Democratic majority. The latest polls indicated that 52 percent of the country opposed reform and 42 percent feared it. Millions of Americans believed that reform would fuel big government, add to the national debt, and lead to tax increases during a recession. Obama's opponents on the far right had made the debate less about uninsured Americans than about "death panels," overspending, taxpayer-funded abortions, unconstitutional government takeovers, and socialism. The debate had begun to destroy Obama's campaign aspirations of bipartisanship. Republican lawmakers stood on the steps of the Capitol and waved signs that read KILL THE BILL! Democratic lawmakers accused Republicans of "fearmongering" and termed them "the party of no." Obama himself blamed Republicans for trying to twist his self-described "centrist" plan into "some kind of Bolshevik plot."

As February turned into March, Obama vowed to do everything he could to pass the bill within the next two weeks, telling one Iowa congressman that he wanted to reform health care even if it cost him a second term. He traveled to Baltimore and debated with the House Republicans at their annual retreat, one against 219. He canceled a trip to Asia, held a seven-hour health-care summit near the White House, and scheduled one-on-one visits with twenty-eight members of Congress to ask for their votes. During a few of those meetings, his pitch sounded more like a plea. "I need this," Obama reportedly said.

Then he discovered Natoma's letter—a "game-changer," one aide called it. His administration had relied on letter writers before, using them for a sentence in a speech, a photo opportunity during a bill signing, or a quick anecdote to offer reporters. But on March 4, 2010, during a press briefing in front of journalists from around the world, Robert Gibbs lifted Natoma's letter above the podium and held it firmly in the spotlight. He asked reporters to wait with their questions and then read the entire letter out loud. "This is a letter the president will likely take with him to meetings throughout this period to remind everyone what's at stake," Gibbs said, and the rest of the administration soon joined him in a public relations blitz. Kathleen Sebelius, the secretary of health and human services, wrote a public letter to Anthem asking it to justify rate increases, to little effect. Speechwriter Jon Favreau worked Natoma's story into three speeches that Obama delivered during the next week. David Axelrod, a senior adviser to the president, lined up television appearances on three major networks to talk about Natoma's letter. "This kind of thing shouldn't happen in the United States of America," he said.

In his office on Capitol Hill, a freshman congressman named

John Boccieri heard Natoma's story and realized she lived inside his district. Boccieri, forty, with boyish good looks, had been agonizing over his health-care vote for weeks. He had voted against the first bill in November 2009 because he believed it would cost the government too much money, and he faced intense pressure to vote no again. He was the first Democrat in fifty-eight years to represent a traditionally conservative district in northern Ohio, and Republicans had hired a plane to fly above his regional office in Canton with a banner that read TELL REP BOCCIERI No. A former minor league baseball player and a pilot in the Air Force Reserves, he had experienced his share of pressure, but never had the stakes felt this high. Constituents picketed outside his office and cold-called him at home. Obama tried to woo his vote with a series of phone calls and invited him to meet in person during a ride aboard Air Force One.

Boccieri's mother had struggled to keep her insurance after suffering from cancer in the early 1980s, and Natoma's story reminded Boccieri of his childhood. He called her to wish her well and talk about her financial struggles. A few days later, he announced that he had changed his mind about health-care reform. He would vote for it. "I was already starting to lean that way, but stories like Natoma's made a huge difference for me," Boccieri said. "It was the final push. Governing is about making hard choices, and this was one of the hardest. I lost friends over this vote, people I've known for years and years. They say it will cost me my job. But some votes become a matter of conscience, and then you have to put aside what may seem like the clear path. I couldn't stop thinking about people like Natoma."

The letter from a cleaning woman in rural Ohio was shifting the biggest debate of Obama's young presidency, so his administration came up with a plan to further capitalize. Why not take a trip on Air Force One to Natoma's hometown for a health-care rally? The president could read her letter, introduce her to the crowd, and make his

case for reform. An assistant at the White House called Natoma to tell
her about the plan.

It sounded great, Natoma said, but unfortunately she wouldn't
be able to make it. The last few days had been a blur, she explained—
chasing a cow, collapsing in the barn, waking in the ambulance,
undergoing tests, and waiting, waiting, waiting for a diagnosis.

Leukemia, the doctors had said. They had given her a 35 percent
chance to live.

. . .

Natoma checked into the hospital in the middle of March for a
twenty-six-day stay, the first stage of a treatment plan that doctors
hoped would last six months. She moved into a room on the eleventh
floor of Cleveland Clinic, a place patients referred to as "Leukemia
World." Doctors administered chemotherapy for thirty minutes every
day, and each time Natoma closed her eyes, envisioned the medicine fighting against the disease, and hummed the theme song from
Rocky. Her older sister, Connie, drove up from Florida, stayed near
the hospital, and helped Natoma apply for emergency Medicaid to pay
for her care.

Natoma was required to wear a mask and remain inside Cleveland
Clinic because every rogue germ posed a deadly threat to her weak-
ened immune system. Volunteers in red blazers offered to push her
around the hospital in a wheelchair. Most of the time, she stayed in
her room, closed her eyes, and imagined she was on her daily walk
around the 3.2-mile nature trail near her house, passing by the dense
beech trees that shadowed the lake, the baseball fields alive with Little League games, and the snack stand where she sometimes stopped
to buy ice cream. On days when she felt well enough, she walked to
a window on the eleventh floor that provided sweeping views of the
landscaped hospital grounds and studied the spring tulips fighting to

break through the soil. It was a beautiful facility, she thought, except that it had so much in common with a prison. For twenty-six days, she was trapped.

Obama decided to come to Ohio to speak about Natoma anyway, and his staff invited Connie to introduce him. Connie hesitated at first, explaining that she knew little about politics and nothing about public speaking. But Natoma encouraged her to do it, and the White House e-mailed a speech for Connie to memorize two days before the event. Connie trimmed the speech with the help of Natoma and a brother who worked as a newspaper editor. She styled her hair and wore a sharp suit, driving to the event in Strongsville, Ohio, while Obama flew in with half a dozen congressmen on Air Force One. A crowd of 1,500 filed into the small space, and the two speakers met briefly backstage. Obama shook Connie's hand, thanked her for coming, and then asked her for an update on Natoma's health.

"She's having a hard time, to tell you the truth," Connie told him.

The president frowned and nodded. He asked Connie to send her sister his best wishes. Then he grabbed her hand and they walked arm in arm onto the stage. Obama waved his hands to quiet the crowd while Connie stepped tentatively to the microphone. Only the top of her head was visible above the lectern. "Hi," she said, looking down to check her notes. "My name is Connie and I am here to introduce the president on behalf of my sister, Natoma, who is sick and can't be here today." She spoke for almost two minutes, summarizing Natoma's letter and glancing back at Obama before speaking again. "It is now my honor to introduce a man who is fighting every day for health-insurance reform that will lower costs and restore accountability to the system. President Barack Bohama!" Connie stepped back from the microphone as her face turned red. It had been a nervous mispronunciation that few people noticed, but it would bother her for days. Obama patted her shoulder and wrapped her in a quick hug. "You did great. Thank you. Thank you," he whispered. Then he handed his jacket and his BlackBerry to an aide in the front row and rolled up his sleeves.

"Hello, Ohio!" he shouted.

He began, as usual, with some lighthearted banter: a joke about the Ohio State men's basketball team and filling out his NCAA tournament bracket; then the customary call-and-response of an audience member shouting "I love you!" and him responding "I love you back!" He thanked a handful of local politicians, reading their names off of an index card. Then he stepped back and surveyed the crowd for a few seconds, his face suddenly serious, and leaned into the microphone to begin his speech in earnest.

"I want to thank Connie who introduced me," he said. "I want to thank her and her family for being here on behalf of her sister, Natoma. I don't know if everybody understood that Natoma is in the hospital right now, so Connie was filling in. It's not easy to share such a personal story when your sister who you love so much is sick, so I appreciate Connie being willing to do so here today. And I want everybody to understand that Connie and her sister are the reason I'm here today."

The crowd remained silent, and Obama spent the next six minutes recounting how Natoma had struggled to keep her insurance despite unfair premium increases. He had given more than forty speeches about health care but none as personal and focused as this. As he reached the climax of Natoma's story, Obama clenched his right hand into a fist and shook it to the rhythm of each sentence. The arena was unusually quiet. "So here's what happens," he continued, bouncing on his toes.

She just couldn't afford it. She didn't have the money. She realized that if she paid those health premiums that had been jacked up by 40 percent, she couldn't make her mortgage. And despite her desire to keep her coverage, despite her fears that she would get sick and lose the home that her parents built, she finally surrendered. She finally gave up her health insurance. She stopped paying it. She couldn't make ends meet. So January was her last month of being insured. Like so many responsible Americans, folks who work hard every day, who try to do the right things, she was forced to hang her fortunes on chance. Just to take a chance. That's all she could do. She hoped against hope that she would stay healthy. She feared terribly that she might not stay healthy.

Unfortunately, Natoma's worst fears were realized. Just last week, she was working on a nearby farm, walking outside, apparently chasing after a cow, when she collapsed. She was rushed to the hospital. She was very sick. She needed two blood transfusions. Doctors performed a battery of tests and on Saturday Natoma was diagnosed with leukemia. Now the reason Natoma is not here today is that she's lying in a hospital bed, suddenly faced with this emergency, suddenly faced with the fight of her life. She expects to face more than a month of aggressive chemotherapy. She's wracked with worry not only about her illness but about the costs of the tests and the treatment that she's surely going to need to beat it. So you want to know why I'm here, Ohio? I'm here because of Natoma. That's why we need health-care reform right now. Right now.

When you hear people say, "Start over," I want you to think about Natoma. When you hear people saying that this isn't the right time, you think about what she's going through. When you hear people talk about, "What does this mean for the Democrats? What does this mean for the Republicans? I don't know how the polls are doing." When you hear people more worried about the politics of it than what's right and what's wrong, I want you to think about Natoma and the millions of people across this country who are looking for help and looking for some relief.

The crowd rose for a standing ovation, and Obama pumped his fist in the air and walked off the stage. During the next few hours, political analysts and television reporters would surmise that they had witnessed a key moment in the debate for health-care reform. It was Obama at his best, they said—eloquent, resolute, and emotional. During his plane ride back to Washington, two more congressmen would commit their votes for reform. His media aides would circulate a video of the speech set to a backdrop of moving orchestral music. He would send out an e-mail to a listserv of thirteen million supporters and write that Natoma was his reminder for "why we have worked so hard for so long" and the "reason I am still in this fight."

But before any of that, before he even left the arena in Ohio, Obama saw Connie backstage and called over to her. He kissed her on the cheek and thanked her one more time. Then he told her to pass a message along to Natoma. Her story was going to impact millions of people, the president said.

. . .

Two days after Obama's speech, Natoma decided to start a diary. She barely had enough energy to write, but she wanted to keep a record of her twenty-six days in Leukemia World. Obama's speech had turned her into an icon. It had caused a Fox News television anchor to call her a liar, deranged lunatics to leave threats on her voice mail, the hospital to position a guard outside her door, and a syndicated crossword

puzzle to feature her as a clue: "Health care figure _____ Canfield."
Seeking some peace, she had unplugged her bedside phone and
declined interviews. The health-care battle mattered less now than
her own long fight ahead: twenty-six days of treatment in Cleveland
Clinic; two months back home to recover; a search for a bone marrow
donor; a transplant operation; and one hundred agonizing days to
determine its success. Even as health-care history unfolded around
her, Natoma focused her diary almost exclusively on the minutia of
her disease. It was the only thing that mattered. On most days, she
could only muster the strength to write one or two sentences in the
diary.

On March 18, the day House Democrats finalized a $940 billion
proposal to extend health-care coverage to an additional thirty-two
million Americans: "You can have sugar cereal in Leukemia World
and not feel guilty!" Natoma wrote. Then, a few hours later: "My nose
is starting to drip blood."

On March 19, as Obama predicted a "tough vote ahead" and made
his final case for reform during individual meetings with eighteen
wavering lawmakers: "I keep telling my family, I am just like a spring
bulb being planted again in the fall," Natoma wrote. "A 12-inch hole is
dug. Then we need a cold snowy winter to act as a blanket. At the start
of spring, life reenergizes."

On March 22, hours after she woke up, turned on the news, and
learned that the House had passed health-care reform by seven votes
and Obama had invited dozens of young staffers to the White House
for a last-minute, revelatory champagne toast: "The Health Bill has
past!!" And then, fifteen minutes later: "The hash browns are hot.
The cereal is crunch. Some day I'll taste these foods again. But I did
take my shower today and it felt great! Not that I care but a fairly large
handful of hair combed out."

A few hours later, she wrote again: "The Drs. came in this afternoon. They sat and looked pretty grave. It seems I have this thing called Philadelphia Chromosome. My odds have dropped down. Now bone marrow transplant is needed for sure. It is 5:44 p.m. What do I do for the rest of the night?"

Later: "11:35 p.m. and brain won't switch off. News of today."

Later: "1:12 a.m. Very dark and quiet. Still can't sleep."

On March 23, Natoma stayed in the hospital while Connie went to Washington to watch Obama sign health-care reform into law. The event was intended to commemorate the bill, but it had also become a celebration of Obama's pen pals. Connie was invited to stand near the front of the room, flanked by two other people who had corresponded with the president: a California businessman seeking insurance for his five employees and an eleven-year-old boy from Seattle whose mother had died suddenly because she could not afford to see a doctor. Six other letter writers were invited to a lunch reception, and Obama planned to thank all of them by name. His supporters considered it a touching and symbolic gesture, but his detractors increasingly ridiculed Obama for using the letters as a cheap political ploy. During his show on Fox News, commentator Glenn Beck mocked Obama with a parody letter from a woman named Gertrude. "In our small town alone, 1,457 people have attempted suicide simply because they are sick and tired of hearing you read letters or talk about the letters that you read every night," Beck said, pretending to read from a letter. "Please, please no more personal stories hand selected by your aides to use as talking points or photo ops. Mr. President, please, for America's sake, tear up those envelopes."

Obama walked into the East Room for the bill-signing ceremony and hugged the letter writers. He stepped up to his lectern and said "Thank you" eleven times to quiet the crowd before crediting lawmakers for their "historic leadership and uncommon courage." He said he was reforming health care on behalf of his own mother, who had battled cancer, and all of the "leaders who took up this cause through the generations." Then, near the end of the speech, he asked Connie to stand and be recognized. "I'm signing it for Natoma Canfield," Obama said.

Meanwhile, still on March 23, Natoma logged her activities in the diary: "Today I took a few sips of milk. Charged cell phone. Read newspaper."

March 26: "Bowel movement. YEAH!"

March 30: "I am really tired but cannot fall asleep. It's 3:41 a.m. I seem to have peed myself 2 times, and now the sleeping pill isn't working. My mouth hurts so bad."

April 5: "Too sick to have any thought."

April 6: "Too sick to think."

Finally, in the second week of April, as she neared the end of her twenty-six-day stay, Natoma began to debate where she should move next. Connie and her husband had invited Natoma to live in their house, a sprawling, forested place with a pool carved into the backyard, but she struggled to imagine living anywhere but home. She decided to make a pro-and-con list, scratching it out on the back of an Ohio Living Will Declaration. Under moving into her own house, she wrote: "Can die at home easier." "Be with the cats." "Might be able to take care of self." Under moving in with Connie: "Biggest worry—dying in their house." Natoma looked over the two lists and made her choice. She would move back to her place in Medina, back to the house her father had built. Connie offered to live there with her, and together they drove away from Cleveland Clinic and moved home.

· · ·

Shortly after moving back in, Natoma woke up in her own bedroom at seven one morning and walked into her kitchen. She poured herself a cup of milk and grabbed a small glass bowl from the top shelf. On the counter was a ziplock bag filled with her daily medications, and she dumped the pills into the glass bowl. These were the pills that kept her alive, but she loathed them.

She had been home for two weeks, long enough for the thrill of returning to old routines to be replaced by a sinking sensation that old routines might be gone for good. Each day brought another onslaught of competing discomforts—nausea, diarrhea, insomnia, and bedsores. Chemotherapy had scarred her mouth with half a dozen open sores, a common side effect, and now white patches covered the roof and floor of her mouth and red abrasions spread across her cheeks, gums, and lips. Swallowing saliva alone was a terrifying task. Gulping down a mouthful of liquid and a series of pills was pure hell, sending shots of pain through her mouth that seemed tantamount to having it sliced open with a razor blade. It had sometimes taken her three days to drink a can of soda or two hours to steel her courage before biting into a piece of watermelon. Suffering through the pills had become the worst part of her daily routine. Doctor's orders required her to take all medication before noon, and the process often lasted four or five hours. Now she looked down at the bowl and counted the pills. Eleven. She counted again. Eleven. She picked up the bowl and carried it to her bedroom, to the living room, and back to the kitchen. Finally, she sat at the kitchen table and reached for a small white pill, the least intimidating, a quarter-inch in diameter, and bounced it in her hand to feel its weight. She lifted it to her face and studied it. "Go down easy, please," she said. She took a deep breath, sipped from the milk, closed her eyes, threw in the pill, and swallowed hard. She grabbed on to the side of the table and squeezed. "Arrghh," she groaned. She opened her eyes and gasped.

Ten pills left.

Each pill came with a scientific name and a full sheet of instructions. There was Prilosec to manage stomach pain, and today she planned to take two since she had thrown up several times the night before. There were two megestrol acetates to prevent her from bleeding, since leukemia had rendered her blood count so low that doctors no longer allowed her to brush her teeth, fearing she could bleed to death after pricking her gum. There was one Gleevec, taken as part of her leukemia treatment; one stool softener; one Claritin because chemotherapy had inexplicably awakened her allergies; one potassium supplement; one oxycodone for pain relief; one trazodone for anxiety; and one zolpidem for sleep.

Natoma looked at the pills and tried not to think about their names, their chemical compositions, or their side effects. They were just colorful little pellets filled with healing power, she told herself. She had tried to shield herself from specifics at every stage of her treatment, never researching her symptoms on the Internet or reading the doctor-recommended leukemia pamphlets. The less she knew, the less she had to fear. She gulped from the milk, tipped back her head, and swallowed. "Ooooh. Ouch."

Nine left.

The glass bowl for pills had once been used for storing M&Ms, which Natoma had eaten religiously before she got sick, half a pack after lunch and half a pack after dinner. But now she couldn't stand chocolate, the way its gooey texture rubbed against the roof of her mouth and lingered on her tongue. Sometimes the mere smell of food was enough to make her vomit, and she especially avoided cooked carrots, meat loaf, Arby's sandwiches, and French fries. On the fridge, Connie kept an itemized list of what Natoma ate each day to make sure she was consuming enough calories. The current list read: "one slice bologna, four sips strawberry smoothie, six ice cubes, two eggs, six crackers, one scoop ice cream, one glass of milk." Natoma reached her hand back into the glass bowl and placed a pill in her mouth.

Eight left.

She gulped down another. Seven.

She groaned again. "I'm already exhausted," she said. She walked into the living room and slumped into a plaid chair with a view out the window and into the front yard. Her skin was pale, and her glasses slid down her nose. She wore gold earrings, a knit cap to cover her bald head, a pink nightgown, sweatpants, and a bathrobe—the only clothes that fit now that leukemia had taken thirty pounds. To keep warm, she draped one blanket over her legs and another over her shoulders. Connie had offered to shop for new clothes at Kmart, but Natoma had declined. "There's no reason to spend the money," she had said. "I'm not going to look good anyway."

Now Connie came into the living room carrying a stack of scrapbooks and photo albums, and she kneeled down next to her sister. Natoma had always kept a meticulous record of her life, and the books were filled with movie stubs, theater tickets, and menus from dinners out. There was a photo album for every year of her adult life, and she opened the book for 2009–2010. Here was Natoma, stout and forceful with a thick mane of unruly brown hair. Here was Natoma dog-sledding through the woods in winter, blowing out the candles for her fiftieth birthday, dancing at a Chinese New Year party, wearing a costume at a Renaissance festival, and leaning over to pet a cow.

"See, I was a person once," Natoma said. "I was a person."

"You're still a person," Connie said.

"No, I'm not. It doesn't feel like it. I'm a disease."

"Well, I think you're a person."

Natoma was silent for a minute, looking at the photos, thumbing through the pills. She reached for the milk. "I hope I get to be a person again," she said.

Six pills left.

Five.

The living room was eerily quiet except for the ticking of a grandfather clock, which pointed its hands to 10:00 a.m. Connie filed her
nails and Natoma looked around the room. There was a framed painting of flowers above the fireplace, another above the entry table, and
a bookshelf displaying a collection of decorative plates. The cordless
phone sat on the coffee table, its ringer turned up to high, just in case
a doctor called with news about their search for Natoma's bone marrow donor. Her three siblings had all been tested in the last week, and
she was waiting to hear if any were a match. She looked down at the
pills and counted. Still five. She stood up and walked out to the front
porch, setting eight peanuts on the windowsill to lure blue jays and
calling over to neighborhood chickens that had wandered near the
street. "Hi, little chickies," she said. The lilacs in the front yard had
started to bloom. She walked back into the living room, grabbed two
small pills, and took them down in one swallow.

Three left. Almost done.

She sat back down in front of the television and watched *Good
Morning America* give way to the local news, which gave way to *The
View*. She had liked to sew and needlepoint before she got sick, but
leukemia had made her fingers numb. She had liked to read, but lately
it made her nauseous. She had liked to make elaborate to-do lists
and keep a detailed journal, but now she could hardly summon the
energy to sign her own name when a form required it. Music was her
only feasible entertainment, so she had started listening to all kinds,
making a mixed CD with tracks from Guy Lombardo, Ludacris, Glenn
Miller, and Alicia Keys. Her immune system was still too weak to risk
leaving the house, and visitors also posed a threat. Once, when she
had first come home from the hospital, a neighbor had dropped by to
visit and wrapped Natoma in a bear hug before talking about a grand-

son who was recovering from whooping cough. That was it, Connie
and Natoma agreed. No more visitors. So the front door stayed closed
and her world became smaller. She sat in her chair, stared out the
window, waited for the phone to ring, and thought about her pills.

Two left.

One.

She tried not to think about death. Hers was a 35 percent chance
to live, she thought, and never a 65 percent chance to die. But sometimes her fears crept in anyway. On the day she had come home from
the hospital, she walked through the front door and her two cats ran
off and hid. She had been counting down the days to seeing the cats,
and their rejection made her sob. They smelled death, she said, and
they avoided her for days. Only after a week spent coaxing them with
treats and baby talk did the cats finally concede to be touched.

Other people had died inside the house. Both of her parents had
passed away in what had become Natoma's bedroom, and a grandmother and an aunt had died in the guest room across the hall. The
ghosts had become a running family joke, and Natoma had once
teased her visitors to "sleep well, but not too well." Lately the jokes
had stopped. Now, when she thought about the dead, she wondered
about their final moments: Had they been comfortable? Lonely?
Peaceful? Scared? Would it have been better if she had died quickly
when she collapsed in the barn? Sometimes at night, pale and small
underneath two comforters, she imagined what it would feel like to
close her eyes and slip away.

The grandfather clock ticked toward noon, and Natoma reached
for her final pill. It was the biggest tablet, and she held it up to her
mouth and shook her head. "This is it," she said. She swallowed and
closed her eyes, squeezing them shut for several seconds. Eleven
pills. All gone. "Thank God," she said. She set down the milk. "Thank

God," she said again. She walked into the kitchen and placed the glass bowl back in the cabinet. It would remain there until the next morning, when she would wake up and fill it with eleven pills again.

. . .

Obama left Washington a few days after the passage of health-care reform to begin a tour of celebratory speeches across the country. He hoped to explain the new legislation directly to constituents, highlighting how it would affect students, small-business owners, and people with preexisting conditions. Instead, when Obama arrived in late March for his first speech in Iowa City, it was another effect of the legislation that confronted him upon arrival: Even here, on a leafy college campus in the center of a tranquil town, political discourse had turned into an angry shouting match, always divisive and potentially dangerous.

Outside the basketball arena where Obama planned to speak, two crowds had gathered on opposite sides of a street, with seven police officers in riot gear forming a dividing line on the two-lane road. On one sidewalk, liberals wore Obama T-shirts while chanting "Yes we did!" and a student from the University of Iowa held a sign inviting Obama to join him at a local bar for Thursday night's $1 you-call-it drink special. On the other sidewalk, middle-aged conservatives and retirees from rural Iowa waved homemade signs showing doctored pictures of Obama and yellow Tea Party flags, which displayed coiled snakes under the motto "Don't Tread on Me."

"This bill is Communism!" one protester shouted.

"Obamunism!" yelled another.

Millions of Americans believed their government had ignored their wishes by forging ahead with health-care reform despite a mounting wave of opposition, and now some of those people had trav-

eled to Iowa City determined to be heard. Polls showed that Obama's
signature bill remained stunningly unpopular. Two-thirds of Americans thought it would cost too much; 44 percent expected the quality
of their health care to decline, while only 18 percent expected it to
improve.

In some extreme cases, the anger had manifested as threats or
even violence. One congressman had received a fax with a drawing of
a noose around his neck, another was warned that a sniper planned to
shoot his family, and yet another received an envelope of white pow-
der in the mail that turned out to be baking soda. A brick was thrown
through the front window at the office of Congresswoman Gabrielle
Giffords, a Democrat from Arizona who said she was taken aback
by the country's new capacity for rage. While Republican politicians strongly condemned the violence, a website for the Republican
National Committee pictured Nancy Pelosi surrounded by flames.
Sarah Palin's Facebook page showed the country's Democratic districts as the targets in the crosshairs of a rifle.

Much of the passion, both for and against, centered on Obama,
and protesters planned a three-day festival of activity to coincide
with his trip to Iowa City. The Tea Party held a warm-up rally the night
before the president arrived, busing dozens of protesters to the airport to greet Air Force One and then assembling hundreds more outside the basketball arena in the hours before his speech. One of those
protesters, a middle-aged man with a grizzled beard, had brought
a bullhorn and a homemade sign that read CHAINS WE CAN BELIEVE
IN. He kept his eyes on the two-lane street, waiting for the arrival of
Obama's motorcade, and raised the bullhorn to his mouth. He cleared
his throat and shouted at the Obama supporters on the other side of
the roadway.

"Now the government tells us that we have to have health care," he shouted. "Every single person's body in this whole country belongs to the government. If you believe in freedom, you need to come to this side of the street."

None of the liberals moved.

"If you don't think it takes 2,700 pages to explain a health-care plan, come to this side of the street."

Still nothing.

"If you haven't given up on our Constitution, on our founders, on the hope and dreams of a free country, then come to this side of the street."

Finally one student walked across. He wore dark sunglasses and carried a poster-board sign that he had made moments earlier. It read THESE PEOPLE ARE IDIOTS. He held it up above the Tea Party protesters, his sign mocking them, while he smirked and listened to an iPod.

Some protesters noticed the student and his condescending sign, and they asked him to leave. More students started to cross the street to join their friend, but the police yelled for them to stand still. The protesters and supporters pushed toward the center of the street. A policeman radioed for backup.

Meanwhile, as the frenzy continued, Obama's motorcade wound through campus and entered the arena through a lesser-known back entrance. The two-lane road would have offered a more direct route. But at a time of such divisiveness, the Secret Service had judged the circumstances and made a determination: The safest plan was to avoid the crowds.

. . .

Natoma and Connie were eating grape salad at their kitchen table when the phone finally rang. The automated caller ID announced

"Clover Land Kleenex," which Connie immediately translated. "It's the Cleveland Clinic!" she said, squeezing Natoma's hand. "Pick it up."

They had been waiting for more than a week to hear if one of Natoma's three siblings was a bone marrow donor match, and time had worn away their eagerness and replaced it with anxiety and concern. Shouldn't they have heard something by now? Each sibling had a 25 percent chance, and sibling matches often led to quick transplants and favorable genetic odds. If none matched, Natoma would be left to hang her fate on a national database, a potentially fruitless search through strangers' DNA that sometimes required months more of waiting, hoping, swallowing pills, and receiving chemotherapy. No, it had to be a sibling, Natoma thought. She was due for a break. Now she picked up the phone and placed it on speaker so that Connie could listen in.

"Hello, this is Natoma," she said.

On the other line, a nurse introduced herself and cleared her throat. "Natoma, I'm calling about your donor search," she said. "I'm so sorry to tell you this, but we have determined that neither your brother or sister is a match."

"But wait a second," Natoma said. "I have two sisters. There's Connie and there's Barbara."

"Oh, I'm sorry. Let me see here. That's right. Okay, hold on," the nurse said, flustered. In the background, she could be heard typing into a computer. Natoma and Connie remained silent and stared at the phone. "Oh, yes," the nurse said. "Here we are. I see. Connie is not a match, but it looks like . . . yes, it looks like Barbara is a match. Yes, I think so . . . Umm . . . Wait . . . I want to make sure. Let me look into this. I'll call you right back."

The nurse hung up, and Connie and Natoma stood up from the

table, both smiling. "I knew it would be Barbara," Natoma said. "I just had a feeling it would be her." Out the window, Natoma watched a deer drink from the pond in the backyard. "Isn't it beautiful here?" she said. She ate a few bites of grape salad, not thinking about the sores in her mouth. Then she reached for her cell phone to call Barbara with the news. Before she could dial, the portable phone rang again. "Clover Land Kleenex," the caller ID announced. This time Connie answered and hit the speakerphone button. "Hello again," she said.

"Hello," the nurse said. "This is hard. It's disappointing. But I'm sorry, no, I was wrong. Unfortunately Barbara is not a match, either."

Natoma banged her hand against the table and looked pleadingly at Connie, who looked back at her sister and shook her head. The nurse broke the silence. "Are you there?" she said. "I know this isn't the news you wanted, but it's okay. It's okay. This isn't the end of the world. We have a database of a million people, and there's a match out there. Now we can move on and begin the next step in the process."

"Oh, darn," Natoma said, finally. "I really wanted it to be Barb. I wanted this to be it."

"We got our hopes up," Connie said.

The nurse apologized once more and then hung up, leaving Connie and Natoma sitting in silence at the kitchen table. The deer was gone. The grape salad stung her mouth. Four pills remained in the glass bowl. The grandfather clock ticked mercilessly toward noon.

"Well, maybe now they'll find you some younger, healthier bone marrow," Connie said.

"Yeah," Natoma said. "I didn't want Barb's old bone marrow anyway."

"No," Connie said. "You want it from somebody better-looking."

"Somebody without wrinkles."

"Somebody famous."

"Somebody rich," Natoma said, and they both tried to laugh.

The nights lasted forever. Neither of them slept. Natoma piled three
comforters on top of herself and stared at the ceiling, walking circles around the 3.2-mile nature trail in her head. The path through
Hinckley Park was one of her favorite places in the world, covering
forty wild acres in a forest not fifteen minutes from her house. It
was where her father had taught her to swim on hot summer nights,
where she had vowed to quit smoking and taken daily walks to clear
her mind while her mother suffered from Alzheimer's. She knew
every bend along the trail, every meadow of wildflowers, every pine,
spruce, hemlock, or maple. Each loop in her head lasted about one
hour. Each night lasted six or seven loops.

Across the hall, Connie kept awake and wondered how her sister was doing. She held her breath and listened, trying to interpret
Natoma's frequent groans, moans, and sighs. Which ones indicated
momentary discomfort and which foretold the next major crisis? It
was always hard to tell. Two months of caretaking had taught her that
oozing mouth lesions could be normal and a paper cut could necessi-
tate a frantic trip to the emergency room. She had read informational
booklets on leukemia and sought advice from dozens of doctors,
making herself a student of the disease, but no amount of information quelled her deepest fear. "I could do something wrong and kill
my sister," she often said. "I could kill her." On the rare nights when
she did manage to sleep, her nightmares were ruled by visions of mistakes she might make or symptoms she might fail to recognize. She
dreamed about the afternoon a few weeks earlier when she had left
Natoma alone to run a quick errand to the library, only to come home
and find her with a sudden infection to the wound around her catheter, forcing her back into the hospital for three days. Connie often
awoke in a panic. Had she done a bad job cleaning the catheter? What
if she hadn't gotten home in time? What if traffic had been bad on the

way to the hospital? As a caretaker, she considered herself both ill informed and inadequate, although neither was true. She was simply new to this; Natoma had been the one who always watched over old and sick relatives. But now the older relatives were dead, Barb was busy with her own grandchildren, and their brother, Ken, had a big job working long hours at the newspaper in Dayton. Connie was the only option left.

A lawyer had given her power of attorney to act on behalf of Natoma, and Connie had spent several days helping her sister apply for emergency Medicaid. To qualify, Natoma had to cash out her IRA and limit the combined balance of her checking and savings accounts to less than $1,700. A few weeks after Connie had submitted the forms, she received a notice in the mail. Leukemia had made Natoma's case an urgent priority, the letter explained, and she had been granted emergency Medicaid. They had not received a hospital bill since.

Connie was sixty years old with neither a job nor children, which had made her sudden move to Ohio logical but not easy. She had always loved and protected her younger sister and now said, often and with conviction, "There is no place else I'd rather be." And yet there were also many moments when she would rather have been anyplace else. Her husband was a pilot, home alone in Homestead, Florida, and she missed their whimsical, recreational flights on the weekends to small-town diners for decadent pancake breakfasts. She missed his tired jokes and how they still made her laugh. She missed his warmth in bed. Alone at night in Natoma's house, there was nothing but darkness and fear—and now a faint, shrill noise coming from the bedroom across the hall.

"Oooh," Natoma cried. Connie sat up and held her breath. Was this discomfort or disaster? She listened for more noise.

"Connie," came a whisper from the other room. Then louder: "Connie!"

She rushed across the hall. "What is it? What's wrong?" she said. "Look," Natoma said, and she held up her arms. They were covered with hundreds of red bumps rising from the flesh, a fierce rash. This malady was new to them. "Okay," Connie said. "Let's figure out who to call." She hurried into the living room and opened a red binder filled with twenty-three business cards, all inscribed with the names of different doctors, nurses, and specialists who had helped treat Natoma during the last two months. Ever since the end of Natoma's in-patient stay, Connie had typically driven her sister to Cleveland Clinic three or four times a week for chemotherapy, radiation, transplant consultations, or various sudden emergencies. There had been the gynecologist appointment that led to surgery, the headache that led to a CAT scan, the slight fever that necessitated a trip to the emergency room, the allergic reaction that resulted in septic shock, and now this mysterious rash. Connie decided to dial the hospital's on-call nurse. The phone rang four times before the nurse answered. "There's a rash spreading all over her arms and legs," Connie said. "It looks pretty bad. Should we come in?"

"Not yet," the nurse said. "Monitor it for fifteen minutes and call me back."

Two minutes later, Natoma walked into the kitchen and held up her arms. Nothing. The red marks had disappeared. The skin felt smooth. "It's weird, but I feel fine," Natoma said. Connie called the nurse and apologized for wasting her time. Then she patted Natoma on the shoulder. "I guess strange things happen when your body isn't your own, kid," she said. "You've got an alien body now." They went back to their beds, stared at the ceiling, and waited for the sun.

Early in the morning, a home nurse came to the house for Natoma's weekly checkup, and the three women sat together at the kitchen table. Connie made coffee while the nurse tested Natoma's vitals and typed the results onto a laptop. "You've gone a little bit backward today," the nurse said to Natoma, who slumped in the chair in her pajamas. She had already made five trips to the bathroom since dawn, and a hazy film covered her right eye. The nurse looked over at Connie. "You look a little tired, too," the nurse said. "How are you doing with all of this?"

Connie thought for a minute. The honest answer was that she had okay days and horrible days. That sometimes, when her sister was out of earshot, she would admit to friends that she felt helpless, that her sister was starting to look a hundred years old, like a ghost, bald and thin and alarmingly dead-eyed, as if ready to slip away at any moment. That just talking to her husband could make her feel weepy. That the long days in the house drove her crazy and she sometimes had to rush out the front door and run an errand—invent an errand— to keep from suffering a breakdown. That she missed her workouts, her friends, her clothes—her life. That her fleeting moments of self-pity compounded her misery by leading to waves of guilt, because of course her little sister had it so much worse, and because of course there was no place else she would rather be.

"I'm just a little worn out," Connie told the nurse.

"You have to take care of yourself, too," the nurse said. "If the caretaker isn't well, that's bad for everyone. I think it might be time for you to have a little time away, a dinner out, maybe a night at home to bond with your husband."

"Thanks, but I'm okay," Connie said. "I'm not complaining."

Natoma interjected. "You should be complaining. Caring for me right now is like caring for a fifty-year-old baby."

"I'm just scared," Connie said. "I'm scared I'm going to do something wrong and kill you. I've never done this before."

"I've never had leukemia before," Natoma said. "It's all new. We're learning together."

"I know. That's true," Connie said, dabbing her eyes with a tissue. "It's just hard. It's hard. But listen, I'm not complaining. You know that I want to be here, right?"

"Yes," Natoma said. "I know."

. . .

A few months after sending her letter to the president, Natoma had begun to receive a flood of mail in return. Each day brought another collection of care packages, balloons, and get-well cards. Some of the mail came from old friends, but most came from strangers who had heard the president's speech about Natoma or followed her story in the news. Natoma sometimes stared at the return addresses—Alaska, Colorado, Wisconsin—and marveled at how people could know about her in states she had never visited. She tried to imagine herself writing to a stranger. Would she ever be so moved by a story to buy a card, write a letter, share her secrets, and search for a far-flung address? She guessed not. When she thought about her mail through that prism, even the most impersonal, cheesy poetry on a Walmart card was enough to induce tears.

Some people sent checks, varying in amount from $5 to $300, and the money paid her electric bill and filled the refrigerator. But more than their money, she treasured the short explanations that people had written on the bottom left corner of each check, assigning them For: _____ "love," "thanks," "inspiration," and "universal health care." Other people had sent bizarre holistic advice, including a packet on New Age Christianity, four typed pages on how to soak in energy through a schedule of continuous sunbathing, and a yoga DVD for beginners. One man from Virginia referred to himself as the Messiah and wrote that he had planted a healing herb for her in his garden and his agricultural schedule indicated that she would be fully healed by June 21. Natoma had laughed at his craziness before taking out her calendar and circling June 21 in red, just in case. "When you have a 35 percent chance you hang on to any hope you can get," she said. She had responded to every letter, tacked her favorites to the wall, and photocopied the checks before cashing them.

The letters were her best medicine, she said, so one morning she set her glass bowl of pills down on the kitchen table and began to sift through a pile of mail. She read each letter once to herself and again out loud so Connie could hear. The first was from a teenage girl in Pleasant Prairie, Wisconsin: "My family has hereditary interconnective disease no one can identify, except to give us noneffective pain killers," the girl wrote. "Tendons are like silly putty. It affects our whole bodies. I have missed a lot of school but I am going to college and my mom worries . . . I tell you all this to thank you for convincing Congress. Thank you from the bottom of my heart for saying what made everything possible."

Next was a postcard from Hollywood, California: "I am going to pray for you."

From Denver: "You are helping make this issue more personal! It helps for people to SEE a real person that they can relate to."

Kansas City: "If you lose your taste for food, try mashed potatoes. For some reason, it was the only thing I could taste during my chemo for breast cancer."

Akron, Ohio: "I am so moved by your bravery."

And now, from Washington. Natoma had recognized this envelope immediately. She had received this same package once already, shortly before her diagnosis. The big manila envelope, the cardboard sleeve, the small envelope protected inside, and a white card embossed with the presidential seal. It was a second letter from Obama.

Over the coming months, Natoma and Obama would continue

to focus on their own arduous fights. Natoma would eventually be matched with a bone marrow donor through Cleveland Clinic's database, throw a re-birthday party in her hospital room, undergo surgery, and spend the rest of the year under Connie's twenty-four-hour supervision. She would be forced to stay away from sunlight and swallow fifteen pills a day while she waited to see if the new bone marrow would save her life or attack her body. It would be months, maybe years, before she knew whether or not she would survive the cancer.

Obama would continue to fly across the country for rallies and speeches, trumpeting health-care reform as a "historic achievement." He would attend dozens of fund-raisers to repay members of Congress who had voted for the bill, and he would campaign on their behalves as the midterm elections neared. He would watch with dismay as the new era of divisiveness continued and the political violence escalated. He would continue to defend health-care reform as a linchpin of his legacy, even as voters turned on the Democratic Party and rival politicians threatened the bill with lawsuits and promises of repeal. He would watch sixty-six Democratic representatives lose their seats in the midterm elections largely because of their votes for health-care reform, including Ohio's John Boccieri.

But now, sitting at her kitchen table, Natoma opened the second envelope addressed to her from the White House and found a lasting testament to how much her brief intersection with the president had meant. "Natoma," Obama wrote. "After all the struggles that you've been through, I know it must be tough to face your latest challenge. Please know that you have inspired me greatly, and you are in my thoughts and prayers." He had also mailed a photograph of himself signing the health-care bill. Inscribed was a short message that Natoma would think back to again and again to fortify her during the hard months to come.

"I couldn't have done it without you," the president wrote.

CHAPTER 5

"Stop and listen to all
the American people!"

Thomas Ritter turned on the television at his home in Plano, Texas, flipped the channel to Fox News, and settled into his usual seat on the end of the leather couch, its back cushion stained from the rub of his hair gel. It was early on a Tuesday evening, which meant Thomas had already begun his weekday routine in the room he called "the man cave." He held a black remote in one hand and squeezed an orange stress ball with the other. Sweet tea and Diet Coke rested in front of him on the coffee table. Conservative host Glenn Beck spoke from the flat-screen TV.

"Obama has trotted out another supposed victim of the system," Beck said, looking directly into the camera. "This one is Natoma Canfield, a breast cancer survivor."

Thomas, forty-six, leaned forward on the couch, jiggled his left knee, cracked his knuckles, and threw the orange ball against the ceiling. His habit was not to watch TV so much as to interact with it. He worked the remote with his right thumb, flipping from Fox to CNN to MSNBC, turning the volume up to hear the analysts he liked and muting it for the others. When none of the channels held his attention, he jumped up from the couch and walked across the room to his computer, where he read political news stories on Yahoo!, downloaded the HR 3962 health-care reform bill, and e-mailed producers to critique their news judgment. He wheeled around to see the TV and then turned back to the computer, carving circles in the carpet. His wife and daughter-in-law kept the glass door to the man cave closed so they could watch reality shows in the other room, but sometimes they decided to watch Thomas instead. He was more entertaining. "What a nerd!" they agreed, giggling. He flailed his arms, tossed off his shoes, and bounced up and down on the couch. Even through the closed door, they could still hear his usual running monologue whenever Obama or one of his aides appeared on TV. "Oh, come on, dude. Come *on*! . . . You know that's not true. You know it! . . . No, no. Now you're lying, dude! You're lying! Wake up. Wake up! Why aren't you listening to the American people?"

Now, on Thomas's TV, Beck was saying, "We're following in the footsteps of Europe, not America. I have never in my life seen anything so outrageous as what this administration is doing."

Thomas was a lifelong Republican, but only lately had politics become his obsession. He set his alarm on Sundays to watch three morning news shows at once—"It just kills me that they're all on at the same time," he said—and sometimes stayed on the couch until he was late for church. On weeknights, the television in the man cave rolled through Fox programming for two or three hours, from Glenn Beck to Sean Hannity to Bill O'Reilly, and Thomas flipped to MSNBC during the commercials so he could "hear what the other side is saying."

Lately he had become incensed by Obama's health-care bill—as much
for the politics surrounding it as for the legislation itself. He had seen
half a dozen polls that all showed a majority of Americans disap-
proved of the bill, sometimes as much as 73 percent, so why, Thomas
wondered, was the president still insisting on passing it through the
back door, searching for a procedural loophole to avoid needing the
traditional sixty votes necessary in the Senate? Why was he impos-
ing his vision on the American people instead of governing on their
behalf? Thomas had lived most of his life in Plano, a suburb of Dallas,
where the high-school football team won state championships, the
malls were measured in square miles, and the three-bedroom houses
came with manicured lawns, rock gardens, and identical stone huts
built around the mailboxes. This here was the heart of America,
Thomas believed. He knew almost nobody in Plano who supported
Obama's bill.

"They're going to do whatever it takes to pass it," Beck said now.
"They are going to go the way of the snakes and the cockroaches. They
are going to crawl out in the cover of darkness and they're going to
pass this, make it happen one way or another.

"Don't you let them do it."

In the last five years, Thomas had seized control of his life and
earned a nickname from friends as "the comeback kid." He had quit
smoking two packs a day, sworn off alcohol, walked away from an
unfulfilling career in restaurant management, recommitted to his
Christian faith, and strengthened relationships with his ex-wife and
two teenage children, Alexa and Jeffrey. He had become a fifth-grade
history teacher in a school serving a predominantly poor, Hispanic
neighborhood and then traveled during the summer to volunteer
in Peru. One afternoon during a singles' lunch after church, he had
fallen for a pretty blonde named Lynette, who was also divorced

with two teenage kids. He had taken her out for enchiladas at On the Border and married her six months later. Until then, everyone had always known him as Tom, but Lynette called him "Thomas," and so that's who he had become.

The transformation made Thomas believe that life essentially boiled down to two choices: be the person things happen to, or be the person who makes things happen. Once a halfhearted Republican who had failed to vote in a handful of presidential elections, Thomas began researching everything from immigration to gun laws to the national deficit and voicing his opinions whenever he could. He called in to talk-radio shows and helped local Republicans campaign for office. He wrote letters to politicians who angered him, sending missives to Vice President Joe Biden about his profane language and to Michigan congressman Bart Stupak about his support of health-care reform. Lately, though, Thomas had been bothered by Obama the most.

"If this passes, they will control every aspect of your life," Beck said now. "That is frightening. It is absolutely frightening."

Thomas had supported Mike Huckabee early on in the 2008 presidential election because of his strong stance against abortion. Later, during the general election, he had forced himself to like John McCain, mainly because he was the last Republican left. As the election dragged on and Obama emerged as the likely winner, Thomas received a steady flow of e-mails from his mother and mother-in-law about the young candidate's background. Obama was a devout Muslim, a foreigner, a racist, and a crook, the e-mails said. Thomas deleted the messages, disregarding them as conspiracy theories. But some of their basic ideas took hold. Obama was not a Muslim, Thomas concluded after doing some Internet research, but he was sympathetic to the faith after living for a few years in Indonesia. He was not a racist, but he had soaked in the racially charged sermons of

Reverend Jeremiah Wright. He was not a crook, but he had sometimes surrounded himself with shady characters while rising to power in Chicago, with its culture of political corruption. "His whole background just made it seem like we had nothing in common," Thomas said. But still, on election night, Thomas had marveled at the televised images of huge crowds gathering around the world and vowed to give Obama a chance. He was a patriot above all else, and he believed that Obama's election was a historic moment that he wanted to take part in. He rushed out in search of an Obama keepsake after Election Day and came home with two local newspapers bearing triumphant headlines: CHANGE HAS COME TO AMERICA and GREAT EXPECTATIONS.

But for Thomas, the aura of hopefulness lasted only a few months. The economy continued to tank, and Obama responded by pushing a bank bailout ($700 billion), an auto bailout ($85 billion), and a stimulus package ($787 billion) while Thomas fretted about the extending reach of government and the escalating national debt. He watched Obama spend three months deliberating how to proceed with two wars, even as the shorthanded U.S. troops continued to fight—including Thomas's own son-in-law, a machine gunner beginning his second tour in Iraq. He saw the economy continue to sputter as Lynette lost her job and then accepted two jobs at once, working seven days a week in a fruitless attempt to keep pace with their credit card debt.

Most maddening of all, Thomas continued to hear Obama and his staff blame the country's problems on his predecessor, George W. Bush. "Oh, come on! Take some responsibility!" Thomas often yelled at the TV in the man cave, and when Lynette came in to check on him, he would continue to rant. What would happen if he blamed all of his problems at work on the teacher before him? What if he said—and now he tilted his chin skyward and imitated Obama—"Oh, the fourth-grade teacher left us with a major mess. We inherited two kids who couldn't read, seven kids with behavior problems, and six bad test takers." How would his principal react to that? "I'd get fired within a month," Thomas said. But Obama and his staff had been deflecting blame and belittling their critics for more than a year, Thomas said. The president had presented himself as a unifier during the campaign, but now Thomas believed the country was more divided than ever, especially over health care. Everyone was either a Democrat or a Republican, a liberal or a conservative, and neither side listened to the other. He believed Obama and his allies had dismissed the Tea Party as racist, Fox as biased, Sarah Palin as dumb, and Republicans as "The Party of No."

Somewhere amid all of the divisiveness and mockery, Thomas believed, entire groups of Americans had been disregarded. People like him had become nothing more than a compilation of stereotypes about the political right, even if reality was much more nuanced.

Yes, Thomas believed the border to Mexico should be closed to protect American jobs and American security, but he also adored the Hispanic students whom he taught and he wanted their parents to be given a path to citizenship. He played football with his fifth graders during recess, tried to speak with them in his lousy "restaurant Spanish," and made house visits to meet their parents and get to know their neighborhoods.

Yes, he loved to watch Fox News on a leather couch in a three-bedroom house that had raised ceilings, a fake fireplace, and a 1940s piano that nobody played, but he was hardly a product of upper-class entitlement. He had been the first in his family to graduate from college, paying his own way through the University of North Texas while working full-time as a waiter at Cheddar's. After college, he had spent long stretches unemployed, living without health care and delaying treatment on a dangerous heart condition until he landed a job with benefits.

Yes, he feared radical Islam and felt uneasy when he saw women shopping at Walmart dressed in the full burka. But one night, a Muslim woman had saved his life. It had happened about seven years ago, when he was at his absolute low point—divorced, lonely, living in an apartment, drinking too much, and floating from one unfulfilling job to the next. He had gone down the street by himself to a bar, drank too much Rumple Minze and Miller Lite, and decided to walk home. About halfway back, he had passed out in the middle of a dark two-lane highway, and the first woman who drove by saw him in her headlights and slammed on the brakes. She was a middle-aged Muslim who happened to live in Thomas's apartment building. She recognized him, loaded him into her car, and drove him home. Thomas woke up the next morning, remembered what had happened, and imagined how easily someone could have run him over. He decided his survival was a tribute to human kindness and a sign from God. He had his last drink later that month, became a regular again at his church, met Lynette, and decided to become a teacher. He and the Muslim woman had become friends. He had researched parts of the Koran on the Internet and tried to understand the faith for himself.

Now, on Fox in the man cave: "I can't think of anything more morally bankrupt than this. All hell is going to break loose."

And then: "We want Americans to go Code Red."

At about 10:00 p.m. on March 16, Thomas stood up from his couch and walked over to the computer. Enough, he thought. He had heard once on TV that people could send e-mails to the president, and now he opened the Internet and went to Whitehouse.gov. The page was dominated by a photo of Obama speaking during his rally for Natoma Canfield in Ohio. To the right of the picture was a small link for "feedback," and Thomas clicked it open. He typed "health care policy," in the subject column and began his e-mail.

Thomas had never needed to type during his years in the restaurant industry, and he still felt uncomfortable with a keyboard. He usually liked to write his notes on paper first, holding the pages in his hands and scratching out words until he had the draft just the way he liked it. Then he would peck the note into the computer, searching for one letter at a time or sometimes giving up altogether and asking Lynette to type it for him. But now it was late at night, his message was urgent, and there was no time for perfection. He hunched over the keyboard and started to type, his fingers struggling to keep pace with his mind. "Dear Mr. President," he wrote.

> I hope you read this and that you stop and listen to all the American people! This bill has caused such a divisive, dirisive, and toxic environment. I teach and watched as excited students were motivated by the promise of hope. Hope that they too could reach the heights of their dreams. I even remember the line we are not blue states or red states but the United States. The reality is that any citizen that disagrees with your administration is targeted and ridiculed. I hesitated to write for fear of some kind of retribution. This is exactly the kind of things you ran against isn't it? I watched you make fun of tea baggers and your press secretary make fun of Ms. Palin which was especially beneath the dignity of the White House. I have hope that you will at least consider that if Congress has to try every strategy possible to pass a bill that it clearly has the majority to pass, and still can't pass with bi-partisan support maybe we should pause and reflect. Do the right thing not the political thing. Suggest a bill that all Americans can support.
> Thomas J. Ritter, Citizen of the U.S.

He read over the note quickly and then called Lynette into the man cave. She followed him to the screen and stood over his shoulder. "What do you think of this?" he asked, and Lynette started to read. She considered herself a Republican because she was opposed to abortion and because everybody they knew was Republican, but the debate over health-care reform bored her. She worried sometimes that her husband's strong opinions could lead to trouble. She had been taught not to talk about politics in public for fear of offending people, and she thought of that now as she finished reading Thomas's note. Did he really want to write an e-mail telling off the president?

"Oh, come on," Thomas said. "It's not like he's ever going to read it."

Lynette shrugged and walked out to the living room to watch her reality shows, closing the glass door behind her. Thomas turned back to the computer and clicked the Send button. His e-mail disappeared from the screen as he wheeled to see the TV in the man cave. He wondered where, exactly, his e-mail would arrive and whether or not anyone would bother to read it.

. . .

The e-mail from Plano, Texas, arrived late at night on the ninth floor of a nondescript office building located a few blocks from the White House, its exact address kept secret for security reasons. An automated computer program scanned the e-mail for threats and sorted it into one of about 75 category folders. Then the message was forwarded to a staff of 50 full-time mail analysts, 25 interns, and 1,500 volunteers—an army built to serve as the filter between the public and its president.

The battle for health-care reform had generated a historic barrage of mail for Obama and wreaked havoc on the ninth floor. During the week in which Thomas sent his e-mail, the White House Office of Correspondence had received 200,000 e-mails, 100,000 letters, and 12,000 faxes addressed to the president. Every letter was tested for radiological and chemical weapons and then packed into a white, twenty-pound box. Ten or twenty boxes each day were loaded into trucks, scanned through metal detectors, and delivered to the correspondence office. The building had its own zip code (20500) and its own postal deliverymen. Mail analysts gathered in conference rooms and cubicles spread across the sprawling ninth floor, which looked more like a temporary office space with its whitewashed walls, gray carpets, and doughnuts sitting on a counter in the break room. The analysts worked from 7:00 a.m. to 10:00 p.m., reading through mail, organizing it by category, and then selecting the ten pieces destined for Obama's desk.

The colossal mail-room operation had been refined over the course of two hundred years, expanding along with the popularity of presidential mail. George Washington and Thomas Jefferson received an average of about five letters a day in the White House, opening and responding to all of it themselves, but the mail increased as the price of postage dropped. William McKinley complained about a "flood of 100 letters" each day in the late 1800s, so he hired an assistant to open them. It remained a manageable, one-person job until March 4, 1933, when Franklin D. Roosevelt was sworn into office during the Great Depression and began delivering a series of intimate radio addresses, his fireside chats. Roosevelt implored millions of listeners to "tell me your troubles," and they responded by sending 450,000 letters to the White House during the next week.

Roosevelt's mail filled two storage rooms in the basement and piled up in the hallways outside the Oval Office, so he hired a temporary staff of twenty-two to read and respond to the letters. He told the newcomers they would be employed only until the mail was no longer a fire hazard, but that day never came. He continued to receive about ten thousand letters a week for the next ten years, and eventually his staff stopped counting mail by the piece and instead measured stacks of letters by the yard. Roosevelt gave a total of thirty-one fireside chats, each time speaking directly to listeners in the second person, using basic language and encouraging feedback. Those who wrote to him came to regard the president less as a distant power figure than as an accessible friend, sending him thousands of birthday and anniversary gifts.

It was a shift in the perception of the presidency that would endure beyond the end of Roosevelt's last term in 1945. Harry Truman received three truckloads of personal mail each day at the White House. John F. Kennedy received 15,655 letters a week. Richard Nixon got 44,563 a week. Bill Clinton, the first president with a public e-mail address, received 1,051,353 e-mails and 2,259,308 letters in 1998 alone.

Each president's legacy was shaped in part by his relationship to the mail. Abraham Lincoln decided to grow a beard because of a letter from an eleven-year-old girl who suggested that "whiskers" would "make you look a great deal better, for your face is so thin." Dwight Eisenhower created early opinion polls by dividing the mail into stacks of "pro" and "con" and using the tally to measure his popularity. Lyndon Johnson shaped his speeches around anecdotes from letters supporting the Vietnam War. Nixon, weary of criticism, wanted to see only positive letters, so his chief of staff sent a memo to the mail room instructing the workers to avoid delivering anything to the Oval Office "that expresses opinions contrary to positions taken by the President."

George H. W. Bush kept a stack of note cards on Air Force One and liked to respond to letters during long flights. Clinton's mail room was overwhelmed during the Monica Lewinsky scandal by protesters who sent thousands of cigars. George W. Bush received hundreds of shoes after an Iraqi journalist threw a pair at him. Ronald Reagan asked his mail staff to deliver between thirty and fifty letters every Friday afternoon and then devoted hours each weekend to crafting his responses. When a precocious seventh grader sent Reagan a letter explaining that his mother had declared his bedroom a "disaster area" and he needed "federal funds to hire a crew to clean my room," Reagan happily played along, sending a three-page reply.

> *Your application for disaster relief has been duly noted, but I must point out one technical problem; the authority declaring the disaster is supposed to make the request. In this case your mother. However, setting that aside, I'll have to point out the larger problem of available funds . . . May I make a suggestion? This administration, believing that government has done many things that could better be done by volunteers at the local level, has sponsored a Private Sector Initiative program, calling upon people to practice volunteerism in the solving of a number of local problems. Your situation appears to be a natural fit.*

But no other president in history had turned mail into a daily science quite like Obama. He placed the mail room under the direction of Mike Kelleher, a friend and aide to Obama during his time in the Senate, and Kelleher created a correspondence office built on organization and efficiency. For the first time, incoming e-mails were automatically sorted and then responded to quickly with a White House form e-mail. Volunteers answered the telephones on twenty-five "White House comment lines," limiting each call to two minutes, talking to two thousand people a day, and pushing a designated red button to transfer suicide calls or threats.

On March 19, a dozen mail analysts gathered in a conference

room at 8:30 a.m. and began sorting letters and e-mails. Most of the
analysts were former Obama campaign volunteers fresh out of college
who now earned $36,000 a year to read through 350 to 400 pieces
of mail a day. They opened boxes of mail and sorted it into piles.
Some were policy-specific notes that they rerouted to government
agencies, dropping them in bins labeled "Justice," "Education," and
"HUD." About 20 percent of the letters were from people requesting
a specific presidential greeting to commemorate a new baby, a military retirement, or a birthday, so the correspondence office sent each
back a form letter auto-signed by the president and first lady. Dozens
of eighty- to ninety-nine-year-olds, for instance, wanted birthday
cards, so the correspondence office sent each back a letter written
particularly for that age group. "You have witnessed great milestones
in our Nation's history," the letter read, "and your life represents an
important part of the American story."

The analysts' biggest job was to organize the incoming mail into
about seventy subject folders—an ever-changing list of categories
that offered a barometer of the nation's priorities. About half of the
letters in February and March of 2010 focused on health-care reform;
by contrast, about half during the end of 2009 centered on the war in
Afghanistan. Six to 10 percent of all letters amounted to fan mail for
Obama, offering support. Other regular categories included Global
Warming, Faith and Politics, Gas Prices, Death Penalty, Darfur, H1N1,
Iran, Jobs, First Lady, Torture, From Inmates, POTUS Health, and
Single Parents.

Every note was responded to with a form letter. Kids were also
sent a picture of Bo, the first family's dog, posed on the White House
lawn. The mail analysts were never allowed to write an individual
reply to a letter. The office instead relied on hundreds of form letters
auto-signed by the president—a polished response for each antici-

pated comment or query. Custom-made letters addressed everything from schoolyard bullying to the potential nuclear threat in North Korea. An Emerging Issues Committee met regularly to predict the next popular mail topics, and a staff of six writers crafted five to ten new form letters each week. Only Obama himself was allowed to respond to a letter by hand.

As the analysts continued to read in the conference room, they searched for compelling letters that were representative of the rest of the mail and pertinent to the news. Each analyst picked three or four such letters and wrote "sample" on the top right corner, designating mail that could be sent to the president. At about 2:00 p.m., a few hundred "sample" letters and e-mails arrived in Kelleher's corner office, and he spread them across his desk.

Kelleher, a quiet father of three who had moved his family from Illinois to the Washington suburbs to work for Obama, had been instructed to remain unbiased in picking the contents of the purple folder. The president had called on his second day in office to request ten letters, explaining that he wanted a representative sample: complimentary and critical, elegant and hurried. So Kelleher had made it his habit to monitor the daily metrics of incoming mail—for example, 40 percent about health-care reform, 40 percent about jobs, 20 percent about Iraq—and reflect that same mix in picking the ten letters. On this day, almost all of the mail dealt with health care, so Kelleher started sifting through the samples for health-care messages that struck him.

Much of the mail was negative and some was nasty. Kelleher grabbed a printout of one typical e-mail from a writer in Plano, Texas, who implored Obama to "stop and listen to all the American people!" Kelleher knew Obama liked provocative letters that made him think, but this note from Texas consisted mainly of raw passion and flashes of anger. Kelleher sat in his office and considered his charge. Here was a representative sample, to be sure. But did it cross the thin line between critical and offensive?

Kelleher grabbed the printout and scrawled the date and his initials at the top—"3/19, MK." It was a contentious time. The president had requested an accurate sample. Kelleher tucked the e-mail from Plano inside the president's purple folder and passed it on to an assistant, who walked it over to the White House.

. . .

By the time Thomas's e-mail was delivered to Obama, the true cost of his health-care reform bill had already become clear: It had triggered the official, ugly end to his campaign vision of accord and bipartisanship. The same president who insisted during his speech on election night that the country "resist the temptation to fall back on the same partisanship and pettiness and immaturity that has poisoned our politics for so long," now found himself at the center of a political climate that he described with the same word. "It's poisonous," he said.

Obama himself had continued to lose patience with Republicans. All his talk of bipartisanship had yielded few results, with not one Republican voting for his budget or his stimulus package, and only one Republican voting for his health-care bill. Obama had gradually narrowed his aspirations for bipartisanship during his fifteen months in office, from two parties governing as one . . . to crafting some legislation as one . . . to garnering a few Republican votes on major bills . . . to inviting Republicans to occasional legislative meetings. He even had argued with Republicans over the meaning of the word itself. "Bipartisanship does not mean that Democrats give up everything they believe in," he had said, and then John Boehner, the Republican leader in the House, had written a letter in response.

"Bipartisanship is not writing proposals of your own behind closed doors, then unveiling them and demanding Republican support."

Far from the conciliatory campaigner of 2008, Obama was feisty in the days after he signed the health-care bill, even cocky. He bypassed the Senate by appointing fifteen new staffers while Republican congressmen were away on recess. He traveled to deliver celebratory health-care speeches and once gloated onstage: "Leaders of the Republican Party, they called the passage of this bill 'Armageddon. End of freedom as we know it.' So, after I signed the bill, I looked around to see if there were any asteroids falling or some cracks opening up in the earth. It turned out it was a nice day. Birds were chirping. Folks were strolling down the Mall. People still have their doctors."

But what people no longer had was the illusion of governmental accord. A new poll showed 47 percent of Americans believed Obama was trying for bipartisanship, compared to 74 percent in the same poll the year before. In a few days surrounding the passage of the health-care bill, congressmen had been called Nazis and niggers. One had been spit on, another had found the gas line cut at his house, and forty-two had received death threats. In an unprecedented move, congressmen had held an emergency meeting to discuss their safety and the Capitol Police had offered twenty-four-hour protection for any lawmaker who requested it.

Obama received threats through Twitter and more in the mail. His purple folder included both vitriol and concerned notes of support. A religion professor named Pat Earle wrote that "for clergy, the first year in a parish or congregation is something of a honeymoon, but the second one is often a time of criticism and censure." Another letter, from a group of five- and six-year-olds, inspired a speech that Obama delivered in Michigan in the spring of 2010.

Some of the letters make you think, like the one I received
last month from a kindergarten class in Virginia. The teacher
of this class instructed the students to ask me any question
they wanted. One asked, "How do you do your job?" Another
asked, "Do you work a lot?" Somebody wanted to know if I
wear a black jacket or if I have a beard—clearly getting me
mixed up with that other guy from Illinois. And then there
was my favorite: "Do you live next to a volcano?"

But it was the last question in the letter that gave me pause.
The student asked, "Are people being nice?"

Well, if you turn on the news today—particularly one of the
cable channels—you can see why even a kindergartener would
ask this question. We've got politicians calling each other all
sorts of unflattering names. Pundits and talking heads shout
at each other . . .

The problem is that this kind of vilification and over-the-
top rhetoric closes the door to the possibility of compromise.
It undermines democratic deliberation. It prevents learning—
since after all, why should we listen to a "fascist" or "socialist"
or "right-wing nut"? It makes it nearly impossible for people
who have legitimate but bridgeable differences to sit down at
the same table and hash things out.

So what can we do about this? . . . If you're someone who
only reads the editorial page of *The New York Times*, try glancing at the page of *The Wall Street Journal* once in a while. If
you're a fan of Glenn Beck or Rush Limbaugh, try reading a
few columns on the Huffington Post website. It may make
your blood boil; your mind may not often be changed. But the
practice of listening to opposing views is essential for effective citizenship.

On March 19, Obama opened the purple folder and recognized a chance to heed his own advice. An e-mail from Thomas Ritter in Plano, Texas, contained searing criticism, but Obama read it and then waited two weeks until he had time to write an unusually lengthy reply. His pattern of responses showed that he wrote back most often to people who disagreed with him in a relatively respectful manner. "If a letter starts out in bold, 'You're a socialist idiot bent on destroying the country,' then it is hard to engage," Obama said. "I tend to respond to ones that still give me the benefit of the doubt of wanting to do the right thing but think I'm just misguided."

He liked the fact that Thomas was a teacher, which made him believe the letter deserved a thoughtful exchange. Obama took ten minutes one afternoon to write, crafting a response that covered both the front and back of one of his presidential note cards in cursive.

> *Dear Mr. Ritter—*
>
> *I received your letter, and appreciate your concerns about the toxic political environment right now. I do have to challenge you, though, on the notion that any citizen that disagrees with me has been "targeted and ridiculed," or that I have "made fun" of tea-baggers. I think a fair reading is that I have gone out of my way to listen to legitimate criticism, and defend strongly the right of everyone to speak their mind—including those who routinely call me a "socialist" or worse.*
>
> *I sincerely believe that the health care reform bill was the right thing to do for the country. It certainly wasn't the smart "political thing"! And I hope that in the months to come, you will keep an open mind and evaluate it based not on the political attacks but on what it does or doesn't do to improve people's lives.*
>
> *Sincerely, Barack Obama*

. . .

Thomas received Obama's response in the mail on a Friday, and he spent the first few minutes in denial. This must be a well-executed prank, he thought—but then he noticed the embossed presidential seal. A low-level aide wrote it, he reasoned—but then he noticed the smudge patterns that indicated a left-handed writer. It was computer generated, he guessed—but then what about those crossed-out words? Only after Thomas looked up samples of Obama's handwriting online did he finally concede. "He actually wrote it," he said. Then he called a few relatives and read the president's response over the phone. His mother and sister-in-law said they thought Obama sounded smug and condescending, and for the first time Thomas found himself defending the president. "Hey, he read it!" he said. "At least he's listening to what we think."

The next morning, Thomas sent another e-mail to the White House. "Wow!! I am speechless!!" he wrote. He apologized for being rude in his original note. "I will keep an open mind and cut you some slack," he wrote. Then he grabbed Obama's handwritten letter and carried it to his car. He had already committed to go to school for a carnival, where the students would toss pies in his face and throw him into the dunk tank. He set Obama's letter down carefully on the passenger seat, intent on bringing it to the carnival to show it off.

He drove out of Collin County and beyond the planned subdivisions, the huge chain stores, the gorgeous new elementary schools, and the public high school with a fountain at the front entrance and an indoor practice facility for the football team. His drive to work had only taken forty minutes when he used to travel on the highway, but the tolls cost $120 a month so lately he had decided to stick to the side streets. He stared out at the flatlands of Texas and mulled over Obama's letter. Maybe the president had a point, Thomas thought.

Had he been overly critical of Obama just because they disagreed on the issues? Had his e-mails or conversations added fuel to the country's nasty political discourse? "I think I can pull back a little bit and try not to get so angry," he said. "I guess reasonable people will sometimes disagree." He vowed to listen to Obama a little more and yell at the TV in the man cave a little less.

Thomas continued to drive until he arrived in a neighborhood dominated by run-down fast-food restaurants and Mexican tiendas. He pulled into the parking lot of a single-story school building constructed in the 1950s, its property bordered by low-income housing and overgrown grass.

Thomas could have taught at hundreds of elementary schools closer to his house, but he had just signed another three-year contract to stay at Elliott Elementary. It had been the first school to offer him a job when he decided to become a teacher, earning his certification at night while working at Chipotle Mexican Grill. Elliott had hired him as a fifth-grade history teacher in August 2007, and the three years since had been the happiest of his life. He loved inheriting a group of fifth graders, including some who struggled to read at their grade level, and then helping them catch up. It made him feel essential. His father had worked for several years as a janitor at an elementary school before he died at age sixty-eight, and Thomas had thought of him as he hung the Ritter nameplate outside of his own classroom door. Teaching made him proud.

And, slowly, he had become good at it. During his first year, he had struggled to control the students during group work, so he had improvised ways to make each unit interactive. Now his classes divided into tug-of-war teams to battle out the Revolutionary War, with Thomas pulling alongside the colonists to stack the odds against the British. They wrote skits to reenact the Constitutional Convention, made panhandling signs while studying the Great Depression, and battled for seats at the front of the bus during their unit on civil rights. To motivate the students before their annual standardized tests, Thomas had dressed up in a *Star Wars* costume and filmed a motivational video. He had promised to shave off his hair if a certain percentage of the students passed. The kids had fallen short, but not by much, and so he had decided to shave his head anyway. Lynette had come to the school one afternoon with an electric razor, bringing along Thomas's son and daughter-in-law to watch. Thomas sat in a chair in the center of his classroom, surrounded by sixty students who shrieked and took pictures as Lynette ran the buzzer across his scalp. "Mr. Ritter! Mr. Ritter!" some of the students had chanted, and when Lynette finished, they rushed up to rub his head. One of them held a mirror for Thomas to look. The trim was uneven, his hair looked gray, and his head appeared unusually round, Thomas had thought. But here he was, surrounded by his family and these students he had come to love, with everyone laughing and posing for pictures alongside him. It had been the best haircut of his life.

With his hair still cropped short, wearing cargo shorts and an untucked collared shirt, he carried Obama's letter into the school carnival, where kids were shouting and running around with painted faces. Thomas showed the letter to his principal and a group of teachers first, many of whom knew his politics. "I can't believe he wrote back to *you*," one other teacher said. She was a hard-core Democrat who often tried to goad him into long arguments that went nowhere, but this time Thomas just smiled. The principal asked Thomas where he would keep the letter and what he would do with it. "I'm still thinking about it," Thomas said.

The students smeared him with pie and soaked him in the dunk tank, and then Thomas pulled a few of his favorite fifth graders aside to show them the letter. At first, it didn't impress them. "So what?" one student said, and so Thomas explained. He had written a letter to the president, the most important person in the country. The president received thousands of letters each day. He had chosen to read Thomas's letter and then taken the time to respond. "Wait, President Obama actually touched this?" the kids asked, and then they reached out to grab the note card, putting their noses to the paper to smell the ink and running their hands across the embossed presidential seal. It was another interactive lesson—a tactile experience. When Thomas was ready to leave, he had to pry the letter out of the students' hands.

On his ride home, Thomas decided what he would do with the president's letter. Friends had suggested he laminate it, frame it, lock it up in a safe, store it at the bank, or maybe sell it to one of the collectors on the Internet who offered $5,000 or $10,000 for an original note written in the president's hand. But instead, Thomas brought the letter back to school with him again on Monday. "You're crazy," Lynette said, teasing him. He stuck a thumbtack through the edge of the envelope and hung it on the wall behind the desk in his classroom, where students could grab it, read it, and show it off to their friends. It stayed there, unguarded, for the rest of the year.

It was a risk, sure. But he was a teacher, and here was one interactive lesson too valuable to pass up. Even during a time of hardship and divisiveness, a man could speak his piece to the president—and the president might even answer back.

 CHAPTER 6

"I don't feel like I belong here anymore."

Just like always, Lusia Gutierrez knew the family's decision would be hers to make alone. Stay or go? Remain in Arizona or leave the state and its strict new immigration law behind? The question tormented her late into the summer of 2010, and now she had less than one month to decide.

At twenty-two, Lusia—or Lucy, as she preferred to be called—felt too young to be a family matriarch, but life had left her little choice. She lived in a large house with eight relatives in Kingman, Arizona. Her mother and her mother's boyfriend spoke limited English, so Lucy had grown accustomed to speaking for the group. It was Lucy who managed the family's checking account, met with the landlord, and negotiated her mother's days off from work—all while raising two sons of her own, working full-time, and taking evening classes at the local community college. Family members sometimes called her *la jefa*, or "the boss," but never before had the burden of responsibility weighed on her quite like this.

Arizona had passed a controversial law in late April to prosecute and deport illegal immigrants, and the measure had transformed Kingman within weeks. Lucy and most of her family possessed U.S. citizenship; nonetheless, they had started to feel like outsiders as Hispanics in Kingman, a conservative town of twenty-eight thousand isolated in the desert of northwest Arizona. More than half of the town's Hispanics had already moved away. A local conservative group had begun referring to itself as "the unofficial border patrol." The new law was scheduled to take effect in late July, and critics argued that it would lead to further discrimination and harassment of Hispanics.

Suddenly Lucy, who had never so much as registered to vote, was translating the political stories for her mother from each morning's newspaper, staying up late to watch the news, and searching online for the full text of Arizona Senate Bill 1070 so she could read seventeen pages of legalese and fine print and then explain it to her family in Spanish. Suddenly her mother was asking her to fly to Chicago to visit a distant relative, search for a cheap house, and test if the Midwest might be a good place for the family to move. Suddenly each night at the dinner table, her relatives were debating their future and looking to her for the answer.

Stay or go?

The only choice was to go.

Her mother's longtime boyfriend, Bobby, was an illegal immigrant. He had crossed the border in the late 1990s, met Lucy's mother through a mutual friend, and lived with the family for the last four years. Lucy had filled out his application for naturalization and drained her bank account to pay a lawyer $2,500 to help with the paperwork, but the U.S. government had yet to respond. Now, under the new law, Bobby worried his deportation was imminent each time he spotted a police car, so he drove ten miles under the speed limit on his way to work at the Mexican restaurant where he made $7.50 an hour as a cook. He always volunteered to work the night shift so he could watch Lucy's children during the day. The boys were three and six years old, and they called him "grandpa." What would she tell them if *la migra* took Bobby away?

But at the same time, the only choice was to stay.

Lucy loved her job as a receptionist for a local cable and Internet provider, where co-workers came to her house for dinner and the boss described her as "like a daughter." It was a small company in a small town, and most of the customers had come to recognize the pretty young Hispanic with a cherubic face and a reassuring smile. They complimented the blond highlights in her dark-brown hair, her silver-studded nose ring, and the flower design on her acrylic nails. Some even brought gifts for Christmas and asked about her children by name. Another receptionist had recently quit during the midst of the recession, and now the company was using three rounds of interviews to thin out two hundred applicants from across the state, many of whom had college degrees. Lucy conducted some of the interviews, each one a reminder of her own good luck. She had been hired at age eighteen while pregnant with her second child, winning the job based on a casual phone interview and a résumé that consisted of a GED and a job in a fast-food restaurant. "I would never get a position like this with the way the economy is now," she said.

Everyone else in her family also had solid jobs: her fiancé, Luis, on the management track at Home Depot; her mother, Demi, as a prep cook at Cracker Barrel; and Bobby at the Mexican restaurant. Together, they earned enough to feed Lucy's two children and her

three younger sisters—ages seven, fourteen, and sixteen—with money
left over to lease four cars and rent a five-bedroom house. Real estate
prices in Kingman had dropped 60 percent in the last four years,
and Lucy had recently qualified for a housing loan of $115,000. She
sometimes browsed foreclosure sales on the Internet and marveled
at the mini-mansions that fell within her price range. Where else but
Kingman, she wondered, could she possibly afford to buy a seven-
bedroom house with a finished basement and a swimming pool?

But they had to leave.

That's what seemingly every other Hispanic in town was already
doing—throwing together a quick garage sale, packing up the car, and
moving to Las Vegas, one hundred miles to the northwest. Kingman's
public school enrollment had dropped by 5 percent; all six of Demi's
Hispanic co-workers at Cracker Barrel had split town. A gigantic billboard across the street from the police station depicted a red, white,
and blue drawing of Arizona governor Jan Brewer, who had champi-
oned the new immigration law, under a triumphant message in bold
type: ARIZONA—DOING THE JOB THE FEDS WON'T DO.

Lucy had read S.B. 1070 several times and tried to differenti-
ate the facts from the rumors that were spreading around Kingman.
Facts: the bill made it a state misdemeanor crime not to carry immigration papers at all times; it required police to determine immigration status whenever there was "reasonable suspicion" that a person
was in the country illegally; it made hiring illegal immigrants a poten
tial felony. But for Lucy, the bill had also come to mean so much more.
It was the false rumors of immigration checkpoints at her local grocery store and policemen sweeping through Hispanic neighborhoods
wearing black ski masks. It was the empowered conservatives who
walked around town wearing T-shirts that read "Why Should I Have
to Press 1 For English?" It was Luis's bosses at Home Depot, who had

taken down a small sign printed in Spanish to welcome customers
to the store because it became too controversial. It was the waitress
at Chili's who suggested Lucy go for dessert at Sonic instead. It was
the cable customer who approached her desk at work angered by his
bill and told her that "we don't want you people here," forcing her to
wonder for a minute if maybe he was onto something, because lately
Kingman had started to feel as hostile and forbidding as the desert
that surrounded it.

But they had to stay.

Kingman was where Lucy had met Luis, where they had gone to
the town's only movie theater to watch *Bewitched* on every one of their
first four dates. They both had lived in rough places before—Lucy in a
trailer in East Los Angeles; Luis across the border in Tijuana while he
attended high school in San Diego—and Kingman sometimes struck
them as the ideal model of small-town America. Their boys went to
good schools. They lived with family. They had two dogs and a fish.
Once a month, they drove forty-five minutes to Laughlin, Nevada,
on a Saturday night to eat at a Chinese buffet and walk through the
opulent casinos. Where else would they move, anyway? Las Vegas was
too big, the East Coast was too expensive, and Lucy had only visited
Mexico once, when she was four years old. She remembered nothing.

But they had to leave.

Just a few weeks earlier, Demi had received a panicked call from
her great-aunt who had been living illegally in Kingman for thirty-
five years. The woman's dog had escaped earlier that morning. An
animal control officer had found it running down a nearby street
and brought it back home to the address on its collar. The great-aunt
was overjoyed—until the animal control officer mentioned S.B. 1070
and asked to see her U.S. identification card. The great-aunt phoned
Demi, who rushed over with her citizenship papers and explained

that in fact she owned the dog, but the animal control officer was not fooled and phoned the sheriff. "We got an illegal," she said. The police came. Two officers placed the great-aunt in handcuffs. She spent a few days in jail before being turned over to immigration services and scheduled for deportation. Her church raised money and hired a lawyer. When that failed to produce results, a longtime member of the congregation offered to marry the aunt, and she agreed. Now she was on track to become a citizen, and Lucy's family had gained a member in Kingman instead of losing one.

Despite the end result, the incident made Lucy wonder: Would her family be so lucky the next time? And the next? No matter how many nights she went to bed convinced her family should leave, she always woke up the next morning equally sure it should stay. Stay or go? Go or stay? How could she trust herself to decide?

One night after the kids and Luis had gone to bed, Lucy sat down at the kitchen table obsessing again over the pros and cons. She spent her days acting as the family stabilizer, projecting calm, but she often sat alone at night in the living room and let her mind race. Life had come at her too fast, she thought. Only seven years ago, she had been a quiet high-school sophomore with good grades and plans to go to college—the daughter Demi referred to as *"mi ángel."* Then suddenly she was pregnant at sixteen, so scared to tell Demi that she kept it a secret until severe morning sickness forced her into the hospital during the second trimester. Her boyfriend, a high-school athlete, had started using meth, and he was beginning his first of several stints at a rehab center in Mexico on the day Lucy gave birth. She had dropped out of high school, worked full-time to support the baby, and gone back to school at night to earn a GED. Next it was college classes, dates with Luis, a growing family, managing their finances, and arranging meetings with immigration lawyers. Now, the biggest decision in family history was hers to make.

"I help everyone else, but who helps me?" she sometimes wondered.

She sat alone at the kitchen table in the dark house. She needed to confide in someone—someone with more experience making decisions. She took out a pad of lined notebook paper and a pen. "To the President," she wrote at the top, because he was the first authority figure that came to mind. She started to write her first letter to a politician, spilling her feelings without pausing to worry about spelling or grammar.

I don't know if you will every read this. I hope you do. I saw a
video of you reading letters and decided to get the courage to writte
to you. I am 22 years old. I know I am very young and still don't
understand many things. I currently live in the state of AZ and as
you know already "immigration" is a tough topic around here . . .
The town I live in is very small. You have probably never heard of it.
It's named Kingman and sits in the heart of Route 66. There is alot
of people that critizise you here and I feel like racism is very strong
here, kind of a anti-obama and anti-multicultural town. You of
course don't live here but I feel like this town is pushing you out
just like they are trying to push me and my family out. I am a U.S.
citizen but I feel like I don't belong here anymore. I feel like I need to
pack up my belongings and move to Mexico. This new immigration
law doesn't take effect until July 29th but to me it feels like it took
effect the minute it was signed.

I know you are a busy man with everything that is also happen-
ing (oil spill, terrorism) and on top of that having a family, every-
one expecting you to fix everything for them. But please understand
I too have a family that expects me to fix everything for them, and
this new law can possibly brake many families apart. Many people
support this law and like to quickly give their opinion and say that

*we need this bill, but they don't live it first hand they don't see how
this "immigration stance" really is and feels. Right after the bill
was signed I went into a restaurant to buy breakfast and I was
greeted by a gentleman who told me "I don't know why they let your
kind in here." Why that comment? Why? Not because of the color of
my skin can they tell me I am not American! Or that I don't belong
here. I was born in American soil, raised in American soil, and
educated in American soil. I can understand why Arizona passed
this law but I feel like it is opening doors to racism and almost
allowing it to happen. I keep my opinions to myself and don't go
around putting signs in my car or screaming it to the world, but I
feel like I need to, like I need to defend myself from anyone who is
trying to attack me and my family. Is that what we have come to?
America? Where is the America I thought I knew? I'm confused
and flustered. I feel like moving from Arizona, but at the same time
I feel like I should stay and raise my head high because I am an
American and I believe that is enough to be proud of.*

Lucy continued to write for almost three pages, surprised by how
quickly the words spilled from her pen. She closed by writing "hope-
ful . . ." and then signing her name: "Lusia Gutierrez, Arizona Res-
ident & U.S. Citizen." Then she put the letter into an envelope and
went to bed, the same old question still echoing in her head.

Stay or go?

It was time to decide.

. . .

Obama knew all too well the loneliness of making what he called
"tough choices," and he was already obsessing over his latest conun-
drum when Lucy's letter reached the White House. He had promised

to make immigration reform a priority during his presidential campaign in 2008, but instead he had essentially ignored the issue while focusing on health care and the economy. The passage of Arizona Senate Bill 1070 forced him into a choice: Let the law take effect on July 29 even though he disagreed with it? Or encourage the federal government to file a lawsuit against one of its own states, an unusual move that would mean fighting Arizona in court?

Other leaders had bombarded Obama with mail on both sides, illuminating little more than the divisiveness of the immigration debate. Felipe Calderón, the president of Mexico, wrote that S.B. 1070 would promote "intolerance, hate and discrimination." Rick Perry, the governor of Texas, hand-delivered Obama a four-page memo advocating tough immigration laws because, he wrote, "on any given day, the Mexican border region is now beset with vicious murders, tortures, kidnappings and armed confrontations."

But lately, Obama's most frequent mailer had become Governor Jan Brewer herself, the architect of S.B. 1070. She sent memos about illegal immigration to the White House on March 11, April 6, May 20, and June 24. Obama never responded, so Brewer made each letter longer and more indignant than the last.

The governor was in many ways an unlikely adversary to face off against the president in a national debate. At sixty-five years old, Brewer wore thick makeup and brightly colored business suits to complement a smile so unshakable that some rivals had termed it "plastic." She had grown up in Hollywood, moved to Arizona, attended dental school, and then run for local office because she was dissatisfied with her children's junior high. She had ascended to Arizona's secretary of state and then into the governor's job in 2009 when then-governor Janet Napolitano left in the middle of her term to join Obama's administration as the head of the Department of Homeland Security. Brewer's first year in office had been defined in part by clunky speechmaking and infighting with her own Republican colleagues. In April 2010, her approval rating was stuck in the low 40s—even lower than Obama's—and pundits had given her little chance of being elected in November.

Then S.B. 1070 landed on her desk, and within weeks of signing it Brewer had a 60 percent approval rating, a regular role on Fox News, and a group of conservatives pushing her to think about running for president in 2012.

She had always taken a hard stance against illegal immigration, advocating the construction of a fence along the border and refusing state benefits to illegal immigrants, but her resolve seemed to harden further as she signed the bill during a small ceremony on April 23, 2010. She stood at the podium surrounded by Republican colleagues who flashed her the thumbs-up while she reiterated her case: Arizona had an estimated 460,000 illegal immigrants, five times the number it had in 1990. Drug violence had worsened in Mexico and spilled across the border. Phoenix suffered an average of one kidnapping a day, the most of any U.S. city. More than 6,000 illegal immigrants were jailed in Arizona, costing the state about $150 million a year.

"We cannot sacrifice our safety to the murderous greed of drug cartels," Brewer said at the bill-signing ceremony. "We cannot stand idly by as drop houses, kidnappings, and violence compromise our quality of life."

After she made her speech, the shockwaves reverberated across the country. On the lawn outside her office, police squads in riot gear separated protesters and supporters, who alternated chants of "We have rights!" and "No you don't!" In nearby Tucson, a Democratic congressman suggested protesting the bill by arranging a national boycott of travel to Arizona, prompting five death threats that forced him to close his office. In Los Angeles, the city's archbishop said Arizona was "reverting to German Nazi and Russian Communist techniques." In Nashville, a group of country musicians canceled tours to the Southwest. In Texas, Idaho, Ohio, and seventeen other states, Republican lawmakers began drafting immigration laws modeled after S.B. 1070.

And finally, in the White House, Obama mulled another polarizing decision in an already divisive year. He had avoided dealing with illegal immigration for eighteen months, and his political aides cautioned him on the drawbacks of doing so now. Why risk more of his reputation when a Rasmussen poll showed that 60 percent of Americans supported S.B. 1070 and only 31 percent opposed it? Why not focus his energy instead on improving the economy, which Americans had recommended as his top priority? Who would support him on immigration reform anyway? Republicans in the Senate had made it clear that they would refuse to partner with Obama, and lately even Democrats had expressed hesitation at taking on another unpopular issue months before they hoped to be reelected.

But Obama said that S.B.1070 undermined "basic notions of fairness that we cherish as Americans," and he considered it too important to ignore. He told his aides he had made up his mind. He decided to meet with Brewer in person at the White House.

The president disagreed with the governor so completely on illegal immigration that he even disputed her facts. The immigration crisis had not become worse, he believed; it had actually improved. The number of illegal immigrants in the U.S. had dropped from 12 million to 11 million in the last three years. Obama had tripled the number of intelligence analysts on the border and committed 1,200 National Guard troops to the cause—4,800 fewer than Brewer had requested. Deportations had increased under his watch. Violent crime had dropped by 30 percent in some counties along the border. According to FBI statistics, the country's four safest big cities—Phoenix, San Diego, El Paso, and Austin—were all located in border states.

Brewer traveled to the White House on a Thursday morning in early June and met with Obama in the Oval Office. She brought a lawyer and an adviser, setting the scene for a conversation with little common ground. Brewer defended S.B. 1070; Obama argued the law would break apart families, encourage racial profiling, and make Hispanics so afraid of police that they would be less likely to report major crimes or assist with investigations. Brewer wanted to deport Arizona's illegal immigrants—"attrition through enforcement," she called it; Obama believed in a "pathway to citizenship," in which illegal immigrants would be forced to register, pay a fine, and learn English before applying for permanent residency. Brewer said the federal government had "failed" on immigration; Obama countered that state immigration laws such as S.B. 1070 would create a "patchwork system" and undercut overarching federal regulations.

The meeting lasted a little less than an hour. Afterward, Brewer and White House officials spoke briefly with reporters, exchanging political niceties through frozen smiles.

It was "a good meeting," a White House spokesman said.

"Very cordial—very, very cordial," Brewer said. "I am encouraged that there is going to be much better dialogue."

One day after the meeting, Lucy mailed her letter from Kingman. Obama received the note in his daily folder of ten letters, read it, and set it aside for safekeeping. Lucy's note confirmed his belief that S.B. 1070 could lead to stereotyping. He did not reply to her letter; he had already decided on a more sweeping response.

Seven days later, Obama called the law "misguided."

Fourteen days later, Brewer filmed a television advertisement near the border, waggling her finger at the camera and saying, "Mr. President, do your job!"

Thirty-three days later, with Obama's encouragement, the Justice Department filed a lawsuit in district court, asking a judge to declare S.B. 1070 "invalid" and insisting that it "be struck down."

· · ·

Forty-six days later, the lawsuit still unresolved, a mother and daughter stood in their kitchen, having the same conversation that had dominated their dialogue for months.

"I'm scared of what will happen if we stay," Demi said, speaking in Spanish that was translated later.

"I know," Lucy said.

"But if we move somewhere else we have to start over," Demi said.

"I know," Lucy said again.

"That scares me, too," Demi said.

Demi had crossed into the United States for the first time nearly twenty-five years ago, and she often marveled at how utterly American her family had become. She still sought out soft mariachi music and Mexican pop to remind her of a childhood in southern Mexico; her children listened to rap and R&B—"anything with bass," Lucy said—and liked to blast the volume until it threatened to blow out the car speakers. Demi loved to spend her weekends preparing ceviche and spicy Mexican dishes loaded with jalapeño; her youngest daughter, seven-year-old Dora, had no tolerance for spicy food and instead subsisted on lasagna, Cocoa Puffs, and microwave pizza.

Most disorienting of all for Demi was the language barrier that had developed inside her own house. She had come to the United States with an English vocabulary that consisted of a few basic words—"dollar," "work," "bed," and "bathroom"—and her skills had improved only marginally in the years since. She had lived, worked, and socialized mostly with first-generation Mexican immigrants who spoke Spanish. Recently, during her shifts at Cracker Barrel, she had picked up more English by listening to country music on the radio, and one day she had summoned the confidence to attempt conversation with her boss. "Don't bother," he had said, waving her off after a few slow sentences. "I can't understand your accent." She had not spoken English at work since. "It makes me feel stupid," she said.

But she also believed English was the language of opportunity for her children and grandchildren, and she insisted they master it before learning Spanish. She encouraged the kids to watch television and play video games in abundance, reasoning that technology could teach them words she still didn't know. Dora and the two grandchildren spoke to Demi in English, and she spoke back in Spanish. They relied on Lucy to translate all that was lost in between. Sometimes, to impress her mother, Dora counted to ten in the gringo Spanish she had learned by watching *Sesame Street*.

For Demi, it was another inconceivable result of the journey she had started early one morning in 1985, when she left her family's farm in southern Mexico with little more than the $250 cash payment for a coyote to guide her across the border. She had never wanted to go to the United States; her father disappeared every few years to work in Colorado, and that was bad enough. But her mother insisted that she go. Demi was fifteen years old, and she had seven younger siblings whose survival depended on her making money in America and sending it home. She rode two thousand miles on a bus to Tijuana with her cousin, and they checked in to a downtown hotel. A coyote picked them up in a van at 11:00 p.m. and led them through a hole in a fence east of San Diego. They ran through the desert and across the interstate. An eighteen-wheeler stopped to pick them up. They arrived in Los Angeles just before 4:00 a.m.

Demi moved into an apartment in East L.A. with an aunt, sharing a bedroom with three other young Hispanic women to trim her rent to $100 a month. She got a job working at a fabric factory where she cut loose strings from clothing six days a week. It was tedious work that strained her eyes, but the boss paid a weekly salary of $170 in cash each Saturday night. Demi had promised to send $100 home to Mexico every week, but she received her first payment and took a bus straight from work to a downtown shopping mall with a few coworkers. In less than two hours, she spent the entire sum on two pairs of shoes, a white dress, a necklace, a boom box, and a few Mexican cassette tapes. Then she went out dancing. It was the most thrilling night of her young life.

She had become addicted to America after that—to the money and the malls and the shoes. To independence. To owning things. Her father came to L.A. a few years later and tried to take her home to Mexico, but she refused. Instead, she stayed in Los Angeles, met a man, married at age seventeen, and gave birth to Lucy and three more daughters. Congress passed the Immigration Reform and Control Act in 1986, granting amnesty to 2.8 million illegal immigrants, and Demi filled out some paperwork and was granted her citizenship within six months. She continued to work at the fabric factory for thirteen years, sending $100 to her parents at the end of each week.

Her husband had always struggled with his anger, and he became more abusive as their marriage wore on. One night in 2001, furious that Demi had ordered pizza without his permission, he punched her in the face during an argument in their driveway. Lucy, then thirteen, watched from the living-room window. She locked the door and called 9-1-1. Her father saw her make the call and ran away. Demi got up from the driveway, hurriedly packed some clothes into the car, and drove with her daughters to stay with a relative in Arizona. The state had been their home ever since.

And now, if Arizona was going to remain home despite the new law, Demi had decided that she needed to learn English. She had put off the task for twenty-five years with one excuse or another—fatigue, full-time jobs, raising a family—but the proposed immigration law had instilled a new urgency. With all of her Hispanic co-workers gone from Cracker Barrel, her shifts as a prep cook were lonely and slow, with only the radio, a dicing knife, and a gigantic tub of vegetables to keep her company. She worried about always burdening Lucy, her full-time translator. Spanish had become symbolic of illegal immigration among some conservatives in Kingman—"One Country, One Language," a popular bumper sticker read—and Demi felt less comfortable speaking it in public. In this state, at this contentious time, Demi believed there was only one sure way to prove herself as a citizen. She needed to master the same fluent, unaccented English spoken by her neighbors.

With that as her goal, she left home one Thursday evening after dinner and drove across town to Mohave Community College for a beginning-English class for adults. She had registered for the free course earlier in the summer with Lucy's help and had spent Tuesday and Thursday nights in the classroom ever since. She walked into the room, passing an American flag and a copy of the U.S. Constitution taped to the wall, and sat down at a desk in the front. Ten adults filled the desks around her—four from Mexico, three from Iraq, two from China, and one from Colombia. The teacher, an Arizona native named Steve, stood at the front of the room wearing thick glasses and a rumpled sweater.

"Hello everybody," he said, careful to enunciate each syllable. "Thank you for coming to class. Who wants to tell us what they did so far today?"

Demi stared down at her desk. She had not been a student since

she left Mexico, and she was self-conscious about her English and
terrified of being called on. But anxiety had also made her a careful student. She carried a cheat sheet in her pocket—"we = *nosotros*,
you = *ustedes*, they = *ellos/ellas*"—and a Spanish-to-English diction-
ary in her purse. Two freshly sharpened pencils sat on her desk. With
Lucy's help, she had already completed every exercise in the class's
150-page workbook, moving almost 100 pages ahead of the rest of the
class. She had come to the community college with her hair gelled and
curled, wearing dress-up jeans, a blouse, and a faux-pearl necklace.
She referred to Steve, reverentially, as "Mr. Teacher."

This evening's lesson focused on the present progressive, a verb
tense that few in class could decode in their native languages, much
less in English. Steve stood at the front of the room and held up a
drawing from the workbook, which showed a white man in a business
suit sitting at a large desk. "Somebody tell me about this picture,"
he said. Nobody answered. Steve looked around the classroom and
locked his eyes on Demi, who continued to stare down at her desk.

"Demi," he said. "In the picture, is Mr. Smith sitting or standing?"

Demi looked up from her desk, staring first at Steve and then at
the picture in his hand. Her face flushed. She studied the image for a
few seconds in silence and then spoke at a volume barely louder than
a whisper.

"Eets a sitting?" she said.

"Okay, yes. That's good," Steve said. "*He* is sitting."

Demi nodded and repeated the sentence slowly. "He ees sitting,"
she said.

The class spent much of the next two hours talking about similar drawings, and later Steve held up an image of a woman eating a
taco. The Iraqis in class had never heard of a taco, so one of the Chinese women mentioned Taco Bell as a point of reference. The Mexi-

can women jumped in to say that actually real tacos were made with homemade guacamole, beef, and rice, at which point the Colombian woman said that, in South America, tacos usually consisted mostly of fish. At the front of the classroom, Steve leaned back in his chair and shook his head in disbelief. "It is amazing that we are having this conversation about tacos around the world here in Kingman, and the best part is we are all speaking in English," he said. "This is how you will get better, by holding real conversations in English."

He dismissed the class a few minutes later, and Demi gathered her belongings and stood up to leave. She walked out of the classroom and found three other Hispanic women waiting for her just outside the doorway. They had become friends during their time at the community college. "Hard class," Demi said in English, and they all nodded in agreement. They stood in silence for a few seconds, and then Demi reverted back to Spanish to make a joke about the awful tacos at Taco Bell. The women laughed, and then they stood in the hallway for the next twenty minutes, gossiping in rapid Spanish.

· · ·

While Lucy continued to weigh her family's decision, she drove around Kingman and looked at houses, hoping to form a clearer picture of what a future in Arizona might look like. She had already qualified for a housing loan of $115,000, and now her daily junk mail included a handful of notices about foreclosure auctions and short sales. "THERE HAS NEVER BEEN A BETTER TIME TO BUY!" one of the mailings proclaimed. Mortgage rates had dipped below 5 percent, meaning Lucy and her family could buy a house on a thirty-year loan and pay only $700 a month—$300 less than her current rent. Fifty houses were put up for sale in Mohave County each day, and sellers had become increasingly desperate.

A real estate agent named Lana Johnson offered to drive Lucy around to open houses, and some days they toured more than ten properties listed at $115,000 or less. Not long ago, it had been impossible to buy a house in Kingman for less than $200,000. But now, each Saturday, Lana showed Lucy another sampling of all that passed for affordable housing in Kingman during the real estate crisis of 2010: a mini-mansion equipped with a Jacuzzi on the front deck, once listed for $350,000 and now going for one-third the cost; a four-bedroom adobe home on a golf course; a house on two acres in Valle Vista, twenty minutes east on Route 66, where sunsets bathed the desert in red and gold.

Late one Saturday afternoon, just when Lucy thought she could no longer be wowed by all that fell within her price range, Lana suggested they see one more house—the best bargain yet, she said. They drove ten minutes outside of town, into a swath of red desert surrounded by purple mountains and clear blue sky. They turned off Bull Mountain Drive onto Jack Rabbit Road, pulling into the driveway of a five-bedroom adobe house surrounded by cacti on an acre of land. The house had sold for $499,000 in 2005, but now it was foreclosed and listed for $110,000. The backyard featured a large, inground swimming pool with a blue-and-white-checkered deck. Pumpkins and watermelons grew under a tree next to the detached garage. A wooden porch wrapped around three sides of the house, providing sweeping vistas across the desert and back into town.

"I can't believe this house could be ours," Lucy said.

"Well, believe it," Lana said. "Because I'm telling you, it can."

Lana had spent the last three years struggling to adjust to the diminished real estate market in Kingman. She had emigrated from Russia in 2000, lived in Los Angeles for three years, and then moved to Arizona to become a realtor in 2004. Where better to start a career as an agent? The economy was expanding at record pace, and western Arizona had become an epicenter of new development. Research trends indicated that baby boomers wanted to move to warm areas, and suddenly Kingman, Lake Havasu City, and Bullhead City had emerged as retirement destinations, forming an area realtors referred to as the Golden Valley.

Lana had netted $2.9 million worth of sales during her first year in 2005—enough to make an income of well over $100,000 and earn a plaque to hang in her office for Superior Sales Achievement. But she had never considered her sales all that spectacular. There had been more than 450 licensed realtors in the Kingman area then, and it had seemed to Lana that all of them made "dreamy money." She had no ties to the community, no client base whatsoever, and yet still she managed to close seven or eight deals every month.

One developer had bought up six thousand acres near Kingman and launched plans to build a community called Pravada, complete with thirty thousand new homes, walking trails, shops, recreation centers, and a gated entrance framed with dozens of towering palm trees. "The good life is now your life," the sales brochure had read.

Five years later, only the palm trees and two half-built model homes stood as a monument to Pravada and the era of extravagance it embodied. Plans for the community had been abandoned; the land was back up for sale. Real estate prices in Golden Valley had dropped by an average of 60 percent since the market's peak in early 2007. More than half of the local realtors had switched professions or gone out of business. Lana was married to another agent, and now instead of taking vacations to Hawaii they stayed at the nearby casinos in Laughlin and sometimes went scuba diving in Lake Mead. They had cut back on expenses and trimmed their own mortgage payment by buying a foreclosed house for $130,000, but lately even that seemed like a stretch. "I don't think any agents have savings accounts these days," Lana said.

She did appreciate one result of the new housing market: Now instead of working with foreign investors or rich retirees, she was showing houses to people like Lucy, first-time homebuyers who tended to be giddy and expressive. She followed Lucy through the five-bedroom house for fifteen minutes, watching her race from one room to the next while she decorated out loud. "This could be the boys' room," she yelled. And then: "Wouldn't this be a great place to host a party?"

"This feels like my house," Lucy said before they left.

"Then we should move fast," Lana said.

A few days later, while Lana encouraged her to put in a formal offer for $109,000, Lucy led her family back to the house to help her make a final decision. Lucy, Luis, and the boys rode in one minivan; Demi, Bobby, and the three girls followed in another. Luis pulled up to the house and a rabbit hopped off the front porch. "Cool!" one of the boys yelled.

The house was locked, but nobody seemed to care. They peered in through the windows and admired the spacious kitchen and the carpeted bedrooms. Lucy walked back out to the pool and wondered if maybe this would be the place where she finally learned how to swim. Bobby examined the frame of the front door and stomped on the porch to test its strength. "*Bien*," he said when the porch withstood his weight, and everybody laughed. The kids ran into the unfenced yard to play tag, and Lucy told them to watch for lizards and snakes. "We're in the country now," she said. Demi wandered around to the back deck, measuring the space with her arms to see if it would fit a table. She wondered out loud: Wouldn't it be wonderful to eat outside under a string of Christmas lights? Could they possibly move in before Christmas?

Lucy joined her mother on the porch, and for a moment they

stood in silence and stared out at the mesas and rock formations in the distance. Demi held on to the banister, looking across the acres of cacti and desert. The sun had begun to set, casting shadows across the land. She had always been taken with the beauty of Arizona, with the endless turquoise sky, the fields of golden brush, and the rocky hillsides, at once so austere and yet so stunning. "*Mágico*," she sometimes called it. She stood on the porch and thought about all of the other places she had lived—about competing for beds with ten siblings in Mexico and sleeping on the floor in Los Angeles and running from her husband and moving with four daughters into a cousin's trailer in Arizona. Now this. It was too much. From across the porch, Lucy looked over at her mother and noticed she was crying.

"Does this mean you like it?" Lucy asked in Spanish.

"It means I love it," Demi said.

A few minutes later, they piled back into the vans and drove toward Kingman. On the way, Lucy called Lana from her cell phone and left a message. She had good news, she said. Everybody in her family had fallen in love with the place. They had made a decision about the house—a decision about Kingman. They wanted to put in an offer. They wanted to stay. "It feels right," she said. So early the next morning, Lana began filling out the paperwork.

.   .   .

S.B. 1070 was scheduled to become law in sixteen hours when a district judge finally announced her last-minute ruling on the lawsuit brought by Obama and the Justice Department. Much of the bill was unconstitutional, Judge Susan Bolton said.

Bolton concluded that the law would interfere with federal immigration laws and create a "substantial likelihood" that some immigrants with legal status would be wrongfully arrested, she said. But even as the judge spoke, Brewer set up a press conference at the Ari-

zona governor's mansion to announce that she would appeal the ruling. "This fight is far from over," she said.

Inside the White House, Obama and his aides conceded that they
expected a long battle, predicting that the fate of S.B. 1070 might
eventually rest with the Supreme Court. What at first had seemed like
a hard-earned immigration victory for Obama began to look more
like defeat as summer turned to fall. Brewer's popularity continued
to skyrocket. She trumpeted her "refusal to back down" and became
a heroine of the far right, creating a windfall of financial donations
to Arizona Republicans and prompting Sarah Palin to congratulate
her for having the "cojones" to take on Obama. The president, meanwhile, tried to appease both conservatives and liberals with immigration policies that instead satisfied nobody. He sent unmanned aircraft
drones to monitor the border and deported record numbers of illegal
immigrants—efforts Brewer called "vastly insufficient." Meanwhile,
such attempts to secure the border further enraged Hispanic voters
who already felt like Obama had failed them.

During the presidential campaign in 2008, Obama had promised to create a "pathway to citizenship" for illegal immigrants during
his first year in office, but instead he had made no progress. Now, in
the aftermath of the fight over S.B. 1070, his immigration overtures
to Congress failed spectacularly. No lawmaker would go so far as to
introduce an immigration bill. All eleven Republican senators who
had once favored reform now opposed it. Obama needed sixty votes
to pass immigration reform through the Senate, and he estimated
that he was at least ten votes short. Even his celebrated DREAM Act,
once considered a shoo-in, bipartisan measure to grant citizenship
for illegal immigrants who'd come to the country as children and
completed two years of college or military service, suddenly looked
like a long shot.

All of it made Obama appear increasingly powerless on immigration, and his aggravation became evident as the months wore on. In September and October, with the congressional midterm elections approaching, he filled his schedule with events targeting Hispanic voters. Each time, he was forced to defend his work on immigration. To a Hispanic caucus in September: "Understandably you are frustrated that we have not been able to move this over the finish line yet, and I am, too." To an interviewer on Telemundo: "You know, it is a very difficult thing to do administratively." To the Spanish-language newspaper *La Opinión*: "I think in some ways there is an unrealistic notion of what I can get done by myself."

On October 25, Obama agreed to do an in-studio radio interview with Eddie Sotelo, the host of a popular program on a Spanish station in Los Angeles. Born in Mexico, Sotelo had crossed into the United States illegally in 1988 and gained legal residence a few years later. He had been pushing national immigration reform to his listeners for the last six years, rallying five hundred thousand people to demonstrate in downtown Los Angeles and collecting one million letters to Congress and delivering them to Washington himself. For the last three years, he had been a vocal supporter of Obama, interviewing the president and his wife on the air and often referring to him as "*un amigo.*"

This time, Sotelo wasted little energy on small talk. He usually conducted his show in Spanish, but he interviewed Obama in English and started by offering the president a choice of topics for the interview. "Multiple choice. Are you ready?" Sotelo said. "A—Immigration reform. B—Immigration reform. C—Immigration reform. Or, D—All of the above."

"I think I'll take D, all of the above," Obama said.

"Okay," Sotelo said. "Many Hispanics feel disappointed in you because comprehensive immigration reform has not passed. What can you tell them?"

"Well, I'm disappointed, too," the president said, and the interview deteriorated from there. Sotelo's questions became increasingly
pointed during the next twenty minutes; Obama remained mostly
on the defensive. Only a few years earlier, late in Obama's presidential campaign, Sotelo had chanted on the air to his listeners: "*Sí se
puede! Sí se puede!*" But now he sounded dejected and Obama sounded
pleading. "If the vast majority of Democrats support this issue, if I
as the president support this issue . . . then the question I have is
why are we spending time talking about us instead of spending time
focusing on getting Republicans to do what's right?" he asked. And as
the interview continued, he seemed more than ever like a president
beleaguered by all that he could not control.

"Change isn't easy," he said. "It doesn't happen overnight."

"I am president. I am not king. I can't do these things just by
myself."

"I just want to repeat: I'm president. I'm not king."

"The notion that we haven't worked hard is just not true."

. . .

A few days after Obama's radio interview was translated into Spanish
and broadcast across the country, Lucy and her family woke up early
for a trip to Las Vegas. It was Demi's fortieth birthday, and she wanted
to celebrate at the Broadacres Swap Meet, a weekly event with live
music and more than a thousand outdoor vendors. The swap meet
catered mostly to Hispanics, and Demi believed it combined some of
the best aspects of the two countries she knew well: the sounds and
smells of Mexico amplified by the diversity and extravagance of the
United States. She had made at least two trips to the swap meet every
year since Lucy was born, and now Lucy usually came along with her
own children, continuing the tradition.

They drove to Las Vegas, waited in line with a few hundred people, paid $1.50 to enter, and walked through the gates. Lucy took ten steps inside and then stopped to lean against a fence and survey the scene. "The whole thing makes me dizzy, but kind of in a good way," she said. Mariachi music blasted from dozens of loudspeakers. The air smelled of fried churros and stale Tecate. Vendors stretched in every direction for a square mile, each small stand protected by a white awning. Salesmen stood in front of their stands and loudly hocked their specialty items: old washing machines, Mexican soccer jerseys, Dickies work clothes, vegetables, mattresses, cell phones, and cowboy boots. Everything was cheap, and everything was liable to become cheaper. All around Lucy people were bartering over prices in Spanish. *"Cuánto quieres? Cuánto quieres?"* they shouted. Lucy knelt down so that her eyes were level with those of her two sons. "Listen to me," she said. "When we start walking again, you hold my hand and stay close."

Instead, the boys tugged excitedly at her arms and started to drag her and Luis toward the vendors. Demi and Bobby waved goodbye and headed off in the opposite direction; they had their own shopping to do, and here they wouldn't need Lucy to act as translator. Demi went in search of studded jeans, and Lucy followed the boys to a series of food vendors. She bought them gigantic churros for $2, the grease and cinnamon leaving a trail of stains on their T-shirts. They washed those down with horchatas, then fresh-squeezed lemonades, then Jarritos pineapple sodas. Luis bought the boys a pack of plastic soldiers—$5 for ten toys—and within minutes of playing make-believe "war" the entire unit had been disfigured, with arms and legs scattered across the ground. The boys started to cry. "No problem," Luis said, and he stopped at the next toy stand and bought another pack.

The swap meet had always been the one place where they splurged. Usually Lucy and Luis each brought $300 in cash, and Luis spent his money on gifts for Lucy while she brought her money back home. This time they had limited themselves to $200 total and saved the rest toward a small down payment on the house. Luis looked at a car stereo system but decided to save his cash instead. Lucy bought a hooded sweatshirt, bargaining it down from $40 to $25. After a few hours of walking around under the Las Vegas sun, they were tired and hungry for lunch. Lucy sat on a bench and called her mother to see if she was ready to leave.

"*Estás listo?*" she asked.

"*Cinco minutos,*" Demi said.

They waited five minutes, then fifteen, then thirty. Finally, just when Lucy was about to call again, Demi and Bobby rounded the corner carrying four shopping bags filled with jeans, toys, a blanket, and kitchen pots. They lugged the stuff for half a mile to the overcrowded parking lot, spent ten minutes searching for their vans, and then drove through heavy traffic to a small Mexican restaurant in a nearby shopping center. They waited for a table, and a waitress seated all nine of them at a six-top in the back of the room. The music was too loud. The service was slow. The ceviche was not as good as Demi's. At the front of the restaurant, a television played political advertisements for the midterm election on a loop. "I'm so sick of those," Lucy said.

Two days later, none of them would vote in the midterm elections. Republicans would gain sixty seats in the House of Representatives and five more in the Senate. The results would be interpreted as a denunciation of Obama, and the president would admit that his relationship with the country had become "rockier and tougher," and that he was "doing a lot of reflecting." Jan Brewer would be reelected as governor of Arizona in a landslide, and exit polls would show that her popularity was tied closely to her support of S.B. 1070. She would speak at an election-night party, surrounded by red, white, and blue balloons, and wave her arms to quiet the chanting crowd. She would reiterate her disdain for Obama and her tough stance on immigration. "Tonight the cavalry has come riding over the hill," she would say.

But right now, for Lucy and her family in the Mexican restaurant, none of that seemed to matter. The kids were cranky and verging on tantrums. The adults were tired and debating who would drive home and who would get to nap in the car. Lucy was compulsively checking the messages on her cell phone, hoping to hear from Lana about their offer on the house.

Lucy stood up from their table and walked over to the cashier instead of waiting for the waitress to bring their check. They still had a three-hour drive to Kingman, and all she wanted was to get back home.

CHAPTER 7

"The Gulf of Mexico has bled a black blood for too many days."

I t was the feeling of utter powerlessness that tormented him most. T. Hailey Thatcher, forty-three, sat in his law office in the suburbs of Jacksonville, Florida, and watched on his computer screen as oil poured into the Gulf of Mexico. The grainy video never changed—sometimes it almost looked like a still photograph—but it continued to mesmerize him nonetheless. The camera showed a geyser of black oil spewing from a pipe on the ocean floor, building into a cloud, and then mixing with the clear water until it painted the entire video screen gray. He watched for a few minutes at a time and marveled at the sheer ceaselessness of it: 625 gallons of oil a minute, 37,500 an hour, 900,000 a day. Hailey felt like he had been gripped by a horror movie, except this one had been playing around the clock for almost a full month now, and still there was no end in sight.

He had barely noticed the first news stories in late April that

foretold disaster—an explosion on an oil rig off the coast of Louisiana, eleven men dead, another sad event unfolding more than a thousand miles from his home. But then oil from the destroyed well began
gushing into the ocean, and executives from British Petroleum said
they lacked the technology to plug a hole one mile beneath the surface. Tar balls washed up in Louisiana's marshes, Alabama closed its
beaches, and Florida declared a state of emergency. A senior adviser
to President Obama called it "the biggest environmental disaster the country has ever faced." Meanwhile, back in Jacksonville,
Hailey monitored weather maps to track the spill's path and fought
off nightmares about drowning in oil. The national crisis had now
become deeply personal, and amid the sprawling scope of the disaster Hailey's obsession remained singular.

Would the oil reach Suwannee?

The ramshackle fishing village in rural Florida had few van-
guards, and Hailey had yet to hear it mentioned in news about the
oil spill. Suwannee was an aging collection of double-wide trailers
located twenty-four miles from the nearest highway on the underside
of Florida's boot, in an area Hailey proudly referred to as the "Red-
neck Riviera." The community had a one-room post office, a Laundromat that doubled as a hardware store, and a tackle shop that also
rented exactly thirty-two movies on VHS tapes. The beat-up welcome
sign on the two-lane road into town proclaimed TH I TERNET—COMING
SOON! But in fact Suwannee still lacked even basic cell-phone service,
which was another reason Hailey loved going there. It was just a little
nothing place, he said. It was also the most important place in his life.

His grandfather had bought two small lots on the Suwannee canal
for $800 each in the late 1960s to use for weekend fishing getaways,
and Hailey had visited the property at least once or twice a month ever
since. His grandfather had taught him how to navigate the marshland,

insisting that he shun fancy navigation systems and learn to find fishing spots based only on "dead reckoning." His father had let him stay up late with the adults by the bonfire, where he stared up at the Milky Way, learned to name the constellations, and listened to the older men tell stories about golf and quail hunting in their slow Southern drawls. Over the years, Hailey had helped plant the nearby pine trees, aerate the lawn, and build the wooden tackle closets just off the dock. Neighbors had become his closest friends. He had always lived somewhere else—in Valdosta, Georgia; Minnesota; and now Jacksonville—but Suwannee was the place he called home. "My soul is down there, simple as that," he said. "I'm Southern bred, Southern born, and the Southern spirit of that whole place is just ingrained in me."

But now, as the spill continued to spread, Hailey wondered what would happen to Suwannee if the oil came—and what would happen to him. The area had been protected as a wildlife refuge for more than thirty years because it was considered one of the most delicate river deltas in the country. Less than a mile from Hailey's family land on the canal, the Suwannee River flowed into the gulf and two habitats melded into one. Spanish moss and palm trees shaded the tidal creeks and river inlets, where bald eagles kept lookout from the treetops and alligators sunned on the banks. Then, as the river opened into the gulf, pelicans soared over limestone islands and the wind whistled through marshlands covered in saw grass. Hailey's family also owned property on a farm and on a lake, and he had lived high up in the Rocky Mountains and traveled across Europe. Only the sheer beauty of the red, yellow, and orange sunsets over Suwannee had inspired him to try his hand at poetry and reduced him to tears.

But for as much as Hailey worried about the oil's effect on the delicate habitat, he worried more about what would be left of the place, the people, and his memories. Suwannee was so woven into the fabric of his life that he couldn't quite figure out who he would be without the place. It was where he had drunk his first few Löwenbräus with the man he called "grandpaul" or "granddaddy," a stubborn World War II veteran from Georgia known in Suwannee only as "Kingfisher." It was where he had taken his soon-to-be wife, Lisa, for a "test trip" not long after he spotted her standing by a jukebox in Valdosta in 1991, because even though he had fallen in love with her in that first moment, he didn't want to fully commit until "she saw me in the place where I'm the most true version of me," he said. It was where he had built up confidence in his sobriety after returning from rehab in 1993, because just being in Suwannee was a natural high, and no matter how many times his buddies reached back into the cooler for another beer, the boat was one place where he never felt the need to drink. It was where he had celebrated graduating from college after ten meandering years and then decided to try for law school despite his C-minus grade average. It was where, after fourteen years of filling out law-school applications and receiving only rejection letters, he had finally gotten a congratulatory note from Florida Coastal in 2005 that left him "shakin' like a leaf on a tree and then bawlin' for fifteen minutes," he said. It was where he had studied to pass the Florida bar and where he wanted to open a branch of his law practice, even if that meant an office with no Internet. It was where he had told Lisa to spread his ashes when he died. It was where, a few months after his grandfather died in 2004, he had spent $40,000 in savings to redo the old man's boat instead of buying a new one, preserving the same hull, christening the new deck with a bottle of Löwenbräu, and renaming the boat *Kingfisher*.

Over all those years, the only real change in Suwannee had been generational: grandfathers passed their trailers on to fathers; fathers passed them on to sons. The trailers and boats and makeshift barbecue grills continued to rust with age, but the wear only added to Suwannee's no-frills appeal. Like Hailey, most of the people who owned the surrounding trailers spent their weeks as lawyers or business owners who earned good salaries, but in Suwannee they liked to drink cheap whiskey straight from the plastic bottle, clean their own fish, and chop their own firewood. A weekend with Hailey in Suwannee came with unwritten rules: no shaving, no showering, and no brushing your teeth. The place was a "rustic, acquired taste," Hailey said, but it quickly grew into an addiction. Families occasionally moved into Suwannee, but almost nobody moved out. Hailey and Lisa did not have children yet—"We're late starters," Lisa said—but they still hoped to start a family, in part because Hailey imagined passing down his granddaddy's old trailer and his mental inventory of fishing spots along the river.

For now, though, Hailey alone had been left in charge of his family's property. His father still came down every month or so, but he was approaching seventy and had started spending more time closer to his home at the family's lake house on the Georgia border. Both of Hailey's younger brothers lived in North Carolina and only visited the gulf coast a few times a year. If anybody in the family was going to do something to protect Suwannee from the oil, Hailey reasoned, he would have to do it himself.

One morning in early May, Hailey sat in his Jacksonville office and made his daily checks on the status of the oil spill. He had started his law practice eighteen months earlier with a friend whom he met in law school, and the two new lawyers had made a pact to work six days a week until the business grew. Hailey specialized in personal injury litigation, representing clients who had been the victims of car accidents or medical malpractice, and much of his new business derived from an advertisement he had placed in the Jacksonville phone book.

"If someone's looking for a lawyer in the phone book, they're not leaving a message," Hailey said. "They are calling twenty or twenty-five offices until someone picks up the phone." So he always spent his Saturdays by the phone in his office, calling home every few hours to check up on Lisa and their five-pound toy poodle, Louise. When the phone didn't ring, Hailey turned on his computer and clicked over to the Internet.

He typed in a Google search for "oil and Suwannee" and found a report that said Florida had placed Suwannee and the surrounding Dixie County under a state of emergency. The newspaper article quoted a county official about his strategy in responding to the spill. "Right now, we're just in monitoring mode," he said. "We're going to pray that it doesn't impact us."

Hailey clicked away from the article and felt his muscles tense. *We're going to pray?* Prayer was not a plan. He picked up the phone in his office, called the headquarters of Dixie County Emergency Management, and reached a mid-level employee.

"So, what's really the plan?" Hailey said.

The employee explained that the Coast Guard had promised to notify Dixie County when the oil was three days away from its shores, at which point the emergency management team would formulate a plan.

"That's it?" Hailey said. "What the hell can we do in three days?"

He hung up the phone and called back to ask for a supervisor, this time trying a more gentle approach. "Look, I can help you," he said. He offered to write notes to federal officials on his law firm's letterhead; to open up his Rolodex and start making fund-raising calls; to round up a group of farmers who would donate hay that would then be used to soak up the oil; to drive down to Suwannee, climb into his boat, travel west until he saw the sheen of oil on the surface, and help sop it up.

"We have it under control," the supervisor said. "We'll call if we need anything."

But the days continued to pass, the oil leaked, and nobody ever called. After a few weeks of waiting, Hailey decided to help the best way he knew how. He would write.

He believed few forces could stir emotion like vivid, poetic writing; the music of the Grateful Dead had been one of the defining influences in his life, and he sometimes recited the band's lyrics to help him understand his own emotions. He liked to labor for weeks over moving toasts for his friends' birthday parties and weddings, and he credited his samples of legal writing for finally getting him into law school. He had always aspired to write about Suwannee—one day, he hoped to make it the setting for a debut novel—and now here was his chance. If he could just make a few politicians understand how he felt about Suwannee, Hailey thought, then maybe he could rally them to the community's defense.

He had always considered himself a Republican, born and raised, but he felt suspicious of politics in general. He followed current events but couldn't have cared less about the "slick characters" that rotated in and out of office. "There's too many politicians in politics, if you know what I mean," he said. So instead of making his letters political, he decided to make them personal, sharing stories about his father and grandfather and the spots on the river where he learned to fish. He sent letters to all eight commissioners in Dixie County, to the sheriff, and to the city manager. He wrote three state senators and three members of the U.S. Congress. And then, one afternoon in late May, because he had come this far already, Hailey decided to write a letter to the president. He called Lisa to tell her he would be home from work a few hours late. He had one last letter to finish from the office, he explained, and he wanted to get this one exactly right.

As he stared at the keyboard, Hailey thought back to one of his father's favorite stories about Suwannee. Hailey's parents had been down at the trailer for a relaxing weekend a few years back when his mother had spotted a bloodstained pelican perched on a roof across the street. A heavy fishing line was dangling from the bird's beak, making flight impossible. Hailey's parents had stared at the bird through binoculars for almost an hour, first curious, then invested, then almost tearful. Finally, tired of watching the bird suffer from afar, Hailey's mother had decided to do something about it. She was almost seventy years old, a Southern belle who loved fancy dresses and formal dishware, but she had gone across the street, climbed up a ladder onto the roof, scraped her hands on the gutter, and then clipped off the fishing line with an old pair of sewing scissors. The bird had waited patiently while she worked and then soared off toward the gulf. It had been one of the most moving experiences of all their time in Suwannee, saving that one pelican. And now Hailey wondered: How many thousands of pelicans were at risk right now?

"Dear President Obama," he wrote.

Never before have I taken the time to write to any of my political representatives in Washington. My deep concern for the health of my state's waters, and more importantly, for a little area I call "my little corner of the world" prompts this writing.

In the mid to late 1950s, my grandfather Paul B. Hatcher began making regular trips from our hometown of Valdosta, Georgia to Suwannee, Florida. In 1968, he purchased two lots there, on a canal, and outfitted our family fish camp. My first trip to the town of Suwannee was most likely in 1973, when I was 6 years old. I am now 43. For the last thirty-seven years, I have grown up in the town of Suwannee, the river bearing the same name, and its people playing a very important part of my life.

My grandfather died in 2005. You see, we were very, very close, my Grandpaul and I. He "learned me" how to find trout on the flats and Spanish mackerel offshore. It was he that taught me how to navigate the channel of Salt Creek, then peel off to the north in between and through the countless oyster bars, behind Cat Island, then up to Double Barrel and Bumblebee Creek. He gently guided me into the back of Moccasin Creek for redfish. Most important, my grandfather also taught me to have a healthy respect for the sea. And believe me, I do.

Now, not only do I have a healthy respect for the sea, but a heavy heart as well. The Gulf of Mexico has bled a black blood for too many days now, and the impact to this precious resource has only begun. What will become of my little corner of the world? What will happen to the places that I caught trout and flounder just last weekend? Will Deer Island's sandy beaches be covered next week or next month with oil? Will the clear waters of summer at Pepperfish Key be clouded over, hiding the grasses where I hunt for scallops? Will the myriad creek mouths be slammed shut with the oil that pours from the Gulf floor? Is BP going to come to Suwannee before the oil and take preventative measures to protect what I have known to be the most beautiful place in my life? Will your administration be proactive over the coming days, weeks and months to protect my special place? To me, and countless others, this little village of fishermen, crabbers and clam men is at least as valuable as General Motors and AIG were to you, and I believe we deserve the same treatment.

And then, what of the Suwannees that belong to millions of others like me? You see, my Suwannee is everywhere. To another, it may be called by a different name, and it may be a different longitude and latitude. The oyster man in Apalochicola. The charter captain out of Destin. The young boy from Panacea who is just now

*learning the sea from his grandfather. The couple who purchased
a vacation home on St. George Island. St. Teresa. Horseshoe Beach.
Steinhatchee. St. Marks. On and on and on the list can, and
does, go.*

*As the highest elected official in our union charged with the duty
of protecting our country, I can only hope that you will do what you
can to safeguard our state and national resources. I will be watching your speeches. I will be following your decisions. I will closely
look at who you choose to assist you with your decisions. I will be
praying that you will soon, very soon, realize that despite what you
claim to be doing, it is not nearly enough. You must do more, and
you must do it now.*

Hailey wrote for almost two hours, so lost in thought that he never
looked up at the clock. By the time he finished the letter, it was after
8:00 p.m. Lisa would be worried, he thought. He read over the final
draft one more time and printed it from his computer. It was good,
he thought—as good as he could do. He looked up the mailing address
for the president on the Internet and then decided to fax a copy to the
White House as well. A fax would arrive at least two days earlier than a
letter, Hailey decided, and right now speed mattered. Two days meant
another few hundred pelicans, another couple million gallons of oil.

.   .   .

Two days after Hailey wrote his letter, Obama left Washington on Air
Force One for his third trip to the gulf coast in a month. Oil had been
leaking into the ocean for forty-five days, long enough for aides at the
White House to begin making inside jokes about fate and Murphy's
Law. Here was the latest evidence that, at least so far during Obama's
presidency, all that could go wrong had gone wrong. An explosion

on a privately run oil rig located two thousand miles from the White House had become a hole in the ocean that no scientist could fix, and now it was Obama who suffered much of the blame. On his first trip to Louisiana to assess the disaster, a rare tornado had grounded his helicopter and forced him to make a speech in sideways rain. Then a terrorist had tried to detonate a car bomb in the middle of New York City, truncating Obama's trip and forcing him to turn his attention to yet another potential crisis. His approval rating had just hit another all-time low, and a CBS News poll indicated that only 35 percent of Americans approved of his response to the oil spill. Even during his best attempts to maintain perspective, Obama had started to sound tired and resigned. "Look, we've gone through a difficult year and a half," he said. "This is just one more bit of difficulty."

Obama and his staff had prepared for what they called the "worst-case scenario" in the gulf, meeting to outline the federal government's response less than forty hours after the initial explosion and then holding similar meetings inside the White House every day since. Typically, the worst-case scenario had in fact come to fruition—only it was much worse than anyone had thought possible. The estimates of oil spewing into the gulf had escalated from 42,000 gallons a day . . . to 200,000 gallons . . . to 440,000 gallons . . . to more than a million gallons. Some of Obama's experts now predicted oil would continue to leak until August, by which time it would have spread across the gulf, around the Florida Keys, and up into the Atlantic Ocean, covering more than half of the country's mainland shores. Millions more people would lose work during a time of high unemployment. Billions of dollars would be lost in an already down economy. If the oil well was not capped soon, Obama said, the spill's devastation would be felt for decades.

"Obviously, this has gone on far too long," White House press secretary Robert Gibbs said on the same day Hailey mailed his letter about Suwannee. "I think everybody is enormously frustrated with that, and rightfully so . . . I think the American people are frustrated. I think the people of the gulf are frustrated. I think the president is frustrated. I think the White House is frustrated."

In the last month, Obama had exhausted what he called the "full range" of his presidential power to respond to the spill, and yet respected strategists in his own Democratic Party had dismissed his efforts as "lackadaisical," "lackluster," and "sluggish." In his weekly press briefings, Gibbs now regularly protested by asking a question of his own: What else could the president do? Obama had met with the families of the eleven men who died in the initial explosion on the oil rig and created a federal commission to investigate the accident. He had activated 17,500 members of the National Guard, sent 1,400 boats, deployed 3 million feet of boom to protect the shore, established 17 command centers, and orchestrated the recovery of 11 million gallons of oily seawater. He had requested a shipment of seafood from the gulf to serve for dinner at his forty-ninth birthday party. He had put on gloves to pick tar balls off the beach, worn boots to tour the marshland with local fishermen, and met with Louisiana's small-business owners over baskets of hush puppies and plastic cups of sweet tea. But still the spill continued to expand, and the criticism of Obama grew along with it.

Loyal aides complained that Obama couldn't win in the game of public perception, no matter how hard he tried. It was his job to orchestrate a levelheaded response that best served the long-term future of the gulf, but he was being judged based on the raw emotions of people who wanted to see immediate results, no matter the cost. Opinion polls indicated that he should take more responsibility for the spill, so he made a speech and said, "The buck stops with me," which then became an invitation for critics to pile on more of the blame. Americans wanted him to show more anger, so he told NBC's *Today* show that he was looking for "whose ass to kick," which sparked complaints that he was forcing emotion and acting beneath the presidency. The public demanded that he hold BP accountable, so he pressed the company for $20 billion in restitution, which a Republican congressman then ridiculed as a "shakedown." He encouraged Americans to vacation in the gulf and was called hypocritical for planning his own regular trip up north to Martha's Vineyard. So he scheduled a vacation to the Florida panhandle, where he swam in the ocean, played miniature golf with his family, and went for a boat ride—activities that some Republicans then dismissed as opportunistic photo ops.

Finally, on May 27, Obama held a rare press conference in the East Room of the White House to address the mounting criticism. He stood at the lectern and winced as reporters asked a succession of hard questions. Would this disaster discredit him like Hurricane Katrina had done to President George W. Bush? Would he fire people in his administration? Did he worry about his credibility?

"Look," Obama said. "If you're living on the coast and you see this sludge coming at you, you are going to be continually upset, and from your perspective, the response is going to be continually inadequate until it actually stops. And that's entirely appropriate and understandable. This is what I wake up to in the morning, and this is what I go to bed thinking about—the spill. And it's not just me, by the way. When I woke up this morning and I'm shaving, Malia knocks on my bathroom door and she peeks in her head and she says, 'Did you plug the hole yet, Daddy?' Because I think everybody understands that when we are fouling up the earth like this, it has concrete implications not just for this generation but for future generations."

Nobody felt that reality more than families who had cherished the gulf for generations—families like Hailey's. Obama received his typed letter about Suwannee in the Oval Office in early June and read it from beginning to end. It was one of the most personal, emotional letters he had received during the oil spill—but this time the president chose not to write back. His schedule was more overwhelmed than ever. The oil had yet to reach Suwannee. Obama decided he needed to focus his attention closer to the source, and he asked his aides to arrange another visit to Louisiana. He wanted to meet with a small group of Southerners who appreciated the gulf as much as Hailey but whose boats were already covered in oil and whose livelihoods were also at stake.

Obama had sometimes tried to speak with small groups of constituents face-to-face as president, hoping it would counteract his feelings of isolation. But usually such sessions only resulted in more frustration. Obama believed that most regular people lost the ability to communicate honestly in his presence. "All they see is the office of the presidency," he said. "People find it hard to be spontaneous with the president of the United States. They may think you're an idiot, but if you're standing there right in front of them, they'll shake your hand and bite their tongue."

He relied heavily on letters precisely because he believed they were one of the few places where he was still told the truth. Most of the writers hardly expected him to read their letters, he said, so they essentially wrote diary entries that he considered "intimate and unfiltered." He had tried to re-create that dialogue by inviting letter writers to the Oval Office only to watch their indignation turn soft or their criticism turn to appeasement. "This setting is too intimidating for a lot of folks," he said. So now he had decided to try something else: to go to them instead, and to meet in the least-intimidating location his aides could find.

Obama flew to New Orleans for that meeting on a humid Friday morning in June and traveled two hours by motorcade to Grande Isle, a town of 1,500 crammed onto a small barrier island and threaded to the mainland via a two-lane causeway. On the drive, the motorcade passed a portrait of Obama on a building with the words "What Now?" painted onto his forehead. The motorcade pulled into a ramshackle bait-and-tackle shop on the edge of the water. Obama rolled up the sleeves of his blue-and-white-checkered shirt, walked through the shop, and sat down at a picnic table out back. An employee brought out two trays of boiled shrimp and potatoes. Five local residents took seats at the table, and David Carmadelle, the mayor of Grand Isle, shook Obama's hand and sat directly to his right. "Thanks for coming, everyone," Obama said.

For the first few minutes, Obama peeled shrimp and listened to the residents introduce themselves. Terry Vegas had been shrimping for forty-seven years, always catching the bulk of his haul in late summer, and now the Coast Guard had prevented him from going out on the water. Floyd Lasseigne was a fourth-generation oysterman who worked the same beds that had been in his family for a hundred years, but now they were coated in oil. Patti Rigaud owned a local convenience store, and her business had plummeted by 85 percent. Butch Gaspard owned the marina, and now 60 percent of his docks sat empty.

"We're born and raised here—back to our grandfathers and grandmothers," said Carmadelle, who had worked as a second-generation fisherman before becoming the mayor. He looked at Obama and then gestured over his shoulder to the ocean. "We made a living right here behind us."

Obama nodded and grabbed another shrimp, so Carmadelle continued to talk.

"I've been averaging two hours of sleep," he said, "just going in and looking at the ceiling fan and wondering what's going to happen tomorrow, and praying to God that no more oil comes on the beach. We help each other here. And we don't have no money, but it don't matter. We help each other. That's what we do. But we worry. And we don't know what's going to happen tomorrow, and that's why we depend on you to make sure that . . . you know, we don't want to be on food stamps. None of us. We want to untie the boat, be able to see our two daughters right here and kiss them in the morning and say, 'Daddy's going to work.' "

By the time Carmadelle finished speaking, he looked on the verge of tears. Obama winced and remained quiet for a moment. When the president spoke again, his voice was serious and his expression solemn. It would be another forty-five days before BP managed to cap the gushing oil well, months before Obama's approval rating began to recover, and years before scientists comprehended the full extent of the environmental damage caused by the spill. Obama's administration would spend the next several years helping to direct clean-up efforts and process insurance claims. Lawmakers would propose new legislation about government oversight and offshore oil drilling. But, back behind the bait shop in Grande Isle, Obama took a deep breath and shared what would stand as perhaps his greatest lesson from the oil spill—a realization that largely defined the first stage of his presidency.

"I will do everything in my power to do right by you guys and everybody along the coast," Obama told the locals at the table. "But even though I'm president of the United States, my power is not limitless, so I can't dive down there and plug the hole. I can't suck it up with a straw. All I can do is make sure I put honest, smart, hardworking people in place."

. . .

A few months later, Hailey left his law office early on a Thursday evening, climbed into the cab of his Ford F150 truck, and started driving toward the gulf. One of his favorite events of the year waited two
hours down the road: a Suwannee men's weekend, a gathering he
organized every three or four months to bring his father and a dozen
friends together for two days of fishing and storytelling away from the
interruptions of jobs and families.

The bed of his truck was loaded down with the typical men's
weekend supplies: cheese straws, pecan pies, zucchini breads, sour
cream pound cake, venison jerky, eight cases of Coke, five pounds of
sausage, and thirty pounds of chicken. Lisa was a talented cook who
studied nutrition and prided herself on turning Hailey into a healthy
eater, but he reverted to old habits on men's weekends, avoiding
vegetables, chewing a little Red Man tobacco, and drinking a steady
flow of soda—or "co-cola," as he called it. He stood at just over six feet
tall with solid shoulders and long legs, but the toll of so many similar weekends had rounded his face and softened his stomach. Most
everyone else in Suwannee had a similar build, and local men took
pride in a good gut. One of Hailey's neighbors had posted a sign on
his dock that had become a Suwannee motto: WE DON'T SKINNY DIP. WE
CHUNKY DUNK.

There was still no oil in Suwannee, but the spill remained the central topic of conversation in town. Weeks had gone by since Obama
last visited the gulf, and news about the oil spill had faded from television shows and newspaper headlines. But in Suwannee, the oil was
still the only story that mattered. The handful of late-summer tourists
who usually frequented the town's lone restaurant and fishing lodge
had stayed away for fear of polluted water, lousy fishing, and contam-
inated seafood. The marina had lost 30 percent of its business since
the spill began. A houseboat-rental company had gone two months

without renting a houseboat. The lodge continued to offer extended low-season rates because of the "Oil and Overblown Media Disaster," an advertisement said. Some fishing guides believed the fish hadn't been biting because of all the dispersants and oil in the water; other guides said the fishing had been fine and anybody who said otherwise had no skill with a rod and reel.

The anxiety in Suwannee revolved mostly around the mystery of the remaining oil and where it had gone. Studies showed that as much as 35 percent of the oil in the gulf remained on the surface of the water, and the rest had been cleaned up, evaporated into the air, sunk to the ocean floor, or dispersed into tiny droplets. Depending on the expert, Suwannee was either unlikely to be affected by the spill whatsoever or likely to be forever altered. Some scientists believed fish populations would diminish; others believed flora and fauna would die on the ocean floor; still others believed a massive storm might yet cover the Florida coast in oil. The scientists agreed only on the fact that it would take years of careful study to determine the spill's exact effects.

Three months after the spill began, Obama's response had proved remarkably effective. His government had built and managed a hierarchy of twenty thousand responders essentially overnight, marshaling experts from across the globe and supplying them with boats, equipment, and oil-dispersing chemicals. BP had paid for everything with little complaint. Commercial fishermen reported record hauls for early autumn. Wildlife experts announced that only 2,300 birds had died as a result of the spill, less than 1 percent of the casualties that had resulted from the *Exxon Valdez* oil spill off the coast of Alaska in 1989.

But Hailey and many others like him remained skeptical. His anxiety had eased a bit since engineers managed to plug the oil well, but he still felt ambivalent about Obama's response. The government had acted in the wake of the spill based on complex science—by bringing in marine biologists and chemical experts to forecast what would be best for the gulf over decades. Hailey, meanwhile, had acted on pure emotion. How would his part of the world be affected *now*? The gulf still felt threatened and different, and he was loath to give anyone credit for anything just yet. "Was Obama's response fast enough? Maybe, but I'm waiting on time to tell," he said. During his handful of trips to Suwannee since the spill, he had spent as much time on the water looking for tar balls as for fish. "Every time I see a sheen on the water, I think: 'That's it. There's oil. It's all over,'" he said. "But then it usually turns out to just be a reflection or sunlight."

Hailey had tried to ease his nerves by committing to his own simple plan: Get to Suwannee as much as possible and enjoy it more than ever. As he drove toward the coast for men's weekend, the city lights of Jacksonville gave way to absolute darkness and he put a live recording from an old Grateful Dead concert into his CD player. He turned the volume up for a Jerry Garcia guitar solo and stared out the front windshield at an empty road and a canopy of stars. The solo lasted forty-five seconds, and when it ended Hailey turned down the volume and wiped at his eyes. "I'm getting more sentimental as I get older," he said. "Something about the combination of this music and the scenery down here always gets me."

By the time he pulled up to his trailer, it was almost 10:00 p.m. and all of the other men either had yet to arrive or had already gone to sleep. Hailey changed into pajamas but then paced between the bedroom and the small living room. "I can never sleep on the first night in Suwannee—just too fired up," he said. He turned on the Weather Channel to monitor the morning tides, polished fishing rods that already looked polished, and set out his outfit for the next morning.

He looked around the trailer; every decoration told a story, he said, and put together that story explained him. There was the framed, uneven drawing he had made in kindergarten of a boy and his boat. There was the taxidermy of his first ten-pound bass, caught in 1999. There were pictures on the refrigerator of him and Lisa playing with their dog in the gulf. There was the book he had self-published about the history of his grandfather's boat, the *Kingfisher*. Every object in the trailer furthered the nautical theme, with couch pillows shaped like fish, sea-breeze-scented shampoo in the bathroom, and Ernest Hemingway's *Old Man and the Sea* resting on the coffee table. The trailer looked much the same as when his grandfather had lived in it, but Hailey still worried he had made too many changes. Sometimes he dreamed of arriving in Suwannee, opening the door, and seeing his grandfather sitting on the couch. "What did you do to my place?" his grandfather said in the dream. "It wasn't good enough before?"

Hailey finally went to bed at two and set his alarm for three hours later, hoping for an early start on the water. When he woke up, his best friend, Charlie Cooper, was also moving around the trailer. The men had met in college at Valdosta State, and now Charlie ran a booming insurance business in Macon, Georgia. They saw each other five or six times a year and almost always in Suwannee. It was where Hailey had helped Charlie through a midlife career crisis and a series of rough breakups; where Charlie had supported Hailey as he recovered from his grandfather's death and his drinking problem. Their relationship revolved around long days of fishing, but Charlie considered himself a "lazy fisherman." A day on the boat was more about ten hours of uninterrupted time for two friends to catch up on careers, families, and old neighbors in Valdosta. "For me," Charlie said, "I'd almost rather sit on the boat and do my fishing for beers in the cooler."

They walked out of the trailer in the predawn darkness and drove
to the bait shop, where Hailey left his truck unlocked and running
in the parking lot. He bought a hundred live shrimp from the same
woman who had worked the counter for forty-six years. Then he and
Charlie headed across the street to the restaurant.

The dining room was already packed at 5:30 a.m., and most of the
patrons were Hailey's friends. He walked from table to table, shaking hands and squeezing shoulders. Every customer was white, male,
and dressed in heavy boots and camouflage. Some wore baseball caps
with fishing lures attached to the bills. Hailey sat down with Charlie and his father, who had driven down from Valdosta late the night
before. A waitress came over to take their order. "Whatcha want,
honey?" she said, even though it wasn't much of a question because
the restaurant, which had never offered a menu, had featured the
same two breakfast choices for twenty years. "I'll take bacon, eggs
over easy, and biscuits with gravy," Hailey said. Then he leaned back
in his chair and started speculating about the day's fishing. The moon
was a quarter full and shaped like a U high in the sky a good sign,
since an old Suwannee fishing legend held that the catch would be
bountiful if the moon looked like a cup capable of holding water. But
the wind chimes across town had been singing, so Hailey wondered
if the water might be rough and choppy. "It's windish and airish out
there," he told Charlie. "Could be tough going."

An hour later, the two friends were out on the water. Hailey wore a
custom-made Kingfisher baseball cap over a pair of cheap sunglasses,
and he smoked a cigarette while steering the boat out of the canal
and toward the gulf. The sun rose off the water, and Hailey cranked
some acoustic Spanish guitar music from the boat's speakers. Hawks
soared overhead, and a light breeze whistled off the water. Within
a few hours, they had found their way into a school of redfish. Each

man fished with two rods, and each rod seemed to entice a bite before the bait so much as hit the surf. Hailey and Charlie pulled twenty-five silver-spotted fish into the boat within half an hour, but none was big enough to keep, so they tossed them back and decided to move on. "Let's see what else we can find," Hailey said.

They found nothing. Neither man spotted a fish during the next six hours, and eventually Charlie put away his rod and started grabbing beers from the cooler. Hailey made a ham sandwich, drank a Dr Pepper, and steered the boat. It was cold for Florida, and they saw no other boats on the water. They had the ocean to themselves. Hailey navigated out to a little sandbar by Cedar Key, where pelicans dove near the boat. Then they watched an alligator slither into Dead Boy Eddy, saw the surf crash onto Lone Cabbage Reef, listened to the frogs sing on the Gopher River, and watched the sun begin to set over Cedar Key. Hailey steered the boat back to the dock with the fish cooler empty. He couldn't remember the last time he had been "skunked" in Suwannee, he said.

"I don't understand it," he said. "We did everything we know how to do, went everywhere we know to go. We threw shrimp, spinners, Gulps. They just weren't biting."

"Couldn't get much worse," Charlie said.

"Couldn't get *any* worse," Hailey said.

Then both men started to laugh because this was an inside joke they both knew well. In fact, life could not get much better. "A bad day in Suwannee is the best day anywhere else," Hailey said. He climbed out of the boat and started barbecuing thirty pounds of chicken on the old grill his grandfather had made back in the early 1960s. Fifteen friends and neighbors came over for dinner, and they dipped fresh oysters into hot sauce for an appetizer. Charlie built a campfire behind the trailer, and everybody pulled up a chair. They passed around a bottle of Ancient Age whiskey, skipping past Hailey, and took turns drinking and complaining about the fishing. Dinner was ready by eight, but Hailey delayed the finishing touches because he wanted to stretch the day out for as long as he could. Finally, just before ten, he passed out paper plates and the men lined up in front of the grill.

Hailey filled his plate last and then joined his friends around the fire. He stood on the edge of the circle and cleared his throat.

"I want to say grace to commemorate this great day," he said. The men took off their hats and set down their whiskey.

"Lord," Hailey continued, "thank you for letting us enjoy another day in Suwannee. God bless our military for protecting our right to be here. Even when the fishing isn't good, we are so lucky just to share this place with each other. Thank you for giving us this incredible piece of the world. Thank you for keeping it beautiful. Thank you for doing everything in your power to keep it safe."

CHAPTER 8

"Nobody is getting the same education."

The start of school at Sixth District Elementary was more than a month away, but already Na'Dreya Lattimore had started "clock watching," as she called it. She went into the kitchen of her family's apartment in the housing projects of Covington, Kentucky, looked at a calendar posted to the refrigerator, and let go a ten-year-old's exaggerated sigh. "Still thirty-nine more days," she said. "Why is summer going so slow?"

A few days earlier, her grandmother had splurged on Na'Dreya's back-to-school outfit, the family's most extravagant purchase of the summer, and now the clothes taunted her from a shelf high in the bedroom closet: shiny white Reeboks, a new JanSport backpack, and pink capris studded with silver beads. Na'Dreya was not allowed to wear the clothes outdoors until the first day of school, but sometimes she changed into them anyway, pranced around the house, and mod-

eled in front of a bathroom mirror. August 25 could not come soon
enough.

Not that she expected fifth grade to be flawless—nothing at
Sixth District ever was—but Na'Dreya assumed school would be an
improvement over this. She lived with her mother, grandmother,
and three younger half brothers in a two-bedroom apartment in
Latonia Terrace, a low-income housing project located across the
Ohio River from Cincinnati. Theirs was an overcrowded unit with no
air-conditioning, so they spent the summer trying to outmaneuver
the heat. Two fans whirred on high, and the unscreened windows
remained open at night, inviting in the flies. The upstairs bedrooms
had become sweltering by the middle of June, so now all six people
usually slept downstairs in the living room, two on an air mattress
and four more curled into fetal positions on a wraparound couch. The
faded white paint in the living room had blistered in the heat, leaving yellow scars across the walls. During the day, Na'Dreya and her
brothers found relief in the shaded alley and splashed around in a
small inflatable pool, which they filled with cold water by attaching a
hose to their kitchen sink.

Na'Dreya and her family had moved into Latonia Terrace about
a year earlier, after what her mother, Lisa, described as an "overdue
series of lucky breaks." They had been living in a decrepit old house
in East Covington and stretching their welfare payments to make the
$600 monthly rent when Lisa saw an advertisement online for the
nearby housing project. "Latonia Terrace is one of Covington's most
sought after neighborhoods," it had read. "You will enjoy a trip to the
local ice cream store and a neighborhood Laundromat. Do you like
to walk your elementary-school-aged children to school and back?
You can do so easily from your new apartment at Latonia Terrace."
Impressed, Lisa had submitted an application and called the Cov-

ington Housing Authority to talk her way up the waiting list. Seven
months later, they had moved into the two-bedroom.

Their rent in the projects was $57 a month including utilities,
which made the place a blessing even if life at Latonia Terrace was not
entirely as advertised. The ice-cream shop was shuttered and so was
the Laundromat. The kids did indeed walk to school, but only because
the family had no car and the bus cost $1.50 each way. The trip was
a 1.3-mile trudge along busy roads, past auto shops and abandoned
houses where dealers sold heroin. One of the adults always walked
with Na'Dreya, eight-year-old Marcus, and seven-year-old Joshua
before stopping on the way back to drop off Isaiah, four, at day care.
Lisa believed the hike helped make her children tough, which she
considered the most essential quality for survival in Covington. "My
kids have more miles on their legs than most people do on their cars,"
she bragged.

They had furnished their apartment in Latonia Terrace with
everything they owned, which wasn't much. There was the wraparound couch, donated by a friend; a few old TVs, giveaways from an
elementary school that had closed for budgetary reasons; a vinyl-top
table missing its vinyl top; a washer and dryer that sat next to the
kitchen sink; a dresser with four drawers, one for each kid, with the
top drawer labeled "Na'Dreya's Stuff Only!" The walls throughout
the house had been left undecorated, and the place had developed a
distinctive smell. "The stank," Na'Dreya called it—an assaulting mix
of stale cigarette smoke, aging meat in the refrigerator, and mess
from the new puppy, who had yet to be housebroken and sometimes
relieved himself on the stairs.

Na'Dreya tried to spend most of her time outside, but there too
she struggled to find her place. Older girls hung out across the street
by the basketball court, clinging to the fence and watching the boys

play shirts versus skins. Younger girls stuck to a playground closer
to the project and drew on the sidewalk in chalk. Na'Dreya, verging
on adolescence but still partial to her favorite Mickey Mouse T-shirt,
belonged at neither spot. She was solidly built and weighed almost a
hundred pounds, with beautiful, coffee-colored skin from her black
father and soft hair and big, doleful eyes from her white mother. She
mainly kept to herself or wandered between the neighboring apartments, playing Nintendo Wii in number 113 or babysitting an infant
in 115. On the faded-brick row of Latonia Terrace where Na'Dreya
lived, the six interconnected units shared everything—the inflatable
pool, food stamps, child care, cigarettes. "This is as close to a real
neighborhood as these kids have ever had," Lisa said.

Covington had two other housing projects, but neither rivaled
Latonia Terrace's record for safety and livability. One, City Heights,
was plagued by gang violence; the other, Jacob Price, was in the
midst of being torn down so that a private contractor could build
mixed-income condominiums in its place. A group of politicians
and business leaders in Covington had concluded that the projects
were eyesores that stunted the city's development and needed to be
demolished, which was also happening in cities like New Orleans and
New York. Lisa had heard rumors that City Heights and Latonia Terrace would also be torn down within the next five years, and she had
reached her own conclusion about the future of Covington's projects.
"This has always been a city of poor people, and now they decided
they want to push all the poor people out," she said.

At least the city's recent attempts at beautification provided occasional comic relief for Lisa and the other residents of Latonia Terrace.
Those tourists who bought horse-and-carriage rides along a particularly littered stretch of river shoreline? "They must like the stink,"
Lisa said. The new Covington "wedding district," where six shops

specialized in selling $3,000 dresses? "Hello! This is Covington in a recession," she said. The glass condo building downtown where yuppies paid $300,000 for two-bedroom condos? "Didn't they hear we got the same layout here going for fifty-seven bucks?"

But Covington's dwindling supply of low-income housing had also become a serious problem for a city where nearly 25 percent of the 40,000 residents lived below the poverty line and 1,200 people considered themselves homeless. In the time since Na'Dreya and her family had moved into Latonia Terrace, the recession had nearly doubled Covington's unemployment rate, which exceeded 12 percent. More people needed cheap housing, and fewer places offered it. The project's waiting list for its 230 units had tripled, and the average wait time had swelled to five or six years. Residents of Latonia Terrace who once could have saved enough money to move into private rentals now considered it too big of a risk to take on high rents and higher utility bills. Just about the only people who moved out were the five or six people each month that property manager Pam Henderson evicted for failing to make payments or violating the no-drug policy. Henderson, now left to deal with residents who refused to leave and prospective renters whom she could never accommodate, had started referring to herself as "the bad guy." She had once lived in the projects herself, and carrying out evictions in the middle of an economic crisis made her feel sick. "When people leave here they're probably going to be homeless," she said. "They're only here in the first place because they've got nowhere else to go."

Except for eight months each year, when Na'Dreya could go to school. It was her one reliable escape—which is why Lisa's heart sank when she picked up the phone on another scorching morning in late July and a school administrator introduced herself. Summertime news from the Covington Independent School District had never been good. In 2008, an administrator had called to say that Na'Dreya's elementary school had closed and she would be switched to another one. A year later the district had trimmed back on music classes, then art, then social studies. And already in the summer of 2010, Covington had announced a delayed start to the school year because of a postponed construction project.

"Yes ma'am, what's the problem?" Lisa said.

"Actually, no problem," the administrator said. "I have exciting news. President Obama just made a speech about education. He mentioned Na'Dreya's name and read her letter."

"Wait a minute," Lisa said, her mind spinning. "Are you telling me that the president of the United States knows my daughter's name?"

.   .   .

Na'Dreya had decided to write a letter to Obama several months earlier, near the end of fourth grade. It had been a typical year for her in Covington Independent, which had recently finished dead last out of Kentucky's 174 school districts on the state's standardized tests. The tests showed that Na'Dreya was reading with the aptitude of a sixth grader while many of her classmates remained stuck at a second-grade level. She had scored in the 80th percentile for math while most of her peers had scored in the low 20s. The district's funding was tied to improving its math and reading scores, so the administration had eliminated extracurriculars and trimmed back social studies to a fifteen-minute lesson once a week. Instead Na'Dreya and her class spent an extra hour a day working on remedial math, going back over problems she had long ago mastered.

Even more frustrating, each lesson was interrupted again and again by behavioral outbursts—kids who stood on desks, threw supplies across the room, punched classmates, or told off teachers. After each disturbance, teachers had been taught to "freeze" class for five minutes so they could deal with the troublemaker while twenty-three other kids sat silently at their desks. "We're always just waiting," Na'Dreya said, and so during one remedial lesson she had busied herself by working on a math problem of her own. Five minutes a freeze. Three freezes an hour. Eight hours a day. Five days a week. "I waste ten hours of my life each week because these knuckleheads can't get their act together," Na'Dreya had concluded.

She had accepted this as inevitable until she came home from school one afternoon and overheard her grandmother, Cindy Sebastian, talking about No Child Left Behind. "What's that?" Na'Dreya asked. Cindy told her that it was a government program intended to ensure a fair education for every child—an explanation that only made Na'Dreya more confused. "Fair?" she had said. How could anyone mistake this for fair? She had heard about school districts where everyone did well and went on to college, but in Covington Independent the statistics indicated an entire population marching into the abyss. Ninety percent of the students came from poverty. Fifty percent graduated from high school. Three percent were considered "college ready."

"Nobody is getting the same education," Na'Dreya told her grandmother, and so she had decided to write a letter to Obama.

She had plenty of practice conversing honestly with adults. Lisa and Cindy had decided long ago to hide nothing from the four kids and to talk frankly about their circumstances, no matter how bleak. "Better to tell them the truth and have it hurt once than to lie and have them peel it off slow like a Band-Aid," Cindy said. She and Lisa often sat down at the vinyl-top table within earshot of the kids, smoked Camels, and rehashed an unedited version of their family history.

Over the years, Na'Dreya had distilled these stories into a simple lesson, one she repeated with a sense of resignation beyond her years.
"The bottom line is that people in life let you down," she said, "and
you can't let that mess with what you're doing."

Cindy had grown up around Covington in the 1960s, attended
private school, married, given birth to Lisa and a son, and bought
and managed a popular bowling alley. Her life was "a middle-class
dream," she said, until she divorced in the early 1990s and Lisa, then
a teenager, rebelled and flew off the rails. Lisa blew curfew, ran away
from home, drank, dabbled with drugs, inked a "hustla" tattoo on her
neck, and started fights at school until she was eventually expelled.
She started swooning over "guys who operated on the edge, who lived
fast," Lisa said, but the men only stayed around until the first positive pregnancy test. Each had been a bigger disaster than the last.
Na'Dreya's father went to jail for a drug offense and then went back
again for repeated parole violations. Marcus's father suffered a mental breakdown and disappeared two months into Lisa's pregnancy.
Joshua's father received two life sentences for pointing a gun at a federal officer. Isaiah's father suggested abandoning the newborn baby
at the hospital for a few weeks to save money on food, diapers, and a
car seat.

Lisa mostly blamed the men, but Cindy mostly blamed her daughter. She had exploded when Lisa became pregnant for the fourth time
with Isaiah, whose father had recently moved to Cincinnati from
Africa. "What?" Cindy asked, incredulous. "You've blown through
every dirtbag on this continent and now you're expanding your search
across the world?"

Resigned to raising four children with no fathers and no financial help, Lisa had packed up the kids and fled to Denver in 2004,
lured to Colorado by a high-school friend and the state's reputation

for generous social services. She was soon arrested at a grocery store
for driving a stolen car that she claimed to have borrowed from a
friend. She spent almost two years in jail, and the kids were divided
between two Colorado foster families. Cindy filed for custody of her
grandchildren, and the kids spent another month with a foster family in Kentucky before being reunited with their grandmother. After
her release, Lisa took a Greyhound bus east to Covington and moved
back in with Cindy and the kids. Na'Dreya had not recognized her
mother at first, and for several months her memories of the separation, foster families, and custody proceedings would "bubble up and
make me angry," she said. Four years of reconciliation had eased the
trauma and made her situation feel almost normal. She had her own
version of a two parent family, and she called Lisa "mom" and Cindy
"mahma." But the experience had created at least one habit that suggested lasting anxiety. Every few days, Na'Dreya would say to Lisa,
"You're doing good, Mom, aren't you? You're doing real good?"

She already had been let down by her father, who would sometimes send her beautiful letters and drawings from jail only to dis-
appoint her as soon as he got out. On his last brush with freedom,
he had promised Na'Dreya "lots of us time," she said, and he sometimes had stopped by Latonia Terrace to pick her up. Then they would
drive to one of his girlfriend's apartments, where he would deposit
Na'Dreya in the living room with a coloring book and a box of crayons,
she said. Once, he had invited Na'Dreya to a downtown performance
of Ice Capades only to stick her in a seat between a new girlfriend and
the new girlfriend's daughter. "They were nice and all, but he's always
disrespecting me," Na'Dreya said. After the show, with Lisa's encouragement, Na'Dreya had worked up the courage to give her father an
ultimatum. "If you want to be in our life, start acting like it," she told
him, and he had treated her better in the months since.

Toughness—the ability to endure devastation and sometimes to cause it—was a necessary commodity in Covington, and one that Lisa and Cindy taught well. They had raised four kids on government assistance by learning to be scrappy—by performing a little community service each week to qualify for a $200 monthly transportation stipend and living together to double their monthly household take on food stamps (about $900) and welfare ($700). Lisa had gone back to school in 2008 to earn her GED and then started attending community college on a government Pell Grant with hopes of one day becoming an X-ray technician. For a while, she had worked as a phlebotomist in downtown Cincinnati and drawn blood from strangers for $7.50 an hour, but the income had caused the government to cut her transportation stipend and halve her food stamps. "They make it so that it's not worth working unless you're making $12 or $13 an hour," she said. She had spent most of the last four-plus years unemployed and drawing various forms of welfare, but Kentucky had informed her that she would be dropped from the program in December. "I'll worry about it when it happens," Lisa said. "You learn to fight through, and hopefully you are smart enough and strong enough to get by."

To make sure her children built up the necessary fortitude, Lisa allowed them to fight each other if they wanted, closing the door to their room and letting them hammer out their disagreements. If one of the kids misbehaved, she licked a few fingers and whapped the child across the back of the neck because it hurt more than a spanking. She and Cindy considered their parenting style "old school," and as a result their kids were tough, smart, obedient, and well mannered. Both Lisa and Cindy supervised their children's mandatory homework time, two hours a night. They marched the kids to school in an ordered, single-file line no matter how extreme the weather and often stayed at Sixth District Elementary for hours to volunteer.

Cindy in particular had become an expert at helping teachers manage their classrooms. Administrators referred to her, admiringly, as "the general," although occasionally her authoritarian ideals had created problems, too. Once, while Cindy was volunteering in Marcus's third-grade classroom, the teacher had decided to pioneer a New Age method for fidgety children, allowing them to sit on gigantic bouncy balls instead of in chairs. Cindy had scoffed and then yanked Marcus off his bouncy ball within the first ten seconds. "I don't send you to school to have fun," she had yelled. "I don't send you here to be comfortable or make friends. I send you here to learn. Now get your butt back in that chair!"

She and the teacher had ended up in a shouting match, but most people at Sixth District acknowledged that Cindy's severe tactics yielded results. The elementary school had given them the Family of the Month award. All four kids maintained good grades and perfect attendance records. Marcus was a talented athlete; Joshua could recite the alphabet backward—and often did whenever he met somebody new. Na'Dreya had taught herself to read and then helped sound out words with her younger brothers. Her teachers had nicknamed her "Angel."

Only once had Na'Dreya gotten in serious trouble with her mother. She was punched in the head by a bully during the middle of a fourth-grade class and chose to tell a teacher instead of punching the girl back. The bully outweighed her and Na'Dreya felt scared, she later told her mother, but Lisa was incensed. "Whenever you get hit, you punch back twice as hard and twice as fast," Lisa had said. "Nobody will respect you unless you learn to stand up for yourself."

Na'Dreya had promised that she would become bolder, and Lisa considered her decision to write a demanding letter to the president a promising first step. Na'Dreya sat down in the kitchen after school and wrote a first draft in pencil and then a second draft in pen. She told Obama about how one of her schools had closed down, "but at least I have a school to go to." Then she continued:

> Nobody is getting the same education. Sometimes I think if you are really smart you get punished. The reason I think that is because there are kids in the class that are bad and the teacher has to stay on them for disrupting the class. Then there are the kids who can't keep up and we wind up having to take extra classes that we do not need. They took away our social studies class and are giving us an extra math class for them to catch up . . . Can you fix this so that everybody can be in the rite class? I know you are busy, but I could really use your help on this.

Na'Dreya believed the president might respond quickly, maybe by e-mail. "I am too young and not allowed to have an e-mail," she wrote. "I am giving you my grandmothers." Then she provided the address and reminded the president that it had "no spaces." Cindy and Lisa sealed the letter in an envelope and Na'Dreya sent it from school. A few months later, she received an envelope damaged from the rain. Inside was one of Obama's signature note cards. "Na'Dreya, thanks for the letter," it read. "I can tell you are a very smart young lady, so keep working hard. Your future is bright!"

Na'Dreya was thrilled, but Cindy and Lisa privately doubted the letter was real. Then they saw Obama's speech on TV, when he stared straight into the camera and nodded his head as if he were speaking directly to them in their living room.

"Na'Dreya," the president had said, raising his fist, "you are right."

. . .

Obama had attended a Hawaiian prep school, and his young daughters, Sasha and Malia, had been enrolled at elite private schools in Chicago and Washington. When he decided to run for president, he had recruited a cadre of experts to teach him about public education. The sum of their expertise had resulted in a basic conclusion. "We need to wake up!" Obama declared a few weeks into his presidency.

He decided to shock the country into action by giving speeches in which he referred to public education as a "national crisis" and a "race to the bottom." He visited six schools during his first four months in office and memorized a staggering series of statistics to repeat in public whenever he could:

The dropout rate had tripled over the last thirty years, and now less than 70 percent of students graduated from high school.

America, once the world leader in college graduates, now ranked twelfth.

South Korean students, already far ahead of their U.S. peers, also remained in school for an extra month each year.

Japanese sixth graders worked on the same curriculum as Americans did in eighth grade.

A study of fourth graders in twenty-four industrialized nations had ranked the United States thirteenth in reading and eighteenth in math.

"Despite resources unmatched anywhere else in the world, we've let our grades slip, our schools crumble, our teacher quality fall short, and other nations outpace us," Obama said.

By the time Na'Dreya sent her letter, Obama had succeeded in awakening the country to the problem; a recent poll showed that only 18 percent of Americans gave the public schools a grade of A or B. But Obama and his staff had been considerably less successful in establishing consensus about how to proceed. He had invested record amounts of government money in public education: $100 billion in the stimulus package; a $3 billion boost in his first budget; $5 billion for early-childhood education; $900 million for failing schools; $50 million for dropout prevention; and on and on it went. Still, despite the investments, education experts remained divided over Obama's ideas and whether or not they could work.

Obama had appointed Arne Duncan as his secretary of education, choosing a friend from Chicago and a regular member of his pickup basketball games. Duncan had run the Chicago schools for eight years and earned a reputation as a reformer who was not afraid of taking drastic measures. He fired lackluster teachers, closed failing schools, experimented with paying students for good grades, and advocated building more charter schools, which are privately run but receive public money.

Like Obama, Duncan had serious concerns with the No Child Left Behind Act, a bill proposed by George W. Bush and passed by Congress in 2001. The bill required states to evaluate students every year by giving standardized tests. Each state created its own tests to measure "proficiency"—whether each student performed at average grade level. Schools that showed progress in raising their proficiency rating had the best chance of receiving federal funds.

The problem, Duncan and Obama agreed, was that schools had begun teaching to the tests, narrowing their curriculum to make sure students were proficient in heavily tested subjects like math and reading at the expense of everything else. Schools tended to focus most on teaching students who were within range of achieving the proficient level, while paying less attention to those who already tested well or were too far behind to catch up. Meanwhile, some schools that drastically improved student performance—by raising a group of fourth graders, for instance, from a first-grade level to a third-grade level—were still labeled failures for having students who performed below their grade level. To counter this problem, some states had created standardized tests with such low expectations that they were par with the bottom 40 percent of the world, relaxing standards until proficiency became attainable.

For more than a year, Duncan and Obama worked quietly on a plan to reform No Child Left Behind and then unveiled their proposal, called "the blueprint," on March 13, 2010. Instead of grading schools simply by testing proficiency, they suggested judging schools based on individual student improvement on the same tests, while also evaluating graduation rates, attendance, extracurricular programs, and efforts to narrow the achievement gap between rich and poor students. They called for all states to adopt common standards for testing, with the lofty goal of making every student "college ready" by 2020.

The most controversial part of Obama's blueprint dealt with the bottom 5 percent of schools, which would be forced to take extreme steps toward reform: fire at least 50 percent of the staff, replace the administration, or reopen under new ownership as a charter school. Trailblazing this model in February, a high school in Rhode Island had fired all ninety-three of its teachers after just 7 percent of eleventh graders passed the state math test. Teacher unions had threatened lawsuits and called on Obama for support. Obama supported the firings instead. "If a school continues to fail its students year after year after year, then there's got to be a sense of accountability," he had said.

Obama and Duncan proposed other ideas that put them at odds with the teacher unions, whose members had voted for Obama by a margin of three to one. Obama wanted longer school days because, he said, "we can no longer afford an academic calendar designed for when America was a nation of farmers who needed their children at home plowing the land." Duncan wanted to pay more to math and science teachers because they were in short supply. Obama favored less job security for teachers and more merit-based pay, a scale in which salaries would be tied directly to student performance. A large number of teachers protested that this idea made no sense since standardized test scores also depended on so many factors outside of their control: disabilities, parenting, early-childhood education, and a recession that had left 40 percent of black adults unemployed at one point or another and their children hungry, stressed, and distracted.

Hoping to win over teachers and generate enough support to push his blueprint through Congress, Obama visited the centennial conference of the Urban League to make a crucial speech about education on July 29, 2010. So far, his blueprint had produced little but discord. The House of Representatives and the Senate had held education hearings but had yet to produce a bill. Experts suspected the deadlock would continue for at least another year. Eight civil rights organizations—including the Urban League—had released a report labeling Obama's plans unfair and ineffective.

Surrounded by these disparagements, Obama strode onstage at the Washington Convention Center to mixed applause. He motioned his hands to quiet the crowd. "We've tolerated a status quo where America lags behind other nations," he said. "We haven't done enough about it. This status quo is morally inexcusable and economically indefensible, and all of us are going to have to roll up our sleeves and change it."

Obama spoke directly to high-school dropouts, telling them that quitting was unpatriotic and inexcusable. He spoke directly to teachers. "I am 110 percent behind teachers," he said. "But all I'm asking in return, as a president, a parent, and a citizen, is some measure of accountability."

Near the end of his speech, Obama spoke directly to students. "An education is not something you just tip your head and they pour it into your ear," he said. "You've got to want it. You've got to reach out and claim that future for yourself, and you can't make excuses." He paused and surveyed the audience before continuing.

> I know life is tough for a lot of young people in this country. Too many of them may feel trapped in a community where drugs and violence and unemployment are pervasive, and they are forced to wrestle with things that no child should have to face. There are all kinds of reasons for our children to say, "No I can't." But our job is to say to them, "Yes, you can."
>
> I got a letter recently postmarked Covington, Kentucky. It was from Na'Dreya Lattimore, ten years old—about the same age as Sasha. And she told me about how her school had closed, so now she had enrolled in another. Then she bumped up against other barriers to what she felt was her potential. So Na'Dreya was explaining to me how we need to improve our education system. She closed by saying this: "One more thing," she said. It was a long letter. "You need to look at us different. We are not black, we're not white, biracial, Hispanic, Asian or any other nationality." No, she wrote, "We are the future."
>
> Na'Dreya, you are right. And that's why I will keep fighting to lead us out of this storm, so that young people like Na'Dreya—people of every race, in every region—are going to be able to reach for the American dream. They are going

to know that there are brighter days ahead, that their future is
full of boundless possibilities.

. . .

A few weeks later, Na'Dreya was scheduled to make a speech of her
own. Lynda Jackson, superintendent of Covington schools, had
invited her to talk about her correspondence with Obama in front
of more than four hundred teachers and staff at the district's annual
welcome-back assembly for faculty. Na'Dreya and her family dressed
up and left Latonia Terrace at eight on a scorching August morning
and walked single file to the high-school auditorium. They were running late and the boys moved lethargically in the heat. "Move it or I'll
step on your feet," Cindy yelled from the back of the line.

When they reached the auditorium, two cameramen and a
reporter formed a circle around Na'Dreya to interview her. A school
official whisked her away after a few minutes and ushered the family to seats in the front row. Na'Dreya sat next to the event's other
keynote speakers: a popular author from Australia, the head of Kentucky's teachers' union, and a beloved member of the school board.
Na'Dreya looked up and surveyed the crowded balcony, where hundreds of adults wore dresses and suits and ties and stared down at a
lone podium illuminated by six spotlights. She buried her head in her
mother's shoulder. "I'm scared," she said. A few minutes before the
assembly began, Superintendent Jackson walked over and knelt in
front of Na'Dreya. "How are you doing?" she asked.

"My stomach is filled with some of those butterflies," Na'Dreya
said.

"You're going to do great," Jackson said. "Just remember that
everyone here is already proud of you."

Jackson, fifty, looked typically elegant with straightened blond hair and a pearl necklace to match her pearl earrings. She had a thick Southern accent, and she wore heavy eye makeup to disguise the fatigue wrought by a job she called "a nonstop battle." School had yet to start, but already the year felt long. Even during summer, she often slept only six hours a night and apologized to her husband for leaving the house before 7:00 a.m. to get to work. In her three years as superintendent, she had come to understand her job as equal parts fund-raiser, caseworker, and teacher. "The truth is I've aged quite a bit in the last three years," she said. "This is a twenty-four-hour job."

A longtime administrator in Covington Independent, Jackson had been one of only two solid applicants for a job few people wanted. Kentucky education experts had spent a decade trying to reform Covington's schools, only to watch them further devolve. By the time Jackson was hired, five of the district's eight schools had no active parent association. Every year one-third of Covington's students changed schools and one-quarter of its teachers quit. More than 23 percent of students were classified as having disabilities, 10 percent more than the state average. A Kentucky budgetary crisis had resulted in a district deficit of $2.6 million—a situation made worse because Covington had a long list of unique expenses: a full-time coordinator to assist more than four hundred homeless students; a fleet of social-service counselors; a family-resource center in every school where students could stock up on canned food for the weekend or borrow a clean school outfit from a clothes closet.

Shortly after she became superintendent, Jackson had analyzed the district's predicament and offered an unusually candid assessment. "We are way beyond excuses," she had said. "We need solutions."

And so, in an exhausting blitz, Jackson had tried to provide them. She considered herself a data-driven reformer whose ideals aligned with Obama's and Duncan's, and she began pioneering their ideas even before they released their blueprint. She cut eleven positions in the district's central office and closed two schools, decisions that squared the budget but made her "enemy number one right away," she said. She hired new principals—mostly young, optimistic workaholics who came from outside the district—and told each to build a "war room" in the school where teachers could analyze student-testing data and plot ways to improve it, one student at a time. The district was made over with a new logo, a new slogan ("Destination Graduation"), a new strategic plan, and a new testing system that measured student improvement three times a year. New teachers took a mandatory bus tour of Covington that wound them through all three projects and then listened to a presentation entitled "Demography Is Not Destiny." Jackson made a habit of visiting classrooms for monthly evaluations, asking teachers to forward her their lesson plans, and personally interviewing each of the district's 250 graduating seniors to learn about their experiences. As a result of her efforts, district test scores had begun to improve slightly, and so had staff and student morale. But, like most reformers, Jackson remained a polarizing figure. She was considered either hands-on or meddling, heroic or naïve. She expected to be scrutinized more closely than ever during the 2010–2011 school year. It had taken her three years as superintendent to institute her own plans, but now the district was hers and she would be judged based on its shortcomings or successes. "Now is the time when we have to start turning it around," she said.

With that as her mission, Jackson walked onstage at the assembly and stepped up to the microphone. "Welcome to the beginning of an exciting year," she said. "We have a new strategic plan that you are going to be hearing a lot about, and we have an even bigger goal: We want to be the best urban school district in the nation."

Jackson introduced the school board member, then the union president, and then the Australian author. As they spoke, Na'Dreya's brothers fidgeted in the front row and eventually fell asleep. Lisa sank low in her chair. "This is why I didn't like school," she said. Finally, two hours into the assembly, Jackson walked to the podium and pointed to the front row. "Today we have a student with us who is not afraid to dream," Jackson said. She called Na'Dreya to the stage as the audience rose for a standing ovation, and Na'Dreya stepped up onto a stool so she could reach the microphone. She stared back out at the crowd, eyes wide and mouth agape.

"Wow," she whispered. Then she fell silent.

The night before, Na'Dreya had spent three hours rehearsing everything she wanted to say: how the teachers were not to blame for her school's problems, and how more parents needed to volunteer in the school like her grandmother did to ensure their kids behaved. She had written it all down on lined paper and tucked it into her back pocket, but now she forgot about the paper altogether. She turned to Jackson and shrugged. Jackson smiled and brought over a copy of Na'Dreya's letter to Obama. "Let's go ahead and read this," she whispered, and Na'Dreya tentatively started to read while Jackson traced each line with her finger. The audience chuckled and then gave Na'Dreya another standing ovation when she finished reading. Jackson hugged her and presented her with a framed copy of her letter and Obama's response. "This is for you, for being brave and speaking up," Jackson said.

A few more reporters interviewed Na'Dreya when she walked offstage, and then Lisa and Cindy took turns carrying the framed letter as the family walked home. They let the boys amble at their own pace. Cindy talked about how Na'Dreya might be able to get a scholarship to college. Lisa stopped to show the framed letter to a friend from

Latonia Terrace. "A girl from the Terrace, huh?" the friend said, and Lisa beamed. Na'Dreya walked next to her brothers and yammered excitedly about her experience onstage. "My mouth went dry, and I couldn't see, and then it was like, 'Uh, uh, uh, Oh no! What's happening?' But then I started to read, and it got easier, and they all started clapping, and I was like, 'Yes! I'm doing it! I can do this!' "

.   .   .

Jackson left the assembly and headed back to her office, hoping to do a little research on her computer. Obama and Duncan recently had announced the states that had won Race to the Top grants, a distribution of $4.4 billion in aid to states that were making the most progress toward implementing Obama's reforms. Kentucky had lost out again, despite making it to the finals and sending five state education officials to give a two-hour presentation in Washington. Jackson wanted to know where Kentucky had fallen short, even though she knew the research would only upset her. She logged on and typed in a Google search for "Race to the Top winning applications."

"This is like a pot of gold," she said, shaking her head, "and our kids really could have used it."

Obama considered Race to the Top one of his administration's smartest ideas and most resounding successes. While his education blueprint idled in Congress, Obama and Duncan decided to use Race to the Top to push states to implement their reforms anyway. Obama had created the program by giving the Department of Education almost $5 billion to spend as part of the Recovery Act, gifting Duncan with the biggest amount of discretionary money ever controlled by a secretary of education. Duncan vowed to distribute the money in grants to states that adopted the blueprint ideas: reforming failing schools, building more charters, and paying teachers based on performance. It was, Duncan often gloated, the perfect time to launch a competitive grant program. States were broke and in desperate need of federal money. Long before Duncan distributed a penny, thirty-two states had changed their education laws in pursuit of Race to the Top funds. Illinois had lifted its cap on charter schools. West Virginia had proposed merit-based pay for teachers. Forty-six states had formed committees and spent months completing applications that numbered upward of 250 pages.

Kentucky had pursued the grant as hard as everyplace else, becoming the first state to adopt Obama's common standards for testing and creating a new system for reforming its most troubled schools. Jackson had hoped her state would push even harder—maybe by considering performance-based pay or even removing its ban against charter schools. Jackson had a full-time grant writer on her district staff, and she considered it "a moral obligation to get every penny possible for these kids," she said. Early predictions showed that Kentucky faced a $1.4 billion budgetary shortfall for 2011, and Jackson expected her district budget to be sliced again. A Race to the Top grant would have given Kentucky $175 million, or more than $1 million for each of its school districts.

Jackson stared at her computer and skimmed winning applications from states like Ohio, North Carolina, Georgia, and Maryland. She watched a video and heard Duncan explain that "the quality of applicants were very strong. We just ran out of money."

It was a feeling Jackson knew all too well. She shut off the computer and stood up from her desk. Another school year would start the next morning, and she planned to wake up at 5:00 a.m. so she could bring coffee and doughnuts to the district's bus drivers. She had always loved the first day of school; her husband, a sports fan, compared it to the feeling of spring training in baseball. Everyone started fresh. Everyone was optimistic. For one day, at least, anything still seemed possible.

.   .   .

It rained on the first day of school, so Na'Dreya and her family splurged on the bus. She stepped out of Latonia Terrace wearing her new outfit and walked across the street along with her grandmother and two of her brothers to catch the No. 33 city bus. Joshua and Marcus splashed happily through the mud, but Na'Dreya zigzagged around the puddles to avoid dirtying her fresh-out-of-the-box "writable" white Reeboks, on which her mother had already inscribed the first message in black ink: "Good luck!!"

The bus dropped them off in front of Sixth District Elementary, and Na'Dreya joined five hundred other students in the gymnasium to recite the Pledge of Allegiance. The vice principal welcomed them to "another great year" and then instructed the students to find their classrooms. All at once, they dispersed throughout the hundred-year-old building, footsteps echoing off the tile floors. Na'Dreya hurried upstairs to a fifth-grade room, picked out a desk in front, and started to look over her new classmates. She noticed her grandmother watching from just outside the classroom door.

"Mahma, you can go," Na'Dreya said.

"I know," Cindy said. "I just want to make sure you're all right."

"Please," Na'Dreya said, waving her hand in a shooing motion. "I'll be fine."

Cindy smiled and left, and Na'Dreya's teacher stood up from her desk and walked over to close the classroom door. Heather Gillman, thirty-six, had been teaching in Covington for eight years, long enough to learn that "the uphill battle starts at the beginning of day one," she said. Her first task was deceptively simple: take roll. The attendance sheet on her desk listed twenty-two students, but Gillman counted only fifteen in her classroom. Three of those fifteen were not on her class list, and one raised his hand to explain that he probably was not on any list because he had moved to Covington only a day earlier. Three more students trickled into the classroom during the next half hour, and eventually Gillman set down the attendance sheet and clapped her hands. "You know what? Forget it," she said. "This is our class, all of you sitting right here, so let's get to it."

She asked the students to start emptying the contents of their backpacks into their desks, but two of the boys had not brought backpacks or supplies. "Don't worry. We'll find you what you need," Gillman said. Each student had also been asked to bring in some communal items for the classroom—hand sanitizer, tissues, paper towels—but only Na'Dreya and one other girl had delivered on this assignment. "No problem," Gillman said. "We'll make do."

Gillman had learned to be resourceful during her years in the Covington schools. She had grown up only ten miles across the river in Ohio but "really a world away," she said. Her parents raised her in a wealthy, predominantly Jewish suburb, and she had attended kindergarten through twelfth grade at Cincinnati Country Day School, a $12,000-a-year private school spread across sixty-two acres in Indian Hill. After college at Arizona State, she had come home to work for her father's sweater-manufacturing business and traveled across Asia and Europe making deals. He had hoped she would take over the company when he retired; she had decided to quit instead. "I hated math and I wasn't making any kind of a difference," she said, so she had followed her mother into teaching, earning a master's at Xavier and then applying for a job in Covington that paid $27,000 to start.

For most of the first year, she had been an emotional wreck. A kid in her class had thrown desks, broken windows, and once needed to be handcuffed. She had eaten lunch in the cafeteria with her students and heard them talk about domestic violence, not having enough to eat, and single mothers who stayed out all night. "It felt like I had become a social worker, and until then I had been so sheltered," she said. But she loved helping kids who desperately needed her. She had since passed up cushier teaching jobs, rented an apartment in Covington, and become a mentor to young teachers enduring their own brutal first years.

The key, she had learned, was to establish control of the class during the first few weeks—a period Gillman and her co-workers referred to as the "honeymoon" because students were still inclined to listen and behave. While Na'Dreya and her classmates organized their desks, Gillman looked around the room and tried to pick out the students she called "players"—likely troublemakers who would disrupt class. Later in the morning, for the first lesson, she outlined her classroom rules: one warning for misbehavior; then a timeout; then a phone call home; then detention. "You get four strikes," she said. "But if you hit somebody, that's all four strikes at once. I never tolerate that, and I mean never. Don't mess with me on that one."

Some other teachers at Sixth District had made a pact never to smile in front of students during the first six weeks as a means of intimidation; Gillman had experimented with that strategy but decided it didn't suit her. "It might be naïve, but I still think learning can be fun," she said. Over the summer, an artist had spray-painted her classroom walls with drawings of Lewis and Clark, astronauts, and the Taj Mahal, so that students were now surrounded by the topics of their lessons. She had gone to Atlanta to participate in a teaching seminar on how clapping and singing could help control a classroom, and she planned to regularly serenade her students even though she considered herself tone-deaf.

Near the end of the day, Gillman explained the first homework assignment. The class was going to put together a time capsule that it would open at the end of the year, and each student was supposed to write down his or her goals for fifth grade and hopes for the upcoming decade.

"This is what I want you to do tonight," Gillman said as Na'Dreya jotted down notes. "Think about where you are right now compared to where you want to be, and then think about how you can get there."

*   *   *

Back at Latonia Terrace, with the future weighing on her mind, Na'Dreya rounded up her brothers, the puppy, and a toddler from next door whom everyone called Mud. "Follow me," Na'Dreya told them as she walked upstairs in their apartment. "We're going to play a game."

"Basketball?" Marcus asked.

"Wrestling?" Joshua said hopefully.

"No," Na'Dreya said. "We're playing college."

College was one of her favorite games and also the one they played most regularly. Marcus and Joshua groaned. They considered college confusing and boring and had been saying so to Na'Dreya ever since she invented the game earlier in the summer. But Na'Dreya was older, bigger, and "sometimes bossy," Marcus said, so they trudged up the stairs behind her. There was nothing else to do, anyway. Some of the other kids from the project were still away at school or day care. Cindy and Lisa were smoking cigarettes on the front porch and hashing out finances, like they did near the end of every month when their welfare money and food stamps had all but run out.

Na'Dreya closed the door to the upstairs bedroom and instructed her brothers to "fix it up real nice like a college dorm." Together they made the beds, tucking in the Spider-Man sheets and fluffing up the SpongeBob pillows. They brought up a desk lamp from downstairs and set it on the floor next to a fake plastic keyboard. Na'Dreya sat at the makeshift desk and instructed her brothers to sit still on the bed. "Class starts in five minutes," she said. "No talking. I'll be right back."

She walked out of the room and came back a few seconds later with one of her mother's old community college textbooks, a stack of scrap paper, and a box of crayons, but her classroom had turned to chaos. Joshua threw a tennis ball toward a miniature plastic hoop and screamed "LeBron!" after each successful shot. Marcus practiced somersaulting across the bed. Mud bounced her head against the wall and implored everyone to "Watch this! Watch this!" Na'Dreya surveyed the scene from the door for a minute, frowning, hands on her hips. Then she stomped her foot and clapped her hands. "Y'all are going to fail out of here if you don't get serious!" she said. "I'm not warning you again. You only get one chance in college."

Her reluctant students sat back down on the bed. Na'Dreya handed each a piece of paper and a crayon.

"The assignment today is to make a ten-year plan and figure out what you want to do with your life," she said. "You all are going to have to make something of yourselves, and it starts now. First, you're going to decide what you want to be in ten years. Then you have to write down what it takes to get there."

Her brothers looked back at her with blank stares, and Na'Dreya rolled her eyes. "You don't know how to make a ten-year plan?" she said. She had long ago committed her own plan to memory: straight A's in middle school; straight A's in high school; admission to MIT; straight A's during college while double-majoring in science and math; a successful career in forensic science and maybe moonlighting as a crime-solver on network TV. She liked to chart out this timeline at least once each week, and she recently had begun journaling about her aspirations in a "dream book" to help her stay focused.

Meanwhile, on the bed in front of her, Mud had resumed bouncing her head against the wall, and Joshua and Marcus had started drawing with the crayons instead of charting ten-year plans. Na'Dreya walked over to the bed and sat next to Joshua.

"Okay, let me help you get started," she said. "What do you want to be when you grow up?"

"A wrestler! A really awesome wrestler!" Joshua said, and to demonstrate he body-slammed Mud into the bed.

"Okay, well what does it take to get there?" Na'Dreya said, taking his crayon. "Let's make a map. First you have to graduate from middle school and high school, right?"

"I guess so," Joshua said.

"Then you have to go to college and major in wrestling and get straight A's, right?"

"Um, yeah," Joshua said.

"So then start writing all that down."

Joshua reached over and tackled Mud, so Na'Dreya turned her attention to Marcus, who was still busy drawing. "What are you doing?" she said. "That doesn't look like a ten-year plan."

"I want to draw a T-shirt real bad," he said.

"That's your problem. You don't pay attention," Na'Dreya said. "You know when you actually go to college you can't behave like this, right? You got to study, read, and go to class all the time. So if you're going to play it now, you've got to do it right. Don't you want to make something of yourself?"

Marcus set down his crayon and looked up at his sister, suddenly serious. "I'm sorry," he said. "I want to go to college and then I want to be a policeman."

"Okay, good. Then go ahead and chart that out," Na'Dreya said.

Marcus went back to drawing a T-shirt instead, so Na'Dreya retreated to her make-believe desk and wrote down her own ten-year plan again. Straight A's. Graduate high school. MIT. Forensics.

Her brothers started bouncing on the bed. The upstairs room was sweltering. Through the open window, Lisa and Cindy could be heard talking to the Latonia Terrace maintenance woman about their fly infestation. But Na'Dreya kept her head down and her eyes fixed on the paper. It was the one place where she was firmly in charge and free to plot out her future.

CHAPTER 9

"I was bullyed in high school and seriously contemplated suicide."

Each teenage suicide induced another flashback, and each flashback brought a fresh wave of stress. By the fall of 2010, Jon Santos had started taking medicine for an ulcer developing in his stomach, and nervous energy compelled him to jiggle his knees, fidget his fingers, and pace the length of his small office at work. He came home each evening to his apartment in downtown Atlanta, dropped his briefcase on the couch, and lay down on the hardwood floor. He called over his tuxedo cat, Tootsie, who rubbed against Jon's forehead as he closed his eyes and blocked out the world.

Here he was at forty-three: happy, successful, beloved, self-assured—and a total mess at the end of each day. He worked as the director of the AIDS Walk Atlanta and spent his time coordinating 10,000 participants and 1,500 volunteers for an event that raised $1 million a year. But lately the more taxing part of Jon's workdays had become his occasional breaks, during which he checked his computer for news updates and read about the epidemic of gay teenagers who were committing suicide after being bullied. Each life lost made him reflect on his own. He had been called those same names. He had felt that same hopelessness. He had imagined killing himself in all of those ways. Jon, who considered himself "straight out of central casting in terms of your usual gay stereotypes," was an emotional man who tended to cry often, and now he had a new reason to grieve almost every day.

He had read about at least six suicides during the month of September alone, among them Billy Lucas, fifteen, Indiana, found hanging from the rafters of his family's barn; Tyler Clementi, eighteen, New Jersey, who jumped off the George Washington Bridge after a classmate live-streamed a video of him kissing another man; Asher Brown, thirteen, Texas, dead from a self-inflicted gunshot wound to the head; Raymond Chase, nineteen, Rhode Island, found hanging in his college dorm room. The details of their stories—rich in loneliness, self-doubt, and religious confusion—made Jon think back over his own life and reach a chilling conclusion. "I was just like them," he said. "It could so easily have been me."

He had been born in a small town just outside of Honolulu, and he described his life as "kind of a mistake from day one." His conception was an accident that surprised his middle-aged parents nine years after the birth of his nearest sibling, and his father felt finished with parenting by then. He was a tough man, a thirty-year veteran of the National Guard, and he wanted Jon to be more aggressive on the soccer field and more interested in playing football. Jon, meanwhile, preferred to ride his bike while wearing his sister's old prom dress or play dress-up with an older girl who lived next door. He appreciated pretty things, like purses and dolls. When he was nine years old, his mother took him to a gas station and Jon stared at the young male attendant. "He has pretty eyes," Jon said, and his mother stomped her foot and reached over with her hand to shush him. "Quiet!" she had scolded. "People are going to think you are *mahu*!"

It was a Hawaiian term for "gay," a slang word with derogatory roots, and Jon barely knew what it meant. But even before he reached his teens, he did know already that there was something different about him. Something wrong, he thought. It was the way he lingered on the men's underwear section of the JC Penney catalogue; the way he swooned over celebrities like baseball player Jim Palmer, diver Greg Louganis, and actor Scott Baio; the way he finally relented to watching sports with his dad during the 1980 Olympics, not because he wanted to follow the games but because he liked to admire the participants; the way, when classmates talked about their schoolyard crushes, Jon always claimed his was on the most popular girl in school, because at least then it would never become a reality.

Peers assigned names to Jon's behavior years before he ever did, and their taunting started in about sixth grade. "Queer." "Fag." "Speedo freak." The name-calling escalated with each passing month. By the time Jon reached high school, he counted a group of six girls as his only friends. Then, in the fall of his freshman year, those girls pulled him aside before lunch. It would be best if he spent more time with boys, they said, because maybe then he wouldn't get teased so much.

The abandonment only increased his suffering. He had nobody to sit with at lunch, so he pretended to busy himself with homework or class meetings during the free period. He started failing algebra because he sat between two bullies who intimidated him. A theology teacher assigned students to write their names at the top of a blank piece of paper and pass it around the room to collect a compliment from each classmate, and Jon's sheet arrived back with a handful of slurs. His peers pronounced his every move a telltale sign of homosexuality—the way he looked at his nails, held a glass of water, or fixed his eyes on a teacher during a lecture. He pretended to ignore their taunts but instead internalized them. "I was a verbal punching bag," he said. "I had no chance of defending myself." He was too afraid to tell his parents because any discussion about bullying would inevitably lead to questions about its cause, and because they took him to Catholic mass every Sunday, where he had learned all too well about the particulars of sin. So instead of confiding in anyone, Jon came home each day after school, closed the door to his room, turned up some Michael Jackson, and obsessed over what seemed like his only way out.

Suicide. How could he do it? A bullet would be too messy and he had no access to a gun. Hanging required creating the fatal weapon with his own two hands, and he didn't have the courage for that. He thought about diving into the ocean, swimming out beyond the breaking waves, and trying to drown himself in the surf, but he was a good swimmer whose body would naturally fight back. He went to the library to research carbon monoxide poisoning, studying how to redirect the car's exhaust fumes back into the vehicle with a hose. That method would work best, Jon decided, but it would also require waiting for the right moment. His mother was a housewife who rarely left him home alone.

Before he had the chance to act, he was wandering around campus during another lonely lunch period when he stumbled into a small building he had never seen before—the school counseling office. A counselor asked why he wasn't at lunch. He started to cry and told her about the bullying. She asked if he was gay; he said he wasn't sure. He told her that he had been fantasizing about suicide. She called his parents and they agreed Jon would visit the counseling office once or twice a week. Jon's mother began to worry about him, which felt good. The counselor encouraged him to join student government, the choir, and a peer-advising group.

High school became better after that—still dreadful, but survivable. And once Jon graduated, his life began to evolve in ways beyond the imagination of the freshman who had contemplated suicide while locked in his bedroom. He went off to Loyola Marymount University in California. He drank too much one night and made out with a male roommate. He admitted to himself that he was gay, and a friend took him to his first gay bar, a West Hollywood dive called Mother Lode. Jon had braced himself for dancing strippers, sleazy pickup lines, and men wearing pink, but instead he found regular guys drinking domestic beer, listening to grunge rock, and shooting pool. "Where are the gay guys?" he had asked, and then it hit him: They were all gay—and they were laid-back and normal, just like him. He met friends and then boyfriends, building a community that helped him stop merely accepting that he was gay and start embracing it. He lifted weights, went to tanning salons, and stayed out dancing on Saturday nights. He took a job after college in the university's student activities office and became the adviser to the campus gay-and-lesbian alliance. A roommate's boyfriend died of AIDS, so Jon became an activist and organized one of the first major AIDS-awareness demonstrations on a Jesuit campus.

One afternoon while still in his early twenties, he came home from the gym, lay down on the couch, and decided it was time to come out to his family. He called his sister first and heard his voice crack as he told her. "We know," she said. She told him a story about how their mother, who had recently died from breast cancer, had found out Jon was dating a male soccer player while away at college, and how she had called a family meeting to say, "Jon is *mahu*. Now we know, and we're going to accept it." And, as Jon spread the news, that's exactly what his family had done. His brother, a former football player who managed a Goodyear tire store, confessed that he had sobbed for an hour after watching Tom Hanks's character die in the movie *Philadelphia*. His nieces tried to set him up with the choreographer of their high-school dance team. His nephews found a photo of his muscled boyfriend hidden in a suitcase, confronted him with it, watched him stumble and blush, and then simply said, "Wow, Uncle Jon, nice work! Your boyfriend is ripped!"

Nearly thirty years after he had first obsessed over suicide, he had a supportive family and a close circle of friends. He had moved to Atlanta in his late twenties, finding a trendy condominium and a meaningful job helping to fight AIDS, which he called "the cause of my life." The idea of killing himself seemed ridiculous now. He wished he could have offered some perspective to those troubled gay teenagers when they were contemplating suicide, but instead he only learned their names from news stories or obituaries, when it was already too late.

Still, he hated the idea of doing nothing. So as news of yet another teen suicide played in loops on the news in late October, Jon decided to do what he often did when something in the world made him feel sick. He opened his computer, logged on to Whitehouse.gov, and started writing an e-mail to the president.

His parents had always taught him to take political action; on the morning of his eighteenth birthday, he had come to the kitchen to find an application for the Hawaiian Democratic Party waiting on his seat at the breakfast table. His job organizing the walk for AID Atlanta involved dealing with city planners, politicians, and policemen, and he had learned that he could pull the levers of government through

sheer doggedness—nagging the councilman with a few extra calls or
dropping by the police station unannounced.

Similarly, he had memorized the phone number for the White
House comment line—(202) 456-1111—during George W. Bush's
presidency and called every few months. He had driven upstate to see
Hillary Clinton at a book signing in the late 1990s, bought her a bou-
quet of flowers, and waited in line for three hours to thank her in person for her work on AIDS. He had flown standby from Atlanta to see
Obama's inauguration in Washington, leaving home at 5:00 a.m. and
returning after midnight. Then, when one of Jon's trips back to Hawaii
coincided with an Obama family vacation to the island, his desire to
get close to the president had compelled him to walk along the beach
and circumvent barricaded roads near the president's vacation home
until two Secret Service agents on Jet Skis revealed their guns and
shooed him off. He had e-mailed Obama at least half a dozen times
already, suggesting that he get rid of chief of staff Rahm Emanuel and
his machismo shtick, see through the war in Afghanistan, and repeal
Don't Ask, Don't Tell to allow gays to serve openly in the military. This
time Jon decided to write a much more personal letter. He had heard
the president condemn gay bullying during speeches, and he hoped
his own story might further solidify the president's stance. "Dear Mr.
President," Jon typed.

> I am an avid supporter, donor, activist and life-long democrat
> who also happens to be gay. I have devoted my life to help-
> ing people living with HIV/AIDS in Atlanta . . . I was bullyed
> in high school as a Freshman and seriously contemplated
> suicide. I think the only things that saved me were a genuine
> fear of how to successfully kill myself and a high school coun-
> selor. Life was bad then, but it slowly got better. I attended a

wonderful Catholic Liberal Arts University in California and learned that "God doesn't make junk!" And, whether gay, straight, black, white, asian, able, or challenged, we are all unique and beautifuil and through all humankind the face of God is seen.

Jon typed the note in a few minutes and included a stream-of-consciousness sentence near the end. "I have written many times, and I don't know who reads these letters—I hope someone does," he typed. Then he signed off with a phrase in Hawaiian, "*Kûlia i ka nu'u*" (Strive for the summit!), and hit the Send button.

Later that day, when Jon got home from work and watched the news, he saw a story about the vice president of a school board in Arkansas who had decided to resign after getting caught writing on his Facebook page that all "queers and fags" should commit suicide. Jon fidgeted on the couch in his apartment, lay on the floor with his cat, and went to bed but struggled to sleep. He had been suffering from a recurring nightmare during the last few months. He was young again in the dream, fourteen or fifteen, and he swam out to sea intending to drown. He had drifted maybe half a mile off the coast when suddenly he changed his mind, but now the ocean had turned stormy and the shore had faded into the distance. The harder he swam toward land, the farther out he drifted. The sky darkened while he thrashed and flailed against the water late into the night.

.   .   .

Across the country in Seattle, another successful gay man followed the news about the suicides and decided to take action of a different kind. Dan Savage, forty-seven, was best known as a raunchy sex writer whose weekly advice column in *The Stranger* was syndicated in newspapers across the country. In the last fifteen years, his media empire had grown to include four books, a college speaking tour, an iPhone application, a weekly podcast, and regular appearances on national TV—all thanks to an expertise in fetishes and innuendo. But Dan was also an ardent activist who had been arrested for his political protesting and regularly used his column to advocate for AIDS aware-ness and the legalization of gay marriage. The string of suicides in the fall of 2010 reawakened his indignation. He vowed to adopt gay bully-ing as his latest cause.

Dan had grown up in Chicago and attended Catholic school, where classmates teased him for loving baking and musical theater. His father worked as a homicide cop in a seedy, gay neighborhood ravaged by AIDS, and he spoke disapprovingly about "the gays." Dan had two brothers, both of whom were athletes and hard-core sports fans. He spent most of his adolescence in an "isolated hell," he said, before coming out to his family just before he turned twenty.

But over the years his life had improved in surprising and hum-bling ways. He had met his boyfriend, Terry, on the dance floor of a Seattle club and now they had been partners for sixteen years. They had adopted a son, and their regular family vacations included snow-boarding in the Rocky Mountains and traveling across Europe. He had been working in a video store in Wisconsin when, on a whim, a friend offered him a job writing an advice column for a start-up newspaper, and now his career had made him marginally famous and allowed him time to direct local theater productions on the side. After a few awkward years, his Catholic family in Chicago had come to accept him and adore his boyfriend, whom his mother said she loved "like a daughter."

The tragedy of suicide, Dan thought, was that each victim never got a chance to see how his life would evolve. The bullying would end. New friends would offer support. Families would become more accepting. "I just wish I could have had five minutes to tell those kids: 'I've been there. It will get better,'" Dan said. He wanted to broadcast that message to other gay teenagers who were considering suicide. He and Terry decided to film a video and post it on the Internet.

They had no idea what to say or how to say it, so they sat against a wall in their living room and talked into a video camera for eleven minutes, recounting the torture they had endured in high school. When they finished and watched the tape, it looked like a hostage video, with two despondent people crying in front of a whitewashed wall. "If they weren't going to commit suicide before, they sure as hell will after watching this," Dan said. They decided to try again, this time talking more about the joys of their current lives and less about the misery of bullying. They brought the camera to a nearby bar, ordered drinks, and asked a friend to film them. Dan and Terry sat side by side in the booth, shoulders pressed together, and looked into the camera. In the hum of bar noise in the background, glasses clinked and other conversations continued. This time, Dan and Terry talked about falling in love, watching the sunset over the Eiffel Tower, and becoming parents.

"Honestly, things got better the day I left high school," Terry said.

"What I'd love you to take away from this, really, is that it gets better," Dan said. "However bad it is now, it gets better, and it can get great, and it can get awesome. But you have to tough this period out and you have to live your life so that you're around for it to get amazing."

"Living well is the best revenge," Terry said.

"There really is a place for you," Dan said. "One day you will find love, and you will find a community, and life gets better."

They filmed for a little less than nine minutes, and later that afternoon Dan posted the video on YouTube, mentioned it in his podcast, and wrote a column asking people to make "It Gets Better" videos of their own. He hoped to amass a collection of seventy-five videos, maybe even a hundred. He checked his e-mail the next morning and found his account shut down because of an overloaded server. He received a thousand videos that first week and ten thousand in the first month. They came from priests and politicians, from straights and gays, from anonymous people in all fifty states and gay celebrities like Adam Lambert, Ellen DeGeneres, and Tim Gunn. A web-design company built a fancy site and a New York firm offered to handle publicity. Dan and Terry's video was viewed 1.3 million times. The collection of "It Gets Better" videos drew more than 30 million views. Similar projects were launched in England, Australia, and South America. Hillary Clinton made a video, and so did Nancy Pelosi. Exactly one month after Dan and Terry were filmed in the bar, Dan answered a phone call from an aide in Washington who suggested he log on to YouTube and check out the "It Gets Better" project's latest submission. Dan opened his computer, and there it was: a three-minute video submitted by the president of the United States.

Dan, once an ardent Obama supporter, had grown increasingly frustrated with the president over the last two years. Obama had offered some "pretty words" about gay issues, Dan said, but he had yet to follow through on his campaign promises of repealing the Defense of Marriage Act or Don't Ask, Don't Tell, laws that prevented gays from marrying or serving openly in the military, respectively. His Justice Department had filed a legal brief that equated the validity of gay marriage to "marriage of uncle to niece" or "marriage of first cousins." Dan had publicly given Obama a grade of F on gay rights issues, and he often said that he had lost faith in what the president offered gay rights leaders. "You get a lot of nice speeches, you get invited to cocktail parties, and we have shit to show for it," he said.

Obama recognized how far his popularity had slipped in the gay community, and he regularly said that he sympathized with its impatience. He had promised during the campaign to be a "fierce advocate for gay rights." Just six days after his inauguration, he had read and responded to a letter from a lesbian army officer in St. Louis who asked that he repeal Don't Ask, Don't Tell, and he had reiterated in a handwritten response that he was "committed to changing our current policy." But now, almost two years later, no progress had been made, and gay rights groups had started bombarding the mail room with thousands of flip-flop cards cut in the shape of beach sandals. High-powered gay donors had visited the White House to express their disappointment. Gay rights groups had shown up to heckle Obama at recent rallies in Los Angeles and San Francisco.

When Obama heard about the "It Gets Better" project, he recognized an opportunity to accomplish two goals at once: deliver an important message against gay bullying while also engendering some much-needed goodwill. His daily folder of ten letters had regularly included missives about gay bullying—the e-mail from Jon Santos in Atlanta and letters from a lesbian teenager in Oklahoma and a gay activist in Texas—and Obama had read them all. Rather than write back to one note at a time, the president decided to issue a public response for all to see. Late in the fall of 2010, he told his advisers to set aside thirty minutes in his schedule. He wanted to film an "It Gets Better" video of his own.

On a Thursday afternoon at the White House, an aide applied some light makeup to help take the shine off the president's face, and two cameras filmed him for three minutes in front of a softly lit background. Obama wore a suit and an American flag pin over his heart and spoke directly into the camera. "We've gotta dispel this myth that bullying is just a normal rite of passage, some inevitable part of growing up," he said. "It's not. I don't know what it's like to be picked

on for being gay, but I do know what it's like to grow up feeling that
sometimes you don't belong. It's tough. And when you're teased or
bullied, it can seem like you brought it on yourself for being different or for not fitting in with everybody else. But what I want to say is
this: You are not alone. You didn't do anything wrong. You didn't do
anything to deserve being bullied . . . Over time you're going to see
that your differences are a source of pride, and a source of strength."

Obama's staff posted the video alongside thousands of others on
the Internet, and Dan watched it that afternoon with a sense of disbelief. Here was the president posting on YouTube, echoing Dan's message and even using some of the exact phrases he and Terry had uttered
while filming in the Seattle bar. "The president had thrown his lot in
with me, the skeezy sex columnist," Dan said. But later that night, as
he continued to think about the president's video, Dan began to wonder if it was just another speech filled with hollow, pretty words. The
next day, Dan went on CNN to talk about the president's video and
his record on gay rights, and he said that Obama would only win his
respect by fulfilling his promise on issues like Don't Ask, Don't Tell.

"The president of the United States has the power to do more
than assure LGBT kids that it will get better," he said. "The president
has the power to make it better. We don't see the actions to back up
the words."

. . .

Jon woke up from a nap one Saturday afternoon in early winter and
walked across his bedroom to his computer. A nasty cold had turned
his eyes a bloodshot red, and his glasses sat low on his nose. The
stress of the last several months had taken its toll on his health; he
still had tan skin, an easy smile, muscular shoulders, and salt-and-
pepper hair that added a hint of sophistication to his look. But he also

had a new belly and some bad habits that made him self-conscious. He tended not to sit down for meals when he was harried or upset. While he continued to pay for a gym membership, he had not worked out in months.

On this afternoon, he opened up the computer, logged on to You-Tube, and typed "It Gets Better" into the search box. He had become addicted to the videos since a few weeks earlier, when he first watched one of Dan Savage and his boyfriend sitting side by side in a bar, and now Jon liked to watch a few dozen at a time and e-mail his favorites to friends. The computer processed his "It Gets Better" search and suddenly a sweeping testament to the randomness of the Internet appeared on Jon's screen. There was a video that Jon had already watched from Barack Obama next to one from the cast of the trashy MTV reality show *Jersey Shore*. There were awkward, basement soliloquies filmed with grainy webcams and heavily produced pieces created by the casts of Broadway shows. Taken as a whole, Jon believed the "It Gets Better" collection was one of the most moving things he had ever found on the Internet. Each video echoed the sentiment of a poster that hung on his bedroom wall: "Every Life Deserves Hope."

The first video he watched this morning was one of his favorites, a rendition of the song "True Colors" sung by the Gay Men's Chorus of Los Angeles. Jon turned the volume up on his speakers and nodded his head to the beat as he watched more than a hundred men perform a version of his favorite song. When the video ended, he stood up from his chair to grab a box of tissues.

"The first video—that's usually when the crying starts," he said.

Next he watched a video submitted by five employees at Google, one of whom was an unshaven young man wearing a Wisconsin T-shirt. "It's not easy to be gay when you have four brothers, because there's so much masculinity in the house," the Google employee said.

"I remember laying on my bed and just feeling this dread in my chest, knowing that someday I had to tell my family, or I had to tell somebody, and that alone was enough to terrify me. But the thing about things getting better is it doesn't just happen once. It's not one day you wake up and you go, 'Oh my God! Things are better.' Things actually keep getting better over and over, and in really small ways. Things got better the first time I said to myself, 'Okay, I admit it. I'm gay.' That was a huge step. Things got better the first time I told a friend and somebody else other than me knew. Things got better when I stood before my brother, and it was like the hardest thing in the world to admit it, and I couldn't even get through the sentence, and I started crying, and he gave me a hug."

Jon reached across the desk for another tissue. "I remember feeling that same kind of dread," he said.

Next came a video from Mike Bloomberg, mayor of New York City: "We want you. New York has always been the place where anyone can go and be who they are supposed to be."

Next a city councilman from Fort Worth named Joel Burns, who had made a speech about his near suicide during the middle of a city council meeting—a speech that had since been viewed 2.5 million times. "I have never told this story to anyone before tonight—not my family, not my husband, not anyone," he said. "But the numerous suicides in recent days have just torn at my heart, and even though there may be some political repercussions for telling my story, this story is for the young people who might be holding that gun tonight, or the rope, or the pill bottle."

By now Jon had forgotten all about the tissues. He took off his glasses, and a river of tears and snot ran down his face. He wiped it away with the back of his hand. "Every video feels like they're talking about me," he said. He only had the energy to watch one more, and he wanted it to be his all-time favorite. He clicked the mouse and actor B. D. Wong appeared on the screen. Wong had become famous for his roles as a psychologist on *Law & Order* and a prison priest on *Oz*, but this video looked as if it had been created by an amateur. Half of Wong's face was lost in shadow, and he hunched over a laptop to whisper into a webcam.

"When I was little, I had a real desire to take care of somebody, to become a parent," Wong said. "The outside world told me that one of the many things I would never do was to be a parent. And so, because of all of this, I took everything inward on myself . . . I questioned myself, and I didn't like myself, and I would have done anything I could have to change myself. What I realize now is that I was kidding myself, because that person that I was was so beautiful and free and had so much to offer people, and so much creativity and joy and life that I am ashamed I ever wanted to change him. One thing that surprised me as I got older was that the world is big enough for everyone, and I just needed to find a place for myself, so that I could be myself and be surrounded by all of the creativity and love that I was generating within myself. Now I want to show you something."

Wong picked up the laptop and the camera started to move, and even though Jon had seen this ending at least a dozen times, he covered his mouth in disbelief. "Shhhhh," Wong said, and then he rotated the camera so it showed his ten-year-old son, asleep in pajamas on his bed. Wong appeared on camera again, beaming, whispering softer now. "It can get so much better!" he said.

Now Jon was an emotional mess, and his sobbing shook the desk and carried out from the bedroom into the rest of the house. His roommate knocked on Jon's bedroom door, looking alarmed. Then he saw the "It Gets Better" videos on the computer screen and gestured with a knowing nod.

"Are you okay watching all this?" he asked.

"Yeah," Jon said. "I think I'm actually good."

.   .   .

How much better did it get? That same weekend, Jon left home at eight on a Friday night to attend a small dinner party with seven of his closest friends. He drove out of downtown Atlanta toward the city's most affluent suburbs, entered a gated community, and walked up to the door of a condo. The party's host was an event planner who had also appeared in shows on the Style Network, and he had prepared for the dinner with typical elegance. Modern art hung on the walls next to flat-screen TVs, and instrumental mood music played from the speakers. Eight bottles of wine waited on the counter alongside plates of grapes and soft cheese. Before Jon could so much as take off his coat, half a dozen fashionably dressed, good-looking men had lined up to hug him.

Twenty-five years removed from the isolation of high school, Jon still had trouble believing that this was his social circle: a reality-TV star, a real estate agent who grossed $10 million a year in sales, an employee at the Centers for Disease Control and Prevention, a life coach, and a wealthy entrepreneur. All were gay, successful, confident, funny, and, Jon said, "absolutely fabulous." He had met most of the men either through his work with AID Atlanta or by volunteering for Joining Hearts, a not-for-profit that raised housing funds for people living with HIV or AIDS. Now Jon had dinner with this group every few months. Once a year, the men participated in a fund-raiser called Atlanta Cotillion, during which they dressed as women and wore dramatic ball gowns, wigs, and jewelry. They sometimes called each other by their absurd drag names—Jon's was a political tribute: Hillary-Michelle Hibiscus Baldwin—and made a habit of mixing their gender pronouns, referring to each other with equal regularity as "he" or "she."

It was with this group that Jon felt most free to be himself, so he poured a glass of white wine, sat down at the head of the dining-room table, and called to the other men to take their places around him. They passed the next three hours the same way they had passed many nights before: by telling horror stories from their childhoods, memories that time had transformed from haunting to hilarious.

Jeffrey, the reality-TV star, was thrown down at his prep school and kicked and beaten in the shower. Another of the men had sent his mother a book about Matthew Shepard, a Wyoming college student who was tortured and killed for being gay, only to receive back a book from his mother filled with Bible quotes condemning homosexuality. Rodney, the real estate agent, had pretended to be straight and even kept a sham girlfriend until he left his small hometown in Alabama for college. "The crazy thing is I think they actually bought it!" he said, as the dining room shook with laughter. "I know! Me! Straight!"

Will, the entrepreneur, had grown up in rural Indiana and summoned the courage to come out to his parents after he graduated high school. He had been boarding a plane with his mother to visit colleges in Colorado when she asked if he was gay. He had nodded yes, only to watch his mother faint and then be rushed to the hospital. His parents had stopped supporting him financially, signed themselves up for intensive appointments with a therapist, and forced his younger brother to switch high schools because they feared he would be teased for having a brother who was gay. Will had paid for his first semester of college on a credit card and then studied in Europe and New York.

"The funny thing is they eventually got over it and now they think being gay is like being cool," Will said. "My mom always wants to talk about who I'm dating. She loves hanging out with all of my gay friends."

"It's amazing how much people really do get over it," said Rodney. "I don't think there's a single gay person who doesn't think about suicide growing up. High school is horrible. Just horrible. But then you wait until you're eighteen and you get the hell to Atlanta."

"Yes, Atlanta. Thank God!" said Chris, the life coach and Rodney's partner for the last ten years. "We're normal here."

Atlanta had the country's fourth-largest gay population, and Jon and most of his friends lived near a neighborhood called Midtown, where it sometimes seemed that gay was all that existed. There were gay bookstores, gay magazines, gay gyms, gay restaurants, and dozens of gay bars and nightclubs—most of them located near the intersection of Tenth Street and Piedmont, which Jon's friend Anna Leary referred to as "the corner of gay and gay." The city sponsored an annual Gay Pride week that drew an average of four hundred thousand people, and during each year's parade, Chris and Rodney threw a party at their downtown mini-mansion and hired two straight rugby players to wear American-flag thongs and work as bartenders.

"They love it! They got incredible tips!" Rodney said. He started to tell a story about how he and Chris recently had returned to Alabama for his twenty-year high-school reunion. They had started drinking early and arrived at the reunion prepared for a night of awkwardness. Most of the other people at the reunion had stayed in the small town to work blue-collar jobs, and now they had teenage kids and beer bellies. Chris and Rodney had better jobs and more worldly experience. Then something strange happened. The old "cool kids," Rodney said, started surrounding him and listening to his stories. By 10:00 p.m., he and Chris were the center of attention. By midnight, everyone was asking them to host an impromptu after party. "We were like gay celebrities!" Rodney said. "We were the fancy gays from Atlanta. I swear to God, they couldn't get enough of us."

Now Jon was laughing so hard that his end of the table started to shake, knocking a wineglass on its side and spilling chardonnay onto the floor, but nobody seemed to notice or care. They refilled the glasses and began a series of toasts: to the rednecks who thought all gays were headed for hell; to the aging high-school jocks and their beer bellies; to dear friends; to Jon and his devotion to fighting AIDS; to being happy and healthy. The wine gave way to champagne and the champagne gave way to white Russians. As the clock neared midnight, Jon stood up from the table and said he should probably head home. He was tired and full, he said, and now his ribs hurt from laughing. "I don't think I can take any more of this," he said, rolling his eyes. "You guys are too much fun."

Before he left, the host took out a camera to shoot some group pictures, and Will raised his hand to propose one final toast. Jon sat back down and grabbed his wineglass.

"To life getting better," Will said. But then he paused and shook his head. "No, wait, that's not quite right," he said, and now he raised his voice so he was almost shouting. "To life getting so much fucking better!" And the men laughed and clinked their glasses one final time.

· · ·

Meanwhile, back inside the White House, life was also beginning to improve for Obama—at an unexpected time and in remarkable ways. Just three weeks after his Democratic Party's self-described "shellacking" in the 2010 midterm elections, lawmakers had returned to Washington for the final session of the 111th Congress. The period was traditionally referred to as a "lame-duck session," and for good reason. Jammed between Thanksgiving and Christmas, it was usually a time for cocktail parties, saying goodbyes, packing boxes, reshuffling staffs, and attending to minor budgetary business. But in the waning weeks of 2010, Obama had other plans.

He told his family to leave without him for a vacation in Hawaii and stayed in the Oval Office to meet with as many as fifteen congressmen a day. He angered some Democrats by making a deal with Senate Republicans to extend President George W. Bush's tax cuts for the wealthiest Americans; but in return, he helped pass a tax package that assured a thirteen-month extension of unemployment benefits. Then, over the next few weeks, Obama and Congress built on their sudden goodwill to realize a number of the president's goals. They ratified the Strategic Arms Reduction Treaty to reduce nuclear weapons with Russia, confirmed nineteen federal judges, signed a free trade agreement with South Korea, required schools to serve healthier lunches to children, and passed a bill to provide $4.2 billion in health care for 9/11 first responders.

As Christmas neared, Obama delayed his vacation yet again to focus on his final lame-duck priority: the repeal of Don't Ask, Don't Tell. The president had promised the gay community that he would overturn the seventeen-year-old law by the end of 2010, and now his credibility was on the line. Don't Ask, Don't Tell had resulted in the discharge of more than fifteen thousand gay service members from the U.S. military, and Obama said he considered it one of the great civil rights injustices of his time. Polls showed that a vast majority of Americans—and a vast majority of military leaders—believed gays should be allowed to serve openly, but translating that public opinion into policy had proved much harder than Obama once expected.

Led by 2008 presidential candidate John McCain, a group of Republicans in the Senate argued that any major change to the military proved too risky during a time of war, and they filibustered a repeal of Don't Ask, Don't Tell in early December. To prepare for one final attempt, Obama commissioned a study by the Pentagon about attitudes in the military and worked to win the support of Secretary of Defense Robert Gates. The Senate scheduled a final vote for Decem-

ber 18, and the White House outreach team encouraged gay activists
to call their senators. Back in Atlanta, Jon e-mailed and phoned a
handful of lawmakers and then posted their numbers on his Facebook page, encouraging friends to do the same. "Please! Please! Do it
NOW!!!" one of his Facebook postings read.

And finally, on December 18, while Obama watched from the
White House, the Senate voted to repeal Don't Ask, Don't Tell by a
margin of sixty-five votes to thirty-one, with eight Republicans joining Democrats to form bipartisan support. The White House scheduled a hurried bill-signing ceremony and invited five hundred gay
activists and military leaders to Washington. Obama hosted the event
in a theater at the Interior Department to accommodate a large crowd
more befitting of a campaign rally than a procedural bill signing.

He stepped up to a lectern illuminated by two spotlights, and
Vice President Biden and a dozen congressmen stood near him on
the stage. Obama stared out at his audience, a collection of important
people in tailored suits who now wiped away tears with their hand-
kerchiefs and lifted cameras and cell phones over their heads. For a
few seconds, Obama let them cheer, soaking in their applause and
beaming.

Later, back at the White House during a comparatively sterile
press conference, Obama would find the words to sum up the repeal
of Don't Ask, Don't Tell during the historic lame-duck session. He
would say that "this has been a season of progress for the American
people," and that "we are not doomed to endless gridlock," and that
"this has been the most productive postelection period we've had in
decades, and it comes on the heels of the most productive two years
that we've had in generations." He would smile when a reporter
referred to him as the comeback kid, and he would agree that, yes, "I
am persistent, and if I believe in something strongly, I stay on it."

But now, in front of the activists and lawmakers assembled at the Interior Department, Obama seemed momentarily humbled by the significance of the moment. He fiddled with some papers on the lectern. The audience began to chant, "Yes we did! Yes we did!" Finally, after a few more seconds of smiling and laughing, Obama waved his hands to quiet the crowd.

"This is a good day," he said, simply. And then, still stumbling: "You know, I am just overwhelmed. This is a very good day."

He spoke for ten minutes, thanking a long list of military leaders and lawmakers before concluding that the repeal of Don't Ask, Don't Tell had been an essential moral cause. "We are not a nation that says, 'Don't ask, don't tell,'" he said. "We are a nation that says, 'Out of many, we are one.' We are a nation that believes all men and women are created equal."

The crowd rose to a standing ovation, and Obama moved across the stage to a desk to sign the bill. He used fifteen ceremonial pens while the flashes from dozens of cameras lit up the room. After the president signed his name one final time, he clapped his hand against the wooden desk and nodded his head.

"This is done," he said.

.   .   .

Jon Santos still had one thing left to do.

For more than a month, he had been preparing to film his own video for the "It Gets Better" project. He had typed up drafts of five different speeches on his computer, each detailing a different moment in his life. He had written about suffering through freshman year of high school, studying the specifics of carbon monoxide poisoning in the library, coming out to his family, and leading the AIDS walk. None of the drafts satisfied him, so finally, in the days after the repeal of Don't Ask, Don't Tell, Jon decided to film a video for the world about a moment so private that he had yet to share it with many of his closest friends. It was a story that Jon believed told the truth of life as an American gay man: equal parts pain and hope. It was a story he had rarely told without sobbing.

He borrowed a video camera from a friend, transformed the conference room at work into a filming location, and sought tips on dramatic lighting and sound from his roommate, a former producer at CNN. On a Thursday morning, Jon closed the door to his office at AID Atlanta and printed gigantic cue cards in large type, taping the speech to three pieces of poster board. A co-worker volunteered to act as his human teleprompter, and together they walked into the conference room. Jon sat down in a plastic chair facing the video camera and used his hands to smooth the wrinkles from his shirt. "I look okay, right?" he said. He hoped to make a three-minute video, but he had reserved the room for two hours.

Jon had chosen the conference room because of its somber backdrop, and now he slid his chair into position directly in front of a piece of the AIDS Memorial Quilt. The quilt as a whole had been built over twenty-five years into a fifty-four-ton cultural sensation once considered for the Nobel Peace Prize, and it included forty-five thousand individual six-by-three-foot patches, each in the shape of a grave and dedicated to a victim of the AIDS epidemic. The piece of quilt behind Jon included patches with photos and poems devoted to eight victims—Jeremy M. Pitt, 1967–95; Ruben Garcia, 1955–95, and on it went. "Make sure the quilt gets in the video," Jon said. "Right-o," said his co-worker, who then adjusted the camera and hit the Record button.

The first three takes were an epic disaster. Jon was so nervous that his fidgeting had become compulsive; his knees and arms and shoulders shook, and so did his voice. The idea of a human teleprompter proved fundamentally flawed. The co-worker's vigorous shuffling of poster board behind the camera made it sound as if Jon was filming in a windstorm. Jon could not read some sentences because the tripod obscured parts of the poster board, so he stuttered and then stalled. After thirty minutes of filming, Jon had done little more than repeat his first sentence a dozen times: "Hi, I'm Jon Santos, and I was taunted and bullied in school."

"If I start over one more time I'm going to lose it," Jon said. "Let's take a break."

He wiped sweat off his forehead, rolled his shoulders, and tried to shake the trembling out of his clammy hands. "I've got to relax," he said to himself, and his co-worker chuckled in the background. Jon took a big swig of Mountain Dew and then looked up at the camera with new resolve. "Let's try something different," he said. "Put the cue cards away. I'm going to try just talking." He looked directly into the lens of the camera and started telling a story from twenty years ago. His voice steadied. He stopped fidgeting.

"When I came out to my dad, he had become kind of a fundamentalist Christian," Jon said. "I told him I was gay, and he kind of quoted the Bible and said it was fine with him that I was gay, he didn't care, but that I needed to be prepared and I needed to be ready to answer to my maker. That was very heavy for me to hear. I took that initially as a rejection from him, a rejection of me and who I was. I was working at the university at the time, and I went for a walk one afternoon and there's this beautiful bronze statue of the Virgin Mary carrying the Christ child, and I guess I was praying. I guess so. And all of the sudden I realized that Sister Peg, a university chaplain, had come over, and she said, 'Jon, my son, you look troubled.' And so I told her that I was, and I told her about the conversation with my dad."

Now Jon had started to cry quietly. His co-worker stood back from the camera and sat down to listen. Jon steadied himself and continued.

"Sister Peg looked at me for a long time, and I'm not sure if she was searching for the right words or searching my face, and then she asked me, 'Are you a good man?' And I said, 'Yes. I try to be.' And she said, 'Are you a man for others?' And I said, 'Yes. I think so.' And she studied me again and then she said, 'No, I don't think you're a good man. I *know* you're a good man. God doesn't make junk. You have nothing to fear, because God is love and you can look God in the face and say, This is who I am. This is me. And that's okay.' "

Jon buried his head in his hands and waved for his co-worker to turn off the camera. The co-worker was crying now, too, and he wiped away a tear and then hugged Jon. "That one was a million times better," he said.

A few days later, when Jon watched the tape, he would find so many imperfections: the way his stomach jiggled when he talked, the shadow on his face, his trembling voice, hunched shoulders, awkward pauses, emotional vulnerability, and inelegant phrasing. "It's a mess," he would say. But he would also see one thing he did like: himself—alive, strong, and happy at forty-three. He edited new sections into the video, added pictures from his childhood, and uploaded the montage on YouTube to join Barack Obama, Dan Savage, and thousands of others. This was his story, imperfections and all, and he was ready to share it.

CHAPTER 10

"We have lived on the street for 3 days."

Her high school seemed like the kind of place that existed only in movies, she thought. Each morning, Jessica Duran, seventeen, woke up in Brooklyn and walked six blocks to a mammoth, brown-brick school packed with almost five thousand teenagers. Half of the students had been born outside of the country, and another two hundred and fifty immigrants enrolled during the middle of each school year. Classes were taught in four languages, including entire curriculums offered in Jessica's native Spanish. On a clear day, if she walked to the far edge of campus where Brooklyn disappeared into Lower New York Bay, she could see Ellis Island and the Statue of Liberty towering in the distance.

Some of the teachers referred to Fort Hamilton High School, or P.S. 104, as the "Dream Factory" because most of its students had been drawn to the United States in pursuit of the same promise. Their families had moved from across the world and settled in the diverse lower half of Brooklyn: the Puerto Ricans in Sunset Heights, the Russians in Brighton Beach, the Chinese in Chinatown, the Italians in Bensonhurst, and the Lebanese and Pakistanis in Bay Ridge, which they instead referred to simply as "Beirut." Families had immigrated in search of better jobs, more money, and good educations for their kids. "We're all chasing that American dream," Jessica said—except lately when she said it, she sometimes did so sarcastically.

Jessica had moved to New York from the Dominican Republic when she was four, taking a crowded flight from Santo Domingo with her mother and infant brother. They had become legal U.S. citizens several years later. Now she was midway through her senior year of high school, a time when she had imagined thinking about celebrations, colleges, and careers. But instead Jessica believed she had become "depressive or something." She slept a lot. Her grades had begun to drop. She had stopped calling friends or writing in her journal.

Their lives in the United States had always been hard, but recently Jessica felt as though her family existed in permanent quicksand: the harder they struggled to gain traction, the faster they sank. Her mother, Isabella, had doubled her shifts as an $8.25-an-hour home-health aide in an effort to keep up with mounting debts, and now she worked seventy hours a week caring for elderly nuns with dementia. The long days had raised her blood pressure and cholesterol, aggravated an old injury in her back, and resulted in regular migraines. But her paycheck increased to almost $500 a week, and the extra money brought some short-term relief.

Then Isabella's mother got sick in the Dominican Republic, and she started cleaning friends' houses on weekends to send some extra cash back home. Then a sky-high electric bill forced her to sell Jessi-

ca's laptop for $600. Then the phone company cut off their landline.
Then the government halved their allotment of food stamps because
Isabella had increased her wages above the limit. Then their low-
income, Section 8 housing agreement required that a small percentage of Isabella's extra earnings go toward rent, bringing the monthly
bill to $540. Isabella had taught herself to speak English during the
last decade by studying Jessica's schoolbooks, but she still tended to
speak her native language when she was angry. Now she complained
in Spanish that there was no way out, that her life had become a cycle
of stress and fatigue. But there was one phrase she often repeated in
English when she returned home late at night from work, a truism
that she had passed on to her children. "You work and work but you
never get ahead," she said. "You never get ahead."

Jessica had offered to find a part-time job to help pay the bills,
but Isabella insisted she focus on school and caring for the house
instead. They lived on the second floor of a small apartment building on Eighty-sixth Street, where most of the nearby stores had signs
written in Arabic. Jessica walked home from school and spent her
evenings helping her little brother with his homework, cleaning the
kitchen, and cooking whatever was left in the cupboards, which lately
had meant boiling a lot of brown rice and flavoring it with honey.

They were devout Jehovah's Witnesses who read the Bible every
night and attended church twice a week to pray for God to watch
over them. Lately more tangible help had come from other members of their congregation. Friends filled the refrigerator with eggs
and milk, loaned them a cell phone, and donated furniture to fill the
two-bedroom, one-bath apartment. A congregant who worked as a
doorman at a fancy Manhattan high-rise had donated the building's
throwaways: a flat-screen TV with a deep scar running across the
right side of the screen, a couch, a dresser, and a bundle of six-foot-

tall fake ferns that now served as the main decoration in their living room. Jessica had found a nice piece of wood sitting in the trash over on Eighty-ninth Street and turned it into a headboard for the bed she shared with her mother. Sharing a bed came with drawbacks—Isabella stole covers and Jessica thrashed in her sleep—but they relied on each other for motivation to get out of bed in the morning so they could leave at seven for school and work.

It was near the end of one of those long days at school in November when Jessica trudged into her government classroom for the final period of the day. She was an average student who received mostly B's and C's, and her teachers sometimes mistook her fatigue for laziness. A quiet kid like Jessica could get lost at Fort Hamilton among the city championship football team, the five hundred and eighty special-needs students, and the English as a Second Language program that made up one-quarter of the school. But government was her favorite class, and she sat near the front of the room as the teacher distributed a work sheet detailing their next assignment.

"Pen Power for Pupils" was the title of the assignment. "Each of you can make a difference via (by way of) a letter. You have the power. You can exercise that power/control via your pen."

The teacher, who had been working at the school for thirty years, went on to explain that this assignment had been a staple of his class for decades. More than most government lessons, this one taught a roomful of recent immigrants how to participate in democracy how to be heard. He said that each student would have one week to write a letter to any organization, which he would then grade and send. Students could write to businesses, magazines, or politicians, he said. Then he raised his voice to emphasize one last point: Extra credit would go to students who received a handwritten response.

Jessica sat in her chair and made a note to herself to write a

fan letter to *Glamour* magazine, which she adored for its photos of
makeup and high fashion. But before the final bell rang, the government teacher held up the assignment sheet and offered one final
piece of advice.

"That tiny voice can make all the difference," he said. He turned
to the chalkboard and wrote down an address for the "Honorable
Barack Obama," before turning back to face the class. "Write about
something that makes you angry," he said. "Write about something
that doesn't seem fair."

Jessica walked out of the classroom, returned home, and took out
her notebook, filled with sudden conviction. Her fan letter to *Glamour* would have to wait. This letter would be addressed to a source of
greater authority, to the honorable Barack Obama himself. And this
letter would be angry.

.   .   .

The only difficulty in writing her letter was deciding where to start
because the anger had built steadily over more than a decade. Her
family's first few years in the country had gone well enough. Jessica's
father had moved to upper Manhattan a few years before she came to
the United States, and they joined him in the predominantly Dominican neighborhood of Washington Heights, where he had secured
an apartment and found a job. Isabella started working as a florist
in New Jersey, where she made $12 an hour and dreamed of open-
ing her own shop. The family paid for sessions with a studio photographer and hung the portraits on their walls. Isabella splurged on a
nice Greek fountain for the living room because the sound of rushing
water calmed her nerves.

Her husband met new friends at work, and he started to stay out
late to use cocaine with them. Soon he had lost his job, and another,

and another. He had always had a volatile temper, and the drugs made him angrier than ever. Gone was the man with a handsome mustache who liked to play baseball and hold the umbrella for his wife. Now he beat Isabella often and slapped Jessica across the head when she tried to take away his cigarettes after hearing an anti-tobacco lecture in her school's D.A.R.E. program. He went to jail three times for domestic violence. The final stint lasted almost two years.

The day before his release he called Isabella, sounding as mean as ever, and said he couldn't wait to come back home and see some of his old friends. She hung up and called a shelter for battered women in Brooklyn, which sent a cab right away. The shelter's coordinator instructed Isabella and the kids to bring one suitcase each and leave in secret so that her husband could not find them. Late that evening, on March 26, 2003, Isabella packed up the children's clothes and left her job, her friends, and most of her belongings behind.

They stayed in a single room in the shelter. Isabella stared out the third-floor window and kept watch for her husband, but he never came. Jessica started failing fifth grade and fighting with her classmates. Her brother, three years younger, chewed compulsively on his clothes. Another woman at the shelter offered to help them, and she took them to church and introduced them to Jehovah. They attended services almost every day, mostly because it gave them somewhere to go.

The shelter evicted them from the room after six months, the maximum stay allowed, and they lived on the street for the next three days. They walked all over Brooklyn during the day while Isabella looked for jobs, stopping to wash up at a McDonald's. At night, they rode the subway and slept under blankets in their seats. The kids were exhausted and confused. "Are we homeless?" Jessica asked. No, Isabella said, and then she told them a story about how they were just

riding the train on a very long trip. The kids looked up at the fluo-
rescent ceilings of the subway cars, the only light in an otherwise
black tunnel, and convinced themselves that they were headed for the
moon.

They eventually ended up on the floor of a friend's one-bedroom
apartment in Brooklyn instead. And then, a few weeks later, Isabella enrolled in a training program to become a home-health aide
and found the apartment on Eighty-sixth Street, where they had
been running in quicksand ever since. They still went to church on
Wednesdays and Sundays, sometimes staying for both of the back-
to-back services held in English and Spanish. Isabella in particular
relied on Jehovah as her stabilizing force. She read a pamphlet from
church entitled *The Secret of Family Happiness: Questions Young People
Ask* and studied it for tips on raising teenagers. She posted a household chore sheet on the fridge, assigning alternating nights for the
children to read to her from the Bible. Sometimes, on the weekends,
she liked to walk by herself alongside New York Bay, where she could
again feel calmed by the sounds of the water.

Her daughter was the exact opposite; Jessica's best method for
coping was to let herself seethe. For a short while she had tried spilling her feelings into a journal, even writing a sunny platitude at the
top of each page in an attempt to rationalize her family's struggles.
"One always gets lost in life but sooner or later you find your way,"
she wrote. And later: "Hope is what moves us forward. Hope is what
makes up happiness." But a page or two into each entry, her handwriting turned sloppy and she abandoned her writing mid-sentence.
She preferred to confront her problems head-on rather than con-
template them privately. She considered herself the prototypical
Dominican—fast-talking, stubborn, and brassy. She was girlish with
big brown eyes, delicate lashes, and coffee-colored skin, but she

sometimes used her solid build to look intimidating. "I don't take nothing from nobody," Jessica said, and she never had.

When her grandmother had forced her to go to church as a toddler, Jessica knocked over candles until she nearly set the place on fire. When she became jealous of her infant brother later that same year, she had waited until her mother was in the shower and then taken the six-month-old out with the trash. "The devil child," her family had called her, but now that willfulness had matured into a righteousness that served her well. She yelled at bill collectors who pestered the family with phone calls, and they appeased her by knocking off the late fee. A woman from church derisively referred to Isabella as poor, and Jessica stood up to scream at her in public. "Some people might be snakes, but I'm an anaconda," she said. "I can be flat-out scary when it comes to defending my mom."

She thought of her mother as she sat down at the kitchen table to write her letter for government class. It was almost 9:00 p.m. and Isabella was still at work. Jessica took two pages of lined paper from the three-ring binder she used for class. "Dear Mr. President," she wrote.

> For years, I have seen how my mother struggles to raise two teenagers in this cruel and harsh world, with the help of no one. This is the reason why I admire my mom and look up to her as my hero.
>
> I'm sure you know, Mr. President, what it feels like being raised without a father, I waking up everyday thinking, "Why me?" why my mom? And the many things I want to do, but I can't, to help my mom.
>
> I have seen for years how my mom works and works, so hard and gets paid barely nothing. She works 5 days a week and every 2 weeks she works 7 days a week. From morning until night. She doesn't get any vacations and she _ALWAYS_ has to go to work, sick

and tired because she doesn't get days off. And if she gets it, she
doesn't get paid. Aside from this, she has to work with people who
sometimes abuse her kindness.

This is why I'm requesting that you pay more attention to home
aid nurses and offer them more oppurtunities and services like for
example days off, increase the salary and get benefits.

A couple of years ago, my mom, my brother and I ended up in a
shelter, here in Brooklyn, due to domestic violence. We have lived on
the street for 3 days until my mom finally found a job and apartment. This is why I'm so concerned on how workers are treated,
how my mom is treated. So Mr. President, what would you do if it
was your mom out there being treated like that? How would you
feel?

Jessica put down her pen and read back over the letter. It was
harsh but true, she thought, and she tried to soften the blow with an
endearing sign-off. "With respect, and love," she wrote. She signed
her name and dotted the "i" in Jessica with a bubbly heart.

Later, when Isabella came home from work and read over the
letter, she couldn't help but chuckle. "*Que afrentado!*" she told Jessica. How confrontational! How bold to write something like that to
the president. But that was her daughter, and the next day Jessica
found an envelope and brought her letter back to school. She handed
it to her teacher and felt a small surge of regret. "How stupid!" she
thought, because now she realized that she had made a miscalculation
in the assignment: Writing a letter to the president all but ruled out
earning the extra credit.

.   .   .

The president said the hardest letters for him to read were the ones
that made him feel remote, even powerless. So many writers needed

urgent help, he said, and yet the act of governing was so slow that it sometimes took years before legislation could actually improve people's lives. A few times during his presidency, Obama had been so moved by a letter that he had written a personal check or made a phone call on the writer's behalf to ensure a fast result. "It's not something I should advertise, but it has happened," he said. Many other times, he had forwarded letters to government agencies or cabinet secretaries after attaching a standard, handwritten note that read: "Can you please take care of this?"

Obama had first become enchanted with politics in the late 1980s because he experienced the thrill of listening to people's problems and helping them win quick results. A year after graduating from Columbia University, he accepted a $10,000-a-year job as a community organizer and moved from New York City to Chicago. He rented a cheap apartment, purchased a used car for $2,000, and spent his days driving around the city's housing projects to talk with residents about their lives. He became familiar with many of the same issues that would flood his mail twenty-five years later: housing calamities, chronic unemployment, and struggling schools.

Obama's fellow organizers in Chicago considered him a master of hands-on, granular problem solving. He was skinny and boyish, a good listener if still a bit naïve, and some of the older women in the housing projects made a habit of inviting him into their homes and cooking for him. He looked around their apartments, kept a log of maintenance issues, and then delivered that list to the landlord. He helped arrange meetings with city housing officials to talk about asbestos problems. He established a tenants' rights organization, founded a job-training program, and led a tutoring group that prepared students for college. When he left for Harvard Law School after three years in Chicago, he had set the path for his future. He wanted to become a politician, in part because it would allow him to listen to people's problems and enjoy the simple satisfaction of solving them.

Now he was president, the most powerful politician of all—and yet fixing problems seemed more difficult and satisfaction more elusive. Sometimes, when he read his ten letters each night, he recalled the simplicity of his job as a community organizer and pined for it.

"The people were right there in front of me, and I could say, 'Let's go to the alderman's office,' or 'Let me be an advocate in some fashion,'" he said one afternoon while sitting in the Oval Office. "And here, just because of the nature of the office and the scope of the issues, you are removed in ways that are frustrating. Sometimes, what you want to do is just pick up the phone and say, 'Tell me more about what's going on and let me see if I can be your social worker, be your advocate, be your mortgage adviser, be your employment counselor.' So what I have to constantly reconcile in my mind is that I have a very specific role to play in this office, and I've got to make a bunch of big decisions that you hope in the aggregate will end up having a positive effect over this many lives. But you can't always be certain.

"Reading these letters can be heartbreaking. Just heartbreaking. And some of these letters you read and you say, 'Gosh, I really want to help this person, and I may not have the tools to help them right now.' And then you start thinking about the fact that for every one person that wrote describing their story, there might be another hundred thousand going through the same thing. So there are times when I'm reading the letters and I feel pained that I can't do more, faster, to make a difference in their lives."

In those instances, Obama sometimes thought his best recourse was simply to write a response. He believed that by sending an embossed note card bearing the presidential seal he could at least give a writer some temporary joy and relief. "It lets them know I am listening," he said. Sometimes, at least in the short term, listening was the most the president could do.

Obama opened up his purple folder one night in the middle of winter and read a handwritten letter from Brooklyn that moved him right away. It was from Jessica Duran, a seventeen-year-old girl who had already experienced domestic violence and homelessness. Her problems seemed to span the full range of his domestic agenda: a struggling economy, the challenges facing public education, a growing immigrant underclass. Obama held on to the letter for more than four weeks and then wrote a short response. "Jessica," he wrote. "Thanks for your letter. I agree your mom is a hero, and I'm a big supporter of better working conditions for home care workers. I know your mom is also very proud of you, so keep striving to be your best!"

Obama knew that many of Jessica's issues would take him years to address through legislation. Others he never could. But he handed off his written response to the staff secretary, who mailed it back to the small apartment in Brooklyn. It was nothing more than a few ordinary sentences, but the act of responding always made Obama feel good. He still liked the satisfaction of providing at least one thing that was immediate and concrete.

· · ·

It had been so long since Jessica received mail that she no longer bothered to check for it. She communicated almost exclusively through text messaging and Facebook. The family's small mailbox belonged to her mother alone—or at least it had until one afternoon in midwinter, when Isabella walked into the house waving a large envelope addressed to Jessica Duran and stamped PRIORITY.

Jessica opened the layers of the package one by one as her pulse quickened, and she ripped into the final envelope that contained

Obama's letter. The embossed note card contained a stamp that read "The White House," and Isabella leaned in closer to see it. "*La Casa Blanca?*" she said, gasping. She had been to Washington once to tour the monuments over a long weekend, traveling by bus and sharing a hotel room with four friends from work, and she ranked the trip among the highlights of her life. Jessica had listened to the story of her mother's trip at least a dozen times, but the repetition never bothered her. She liked hearing about the buildings and the statues; she had never traveled in the United States beyond New York.

They stood together at the kitchen table to read and then reread the letter. Jessica translated it for her mother; Isabella marveled at how, once again, her daughter's boldness had yielded results. She told Jessica to hide the letter someplace safe in the house, but Jessica shook her head. She was taking it to school the next morning, she said, in part to cash in on some extra credit.

She had planned to keep the letter in her backpack until government class, but early in the morning she showed it to one of her favorite teachers, who showed it to another teacher, who made copies for his students, who distributed it to their friends throughout the hallways. By lunch, Jessica was a school celebrity for the first time in her life. By late afternoon, she had been called in to see the principal, a woman she had never met, who stood up from her desk in a fancy suit, wrapped Jessica in a bear hug, and said, "You are what Fort Hamilton is all about." By seventh period, her government teacher had begun referring to the letter as a highlight of his fifty-year career. He had encouraged Jessica to think about studying politics, to keep using her voice, and she had practically skipped home against the cold, buoyed by so much more than just extra credit.

The euphoria lasted twenty-four hours. She came home from school the next day to find her mother sitting at the kitchen table with two co-workers on their lunch break from the nursing home. Isabella wore purple scrubs and sneakers, and her hair was pulled into a tight braid. She caught her reflection in the mirror and traced the creases near her mouth and the dark circles around her eyes. "I look old," she said. "I look sick and tired."

She and her co-workers had spent this morning the same way they spent every morning: caring for more than a dozen nuns in their eighties and nineties. The home-care workers did the chores relatives were either unable or unwilling to do. They checked for bedsores, scrubbed out bedpans, changed diapers, did laundry, cleaned dentures, drew baths, lifted and washed bodies, blended liquid meals, and spoon-fed the patients. The nuns were mostly impassive, and sometimes they smiled and made conversation. But on the worst days the dementia, pain, and aging could turn even the sweetest patients mean, and they sometimes spit back food, threw utensils, and cursed at Isabella for speaking in broken English. She always ignored the insults while in the room—"They are just unhappy and sick," she told herself—and waited to spill her frustrations during lunch break.

"Home care is the last job. The floor. The last job," she said now, in her living room.

"We work like donkeys," said Sofia, a home aide for thirteen years.

"We work like idiots," said Delfina, a home aide for eight years.

The three women had bonded through shared suffering. Sofia, who emigrated from Ecuador, was almost sixty and battling chronic bronchitis, but she continued to work double shifts. Delfina, who had a sick husband and a daughter in college, endured an even worse schedule. She worked ninety-six hours a week, splitting her time between two home-care companies and taking one day off every two weeks. She had moved to the United States mainly to provide her daughters with better educations, but now she was sending her eldest to college back home in Peru because that was the only university they could afford. Even that required a $600 payment every month, or about the equivalent take-home from one ninety-six-hour workweek on minimum wage.

Isabella had made exactly $19,301 dollars in the last calendar year. She had no savings account and no credit cards because she believed debt would only compound her problems. She lost $15 from each paycheck for automatic dues to a home-care union, although it seemed to do little on behalf of its workers. The aides received the same hourly wage on weekends as they did during the week, and only one of their two allotted weeks of vacation came with pay. The standard raise averaged twenty-five cents an hour for every two years of service. Isabella sometimes joked that her job would eventually pay her double figures—if only she could stick it out for another fourteen years.

She had looked for other jobs—they all had—but the flower shops in Brooklyn paid minimum wage and janitorial and cleaning positions seemed impossible to find. Isabella blamed some of her problems on her imperfect English, which had been adequate to pass a U.S. citizenship test in 2009 but not good enough to earn a low-wage job in the country's most populated city during a major recession. She had started taking an English class to improve her chances, riding the subway to a community college on her rare nights off.

"Maybe I die before I get another job," Isabella said now, in the living room.

"Maybe we all die in two years," Delfina said, laughing.

"I can't work to sixty, seventy years old," Sofia said. "I feel like sixty or seventy now."

"We get no break, no sick day, no nothing," Isabella said.

"No vacation plan," Sofia said.

"We get a vacation plan," Delfina said, pausing for comedic effect. "Our vacation plan is, 'Okay, no money for you!' "

The women started to laugh, first chuckling and then doubling over in hysterics, and for a minute the exhaustion disappeared from their faces. Isabella gasped for breath and then looked up at the clock. Their unpaid, thirty-minute lunch break ended in three minutes. The women filed out of the house in their scrubs and walked back to the nursing home, back to the laundry and the bedpans and the dentures, back to $8.25 an hour.

Jessica watched them go with a determined stare. She had stayed quiet during her mother's conversation, but she had listened to every word and formulated a plan. "I have to do something to help," she said, and she decided to start that afternoon.

. . .

An hour later, Jessica began looking for a job of her own. She wanted to work in retail, and preferably someplace trendy, so she made plans to go to the most fashionable area she knew: Fifth Avenue in Manhattan, a worldwide destination for high-end shopping. She gathered $12, all the cash in the house, and invited three girlfriends to join her for the trip into the city. She called her mother to say she would be home by six and hung up before Isabella could press for details or dissuade her from going.

Isabella had been strict ever since she moved her family into the shelter, ruling the household with such intimidation that her children sometimes referred to her as Darth Vader. She insisted on meeting and approving of all of Jessica's friends, and those awkward interviews had resulted in only about a 25 percent success rate. Isabella tended to approve of church friends more easily than school classmates, so Jessica spent most of her free time with four girls from her congregation. The entire group had memorized Isabella's rules: home by 11:00 p.m.; call every two hours; no drinking, no drugs, and no pictures in tight-fitting dresses posted on Facebook. Jessica was not allowed to date until she turned eighteen, when Isabella said she would begrudgingly accept dating only as a path to marriage. Jessica was not allowed to walk alone in the city at night. Until recently, she had not been allowed to have a job.

She had wanted to work ever since she turned fifteen—to help her mother pay the bills, sure, but also to buy things for herself. She wanted to watch cable television at home for the first time since 2003, purchase her own cell phone, stock up on fancy makeup, and pitch in toward the rent on a bigger apartment where she could sleep in her own bed. Her mother always had refused. "I want to protect you," Isabella had said. But lately her maternal desire to protect had collided with her desire to provide. The fridge was verging on empty except for a few packages of chicken gizzards bought for seventy-five cents a pound. The electric bill and the rent were overdue. Isabella could not work enough hours or make enough money to keep pace with the debts on her own. Recently she had conceded to Jessica: "I could use a little help."

Jessica's first few trips to look for part-time jobs around lower Brooklyn had resulted only in rejection; most stores were not hiring, and those that were required employees to be eighteen or older. Jessica hoped Manhattan would offer more stores, higher salaries, and better opportunities for getting to know "the business-type people," she said. Before she left home, she dressed up in a purple blouse and her favorite pair of white hip-hugger pants, which she had bought on sale for $10 at the Gap. She applied generic brands of concealer, eye shadow, mascara, and blush. Then she tucked a high-school ID card into her pocket and wrapped a green cloth around her neck as a makeshift scarf. She had run out of deodorant a few days earlier, so she sliced open a fresh lime and squeezed it under her arms, squirming when the cold liquid hit her skin. "We Dominican people have some crazy remedies," she said. "You learn to use what you've got."

She met a friend from church and together they walked down to the subway and boarded an R train for Fifth Avenue. It was one of the slowest train rides in the city, spanning twenty-seven stops and lasting at least an hour, and Jessica passed the time by rehearsing for the job interviews she hoped awaited on Fifth Avenue. "Ask me practice questions," she told her friend as they clung to a metal pole in the rickety train.

"Okay," the friend said. "How many hours each week do you want to work?"

"I would love to work as many hours as I can after school and on the weekends, so probably twenty-five," Jessica said.

"And when can you start?"

"Umm, today?"

"Okay, good. And how much do you want to make?"

"I will take anything," Jessica said, but then quickly changed her mind. "No. I would like to make at least $7.50 an hour."

They got off the train at Fifth Avenue and met two more friends from church who had come to support Jessica. The sun had started to descend below the skyscrapers, and cabs honked and swerved at the beginning of rush hour. Jessica zipped up her black coat and walked from the subway station to Ann Taylor. She idled with her friends on the sidewalk and looked in through the front window. Employees wore suits and smiled at women who carried heavy shopping bags. Mannequins in sparkling dresses stood at the entrance. Two chandeliers framed the store's checkout counter, behind which a stylish, middle-aged woman folded clothes and looked back out the window at Jessica, who now looked down at the sidewalk, shaking her head, all confidence gone.

"Everybody in there is so dressed up and fancy," she said. "There's no chance."

Her friends pushed her through the door, and Jessica walked reluctantly to the front counter. She looked up at the chandeliers, then back down at the floor. She pretended to admire a black-and-white skirt hanging near the register while the saleswoman watched. "Hi," Jessica said, finally. "I'm wondering if maybe you guys might be hiring? I'm hoping to get a job."

The saleswoman smiled back. "Do you have a résumé?"

"No," Jessica said. "Right now I don't have a computer."

"Oh, well, that's okay," the saleswoman said. She reached under the counter, pulled out a stack of about a hundred applications, and handed one to Jessica. "Fill this out, bring it back, and try to get us that résumé. We are not hiring now and might not be for a while, but we would be happy to keep your application on file."

Jessica thanked her and stuffed the application into her purse. Then she walked back out on Fifth Avenue, where she heard variations of the same answer for the next two hours. At Cole Haan, where she asked the guard at the front door if the store was hiring and the guard ushered her right back out: "Sorry. We won't be hiring again until at least this summer." At Kate Spade, where she waited in line behind a woman paying $1,400 for a polka-dot skirt and then tried to flatter the manager by complimenting her makeup: "That's sweet of you, honey, but you can't work here until you're at least eighteen." At Armani, where techno music blasted from the speakers and a disco ball reflected off the tile floor: "It's a bad time of year to find a job." At Victoria's Secret: "How old did you say you were again?" At Juicy Couture: "We actually just ran out of applications."

After two hours spent walking up and down Fifth Avenue, Jessica had yet to find a single decent lead. Now it was almost 7:00 p.m., and Isabella called to tell her daughter to come home. Jessica huddled with her friends to determine their next move. "I want to try one more store," she said. They walked up the street to Sephora, a luxury beauty and makeup supplier, Jessica's self-described "candy land." She took a deep breath and approached the manager of the store. "I love this place," she said. "I'm great with makeup. I would love to work here."

The manager nodded and handed her an application. "Just warning you," he said, "we have a pretty big waiting list right now."

Jessica stuffed the application into her purse, where it joined nine others, and walked across the store to meet up with her friends. "It's hopeless," she said, pouting, and her friends gathered around to cheer her up. They splotched samples of red makeup on her cheeks, layered on some thick mascara, and took pictures with their cell phones. They borrowed tweezers from the Sephora manager, asked for free samples of half a dozen different kinds of makeup, and spent forty-five minutes idling in the store without spending a dime. By the time the store was about to close, Jessica was laughing hysterically, her friends were rolling on the floor, and a humorless security guard was hovering nearby to keep a watchful eye. No, Jessica joked as they emerged onto Fifth Avenue, she would not be getting that job.

As the girls headed back to the subway, televisions along Fifth Avenue showed Barack Obama making his State of the Union speech in Washington. He talked about the recovering economy and about "winning the future," shaking his fist as he reached the climax of his speech. "We may have different backgrounds," he said, "but we believe in the same dream that says this is a country where anything is possible, no matter who you are, no matter where you come from. From the earliest days of our founding, America has been a story of ordinary people who dare to dream."

Jessica walked past the TVs without turning her head and spent her last money on the subway ride home. She entered her dark apartment and climbed over her mother into bed. As she closed her eyes, her vision for the future was simple, and so was her dream. She wanted a job. She wanted out of the quicksand. She wanted to believe that anything was possible when she woke up in the morning.

. . .

A few weeks later, Obama walked into the Oval Office early on a Monday afternoon and sunk into a leather chair in front of the fireplace. He had made the office his own over the last two years, decorating the shelves with family photos and sometimes plopping his feet on the wooden desk given to the White House by Queen Victoria in 1880. But when Obama glanced around the room, he also saw so many reminders of the history and gravity tied to his position. There were portraits of Abraham Lincoln and George Washington; inscriptions from Martin Luther King Jr. and Franklin Roosevelt; and a presidential seal decorating both the ceiling and the carpet. He leaned forward in the leather chair and lifted his hand to massage his forehead.

"People used to say I looked young for my age," he said, chuckling. "But now I'm president, and everybody just thinks I look old."

It was Valentine's Day, but Obama had yet to experience much of the holiday affection. Over the course of the morning, he had already unveiled his proposed budget for 2012, flown by helicopter to Baltimore to visit a school, and held meetings about the economy and national security. The day marked a two-year anniversary for his economic stimulus package, and yet the national unemployment rate remained above 9 percent for the twenty-first consecutive month. Leaders from both sides had already begun lambasting his proposed budget; Republicans believed it would do too little to trim the national deficit while Democrats argued it cut out too much. Politicians had released statements saying that Obama's plan would "hurt low-income people," "continue to destroy jobs," and "accelerate our country down the path to bankruptcy." Even Obama had seemed conflicted about the budget, saying that it required "cutting things I care about deeply," and that "there are always more people who could use some help across the country than we have resources."

Earlier in the day, during his visit to a middle school outside of Baltimore, Obama had stood in the cafeteria behind a black rope and answered questions about his job from seventh and eighth graders. It was an unusually casual atmosphere for a president. Preteen girls giggled and boys with shaggy haircuts tried to hand him cards for Valentine's Day. He spoke into a hand-held microphone and joked about his daughters and his dog before offering to take two questions, even though it required departing from his script. "I'm not supposed to do this," he said. He called first on a lanky kid wearing a red jacket, who stood up and asked what seemed like an easy question.

"What's it like to be president?" the boy said. Obama drew a breath and paused before giving an answer that quieted his crowd.

"You know, umm, uh, some days you are burdened by some really tough decisions. Some of you may have family members that are in Afghanistan, for example. I'm the commander in chief, so I'm responsible for sending those men and women over there. Some of them get hurt. Some of them get killed. So you feel a responsibility that is profound. I'll be honest with you, there are certain parts of the job that are kind of tough. Like, I'm kind of in this bubble. I can't go anywhere . . . I can't be spontaneous, and that kind of gets on your nerves."

And now, two hours later, here he was at the Oval Office, inside the bubble. A White House photographer sat on one side of the room, because it was his charge to follow Obama everywhere. A stenographer stood on the other side and took notes, because White House policy mandates that the president's words be recorded and preserved for the historical record. Outside the door, Obama was cordoned off by a secretary in the inner lobby, another secretary in the outer lobby, two military officers at the West Wing door, three security huts outside the building, and a wrought-iron fence on Pennsylvania Avenue that was guarded by armed members of the Secret Service and the Capitol Police. Obama sat in his leather chair, thinking about the other side of the fence.

He had never written a letter to a president himself. In fact, he had never even considered it. "I think the presidency always felt very remote to me," he said, and it still felt that way now. He sometimes marveled at the idea that his office received twenty thousand letters or e-mails every day. "I'm always very proud of people who take the time to write, even if sometimes what they're saying about me isn't very cheerful," he said. "The fact that we live in a country where people can just decide 'I'm going to give the president a piece of my mind,' I think it says something about our democracy that's unique."

After two years in office and more than five thousand letters in his purple folder, Obama had come to anticipate a few of the lessons in his nightly reading. "Half the country is objecting to something I'm doing and half the country is supporting me," he said. "People go through some tough stuff, and they suck it up and try to make the best of it." But what still surprised him each night—what compelled him to sometimes read letters aloud to his wife—was the intimacy and candor.

"I think a lot of people write not expecting that I will actually read them," Obama said. "In some ways, I think it is an exercise for people to express some really deeply held feelings. Sometimes people feel desperation, and they don't know who else to write."

A secretary opened the Oval Office door, glanced at a grandfather clock in the room, and then looked at Obama. "Mr. Pres—" she said, but Obama nodded his head and cut her off. "I know," he said. He stood up from the leather chair and stretched his back. He had more meetings to attend, more problems to address. He would spend the next five hours in the Oval Office and then rush over to the White House residence to eat dinner and put his daughters to bed. At about 8:00 p.m., he would settle into a couch with his homework packet, a black binder loaded with security briefings and legislative memos. He would reach first for a thin purple folder.

Inside was everything he had come to expect, and everything he had come to rely on. "My heart is breaking," began one typed note from the aunt of a soldier in Afghanistan. "I am writing to request your help," wrote an unemployed single mother in Hawaii. There were letters from rural Oregon and downtown Detroit, missives about the budget and handmade Valentine's Day cards. There were confessions of support and criticism; offerings of inspiration and devastation. There were ten stories from the other side of the fence. Obama reached for the first piece of paper and started to read. "Dear Mr. President," the letter began.

 EPILOGUE

JESSICA DURAN turned eighteen but still struggled to find a job.
She went back to Fifth Avenue twice with no success and eventually
expanded her search across New York City. "I've been to like a hundred stores and gotten nothing," she said midway through 2011. "But
there's got to be a part-time job somewhere in this city, and I'm going
to find it."

JON SANTOS posted his "It Gets Better" video on the Internet,
and more than four hundred people watched it in the first month.
Friends and strangers wrote to comment about the video on his Facebook page. "You were never junk—always a sweet and loving soul,"
one friend posted. Another wrote: "Thank God you were resolute
and determined to go on and do great works." Jon was most moved,
though, by e-mails he received from some of the high-school class-

mates who had bullied him. One apologized for his "adolescent igno-
rance" and said he "couldn't imagine what it must have been like for
you throughout those years." Then he commended Jon for his perse-
verance.

The "It Gets Better" project as a whole continued to add dozens
of new videos each week that were viewed more than three million
times. Obama occasionally referenced the movement in his speeches.
Dan Savage took a break from his job as a sex columnist and wrote a
book about his favorite videos.

Halfway through NA'DREYA LATTIMORE'S fifth-grade year in the
Covington Independent School District, her grandmother and legal
guardian, Cindy Sebastian, vowed to enroll her somewhere else for
junior high. Despite the temporary buzz created by Na'Dreya's letter,
her family believed that Sixth District Elementary remained plagued
by many of the same old problems: classroom fights that went unpun-
ished, incessant behavioral interruptions, and remedial curriculum
that left more advanced students feeling bored and neglected.

"It's to the point where I'm tired of fighting it," said Cindy. "I
went down to the district office and told them that Na'Dreya and her
brothers are all going to switch schools in the next year. These problems have been going on since forever and nobody can do anything
about it."

Cindy had started talking to some administrators at area private
schools about Na'Dreya's letter from Obama, hoping it would win her
a full scholarship. "We still don't have the money to pay for anything,"
she said. Lisa, Na'Dreya's mother, had briefly taken a job at Arby's
making $8 an hour only to quit a few months later after the store cut
back her hours. She had spent her paychecks sprucing up their apartment at Latonia Terrace, buying an eight-piece furniture set for the

living room and turning a storage area into a bedroom for Na'Dreya. It was Na'Dreya's first bedroom of her own, and she hung a framed copy of Obama's letter on the wall.

T. HAILEY HATCHER spent New Year's Eve 2011 in Suwannee, Florida, and then continued to visit his family's fishing camp about once a month. He never found oil, but he also rarely found fish. It had been cold and blustery, bad conditions for fishing. "It might be nothing," he said. But he also wondered if it was something—the latest impact from the oil spill. He eventually reached the same, unsatisfying conclusion agreed upon by most scientists: Only time would tell.

LUCY GUTIERREZ was outbid for her dream house in the desert just outside of Kingman, Arizona, but she fell in love with another place a few months later and purchased it for $137,000. The four-bedroom house sat on a quiet cul-de-sac in a fancy neighborhood, surrounded by a big yard and within walking distance of Kingman's best schools. Lucy and her family moved in at the beginning of 2011, painted the walls, and made the house their own. "This is going to be home for a long time," Lucy said.

Arizona's Senate Bill 1070 remained tied up in the courts. Governor Jan Brewer filed a counterclaim against Obama's lawsuit, demanding $135 million from the federal government to compensate Arizona for the cost of detaining illegal immigrants. Both sides continued to predict that the fight would eventually end in the Supreme Court.

Meanwhile, Lucy continued to suffer occasional prejudices and marvel at what she called "all of this ugliness and hate." Across the state in January, an unstable gunman opened fire while Congresswoman Gabrielle Giffords spoke to a small crowd outside of a grocery store in Tucson. Giffords survived a shot to the head, but six other people died and sixteen more were injured. "The anger, the hatred, the bigotry that goes on in this country is getting to be outrageous," said Clarence Dupnik, the sheriff who investigated the shootings. "And unfortunately Arizona I think has become the capital. We have become the mecca for prejudice and bigotry."

A few months after he received his letter in the mail from Obama, THOMAS RITTER decided to quit following politics cold turkey. He was spending too much time in the man cave watching Fox News, he said, and all of it only amounted to more frustration. "It seemed like I had gone too far," he said, "so now I'm going to watch reality TV with Lynette in the other room."

That plan lasted only a few weeks. The midterm elections sucked Thomas back in, and he celebrated Republican gains in Congress but bemoaned Obama's productive lame-duck session. "Why do we have to make all of these changes so fast?" he said. He made a New Year's resolution to follow politics only in moderation, and he and Lynette decided to focus on getting closer to God, saving money, losing weight, and eating less fast food. They also agreed to grant themselves one exception: They would still eat doughnuts together on Sunday mornings in front of the political news shows.

And even as the calendar turned, Thomas continued to hang Obama's letter unprotected in his classroom, allowing students to hold it whenever they pleased.

NATOMA CANFIELD received a bone marrow transplant at Cleveland Clinic in the spring of 2010, spent sixty-five more days in a bed at the hospital, and then returned home to live under the careful supervision of her sister, Connie Anderson. Over the following months, Natoma's daily dose of medicines ballooned from eleven pills to twenty-one. Her muscles atrophied. She lost more weight, then took steroids and suddenly gained sixty pounds. "Everything hurts," she said a few months after the transplant. "I don't remember what it feels like to live without pain."

But she continued to survive as the days passed, and her blood tests showed incremental improvement. By late August, some hair had grown back. By October, doctors felt confident enough to declare her transplant a success. By November, with the midterm elections approaching their climax, Natoma read the newspaper and tracked the results on the news. She saw Republicans gain sixty-six seats in Congress, largely because of their unified opposition to health-care reform. She watched her congressman, John Boccieri, lose his job amid criticism of his health-care vote, just as he had feared.

The new House of Representatives voted to repeal the health-care law a few months later—an action that was only symbolic, because Obama and the Senate continued to support the bill—and a television reporter from Cleveland came to interview Natoma. He asked how she felt about reform now that it was so maligned. "It's a bill that will still help a lot of people," Natoma said, and friends who watched marveled less at what she said than at how she looked when she said it. Her skin glowed. She wore makeup for the first time in months. She had gone to the mall a few days earlier to have her ears pierced and splurged on $50 earrings.

"We call it the lipstick factor," Connie said. "That's how we knew she was starting to feel better."

Connie scheduled a trip home to Florida shortly after the holidays to spend a few weeks with her husband for the first time in a year. Natoma, meanwhile, stayed home in Ohio with plenty to celebrate. A year after receiving a diagnosis of leukemia, her doctors now believed she would beat the disease. "I'm going to be a member of that lucky 35 percent," Natoma said.

After her son returned from his tour in Afghanistan, POLLY CHAMBERLAIN visited him in Maryland once every few months. Doug Toulotte seemed more serious than Polly remembered—in part because Doug and his wife, Krissy, continued to have a difficult year even after he came home. He continued to apply for jobs with the FBI and the Baltimore Police Department, advancing through the interview stages. But the hiring process dragged on for months, and he kept working security at Home Depot. The job helped pay the bills on their new house but left him yearning for work with greater purpose.

His brother, Ben Toulotte, committed suicide in October. That same week, one of Doug's roommates in military training died during combat in Afghanistan. Doug and Krissy went to the funeral at Arlington National Cemetery. Doug walked through the white headstones and visited the graves of three other friends from the marines. Krissy kept her eyes locked on the new widow, whose wedding had been the same month as hers to Doug, and thought about how lucky she was to still have him. Not long after, they finally rebooked their delayed honeymoon and spent nine days in Hawaii.

STEFAN JOHNSON finished his first semester at La Salle University with a 3.1 grade point average, continuing to pick classes with a focus in politics and communications. He liked the school but sometimes talked about transferring to Villanova, which had a stronger student government and a more active Democrats club. He looked into transferring and decided it would only be possible if Villanova matched the full scholarship he had received from La Salle.

Even with the scholarship, paying for school remained a daily struggle during Stefan's freshman year. A woman from church volunteered to purchase his books, and Stefan saved up some money by working two jobs—one after school at the university's ministry office and the other on weekends at the Cathedral Basilica of Saints Peter and Paul, where he helped coordinate masses.

His mother, Monica, lost her unemployment again on the last day of 2010, and she applied for twenty-five jobs over the next two weeks. Finally, in the third week of January, she was called in to interview for a desk job in the city's parking enforcement department. The interviewer happened to be an old friend, who offered Monica a job. She accepted on the spot without asking for specifics about hours or salary. "It will be better than zero, and that's all that matters," she said.

Stefan took the train across the city to congratulate Monica in person—which surprised none of his new friends at La Salle. They teased him for going home too often. He laughed it off and continued to check on his mom in South Philly every few weeks.

JEN CLINE'S husband, Jay, was officially granted Chapter 7 bankruptcy shortly after his trip to court, and they spent much of the year trying to seize their chance at a fresh start. Jen doubled her class load at the community college, receiving straight A's and staying on track to graduate as a registered nurse in 2012. Jay started installing pool tables in addition to swimming pools, hoping to earn a little extra cash. On one of the family's weekend drives to escape Monroe, Michigan, Jen and Jay spotted a five-bedroom house in the suburbs listed at $89,000 and dreamed of making an offer.

But Jen's unemployment payments expired late in the fall of 2010, and Delta cut Jay's hours during the slow season. They received bills totaling $3,500 for the deductibles on an emergency surgery and the final dosages of Jen's cancer medication. "We're falling back into debt again," Jen said in late October. They could think of only one way to come up with the money, and they debated for days whether or not to take it.

An autograph collector from New York had read a newspaper story about Obama's note to Jen and offered her $3,000 for the president's letter. She had declined, but the collector continued to call, raising his offer by $500 each time. Finally, in early November, he called to make what he said was his final offer: $7,000 in cash. Jen and Jay ran the math and decided they could pay off their medical bills and still save enough to make a small down payment on a house. "It's the right thing to do for the family," Jen said. She agreed to the deal, asked relatives to watch her two boys, and made plans to drive to New York with Jay to make the exchange.

They rode in silence for most of the ten-hour drive while the letter rested in her lap. Then, when they finally crossed into New York, Jen started to cry. The letter was her most prized possession, she said, the highlight of her adult life. "It's like selling off a piece of my soul," she sobbed. Jay suggested they turn around. "It's just money," he said—but it was also a down payment toward their dream house, a way to pay medical bills, and the freedom to splurge on a nice Italian dinner for their first anniversary. Jen shook her head and told him to drive on.

They pulled into the driveway of the autograph dealer's five-bedroom house in the suburbs of New York City, and he handed over a cashier's check for $7,000. Jen stalled before completing the deal. She went into his house to make a copy of Obama's note and lingered at the kitchen table to read over the original letter one final time. "Things will get better," the president had written—and maybe now they would. She handed over the note card with the embossed presidential seal and got back in the car for the long drive home to Monroe.

AUTHOR'S NOTE

Above all else, this book is owed to the ten families who let me into their lives and trusted me to share their stories. I traveled around the country to spend time with each letter writer, and those reporting trips provided the foundation for this book. I was a firsthand observer of most scenes. I was present for all dialogue except in a few instances when I confirmed conversations with those involved. People granted me access to their e-mails and diaries, and I relied on those documents for background information and quoted directly from them in a few cases. Excerpts from letters are reprinted exactly as they were written and sometimes contain misspellings or grammatical errors.

It is not an easy thing to welcome a reporter into your life. These people shared the intimate details of their backgrounds, introduced me to their friends and families, and allowed me to shadow them everywhere for days at a time. I followed them to bankruptcy court, job interviews, fishing trips, doctors' offices, classrooms, and welfare appointments. I spent long days in their houses even when they were sick, tired, or just plain beaten down. They had every right to tell me to get lost. And yet, in every case, they accepted my presence with grace, patience, and good humor. I am humbled by their generosity and touched by their courage. I hope this book does justice to both them and their stories. I also hope my relationships with many of them continue to endure long after this book gathers dust.

In two instances, I changed the name of a writer's relative in order to protect the person from possible deportation (in chapter 8) and possible job loss (in chapter 10). Every other detail in the book is fact.

I would never have been able to access some of these letters without cooperation from inside the White House, where several people devoted time in their busy schedules to help my reporting. Barack Obama agreed to a one-on-one interview in the Oval Office on February 14, 2011. Many of his comments in the book come directly from that session, while the rest come from public remarks, speeches, or press conferences. Several members of his administration helped me understand the issues he confronts every day. I visited the White House mail room in 2010, toured the facility, and spoke to several employees. Moira Mack and Lauren Paige in the White House press office cared about this project even when hundreds of more immediate demands competed for their attention. Moira continued to meet me for coffee even though she never drank any. Lauren helped me track down difficult sources with both efficiency and good humor. This book is so much better because of their help.

Hundreds of articles and a handful of books helped me better understand Obama's policies and provided some context in understanding the president's interaction with the letter writers. I particularly relied on *The Washington Post*, *The New York Times*, and *The New Yorker* for their coverage of political issues. The book *Dear Mr. President*, written by a former White House mail-room employee named Ira Smith, provided a few great anecdotes and some historical context.

On a more personal note, I would never have managed the confidence to take on this project—much less finish it—without the support of my parents, Becky and Warren, and my brothers, Craig and Alec. They read and improved each chapter as the book came together; Dad made sure I adhered to grammatical rules that nobody else knew existed. More than anything, they listened to me talk about this project and these people for hours at a time. They are the most generous listeners I know. I'm so thankful for them.

The original idea for this project began with an article in *The Washington Post*, but I am indebted to the paper for much more than just that. The *Post* has given me one dream job after another for the last seven years. There are not many other places where an intern who overwrites stories about high-school volleyball can cover the president a few years later. Many people at the *Post* have gambled on me and made me a better journalist. I owe special thanks to Lynda Robinson, an editor I trust and relied on for editing and insight during this project; Kevin Merida, a rare boss who also acts like a friend; and Emilio Garcia-Ruiz, without whom I never would have covered high-school volleyball, much less anything else. My direct editor at the paper, David Finkel, did nothing but help shape the idea for this book, teach me about the publishing industry, and inspire me to become a writer who gets at the Thing.

A handful of lifelong friends also read early versions of this book— or heard me talk about it so much that every page will feel familiar.

Chico Harlan read on the plane even as he moved across the world. William Wan edited and sent pages Priority Mail while visiting his in-laws. Adam Kilgore spent his vacation editing on my couch. Louis Goldstein invited me to stay on his couch while I reported, although in retrospect I'm not sure that was much of a favor. So many others have buoyed me with their support and kind words, but here are a few: Isa Barillas, Ellen Barry, Gail Barry, Doug Beckman, Greg Bishop, Joanna Ceciliani, Dave Fahrenthold, Bill Geary, Bert Kaufman, Denison Levy, Rick and Erin Maese, Jeff Passan, Phil Rucker, Eric Saslow and family (although his full support likely depends on whether or not Rachel Maddow ever mentions this book), Darryl Slater, Karen Steinbock, Miriam Stone, and Kevin and Jen Van Valkenburg. My uncle, Chips Barry, passed away while I was reporting; I often missed him and his enthusiasm.

I was incredibly lucky to write some of this book while teaching at the University of Montana, a great journalism school in a breathtaking place. If there's a better daily routine than writing with a view of the mountains and winding down with a pint of Cold Smoke, I have yet to find it. Thanks to the students who helped energize me; to the family of T. Anthony Pollner for bringing my wife and me to Missoula; and especially to Carol Van Valkenburg, the Banvilles, and the rest of the staff for making us feel so welcome.

While writing this book, I had the privilege of working with many talented people for the first time. Esther Newberg, my agent, became an advocate and a friend. I could never have navigated this process without her. Bill Thomas not only edited this book; he also spent the last three years reading my obscure newspaper stories, sending kind e-mails, and instilling in me the confidence to take on this project. Few people have been so generous with their encouragement and time. I am indebted to many others at Doubleday, especially Karla

Eoff, Coralie Hunter, Rachel Lapal, Emily Mahon, Jillian Wohlfarth, and Amelia Zalcman.

My greatest gratitude is contained in the book's dedication. My wife, Rachel, made sure this book had balance and heart, the same qualities she brings to everything. As always, she listened to every word.